Parish Life in Eighteenth-Century Scotland

Parish Life

in

Eighteenth-Century Scotland

A Review of the Old Statistical Account

MAISIE STEVEN

Foreword by Alasdair Steven

SCOTTISH CULTURAL PRESS

First published in 1995 and
reprinted 2002 by

SCOTTISH CULTURAL PRESS

Unit 13d, Newbattle Abbey Business Annexe
Newbattle Road, DALKEITH EH22 3LJ Scotland
Tel: +44 (0)131 660 6366 • Fax: +44 (0)131 660 6414
Email: info@scottishbooks.com

website: www.scottishbooks.com

The publisher acknowledges subsidies from the Scottish Arts Council
and the Russell Trust towards the first printing

BRITISH LIBRARY CATALOGUING IN PUBLICATION DATA
A catalogue record for this book is available from the British Library

ISBN: 1 898218 28 5

Printed and bound by Bell & Bain Ltd, Glasgow

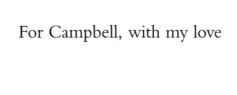

For Campbell, with my love

Editor's Note

The footnotes at the end of each chapter relate to the relevant volume and page number from the *Old Statistical Account*.

Place names used throughout generally refer to those in use during the eighteenth century. If they are markedly different from present day usage, then the twentieth-century equivalent is also shown.

Contents

FOREWORD

How extraordinarily lucky we are in Scotland to have had the remarkable compilation of facts, figures and relevant commentary, called from the outset the *Statistical Account*, produced and published for us two hundred years ago.

It could only have been organised by someone who was energetic, knowledgeable, influential and moneyed and Sir John Sinclair of Ulbster in Caithness was all these.

His research required to be done through intelligent and diligent co-operators in every one of Scotland's 938 parishes. The only possible body of participants were the ministers of the parishes; Sinclair sent each one a circular with 166 queries on local conditions in relation to the national welfare. Half a century before the penny post, individual communication was so expensive he could not have afforded to do this except that, as an MP, he had the privilege of parliamentary franking. He hoped to 'found a system of political economy, on a minute and extensive investigation of local facts.' In this he failed. His great work did not 'lead to systematic reforms and changes'.

He adopted the new word 'statistical' from mainly German sources, where it came in more precisely for the collection of numerical facts for government or state use. Sinclair's interests went well beyond that. He aimed to promote the happiness and improvement of all within human society, and it is in concentrating upon this fundamental element of his survey that Maisie Steven (same surname as mine, but unrelated) has drawn from the twenty volumes a single volume that highlights vividly the everyday lives of the Scottish people in that crucial last decade of the eighteenth century – a period that has been increasingly hailed with recent years as the time of 'Scottish Enlightenment'.

This is nothing if not an animated book. No one can read anywhere in it from agriculture to occupations or mode of living without stimulation from the trenchant ideas and ideals shown by nearly a thousand thinking Scots two centuries back. The author may lament that she is not a historian, but needlessly: if she had been she might have developed an interesting historical thesis, but here we have something for every reader not only about history but exuberantly about life.

This is a gem-studded compilation that reveals our ancestors as no other single book could do so pithily and profoundly.

Alasdair Steven

BIOGRAPHICAL NOTE

Maisie Steven is by profession a nutritionist/dietician who formerly worked in hospitals, both in Scotland and Canada, and also in food research and community health. For eight years she was a lecturer at Queens College, Glasgow (now Caledonian University). She has written several papers on nutrition and health and in 1989 won a major award from the International Foundation for the Promotion of Nutrition Research and Education, for a paper entitled 'Strategies to Influence Nutrition Behaviour'. She is the author of *The Good Scots Diet: What happened to it?* (1985, Aberdeen University Press), a history of diet and health in Scotland. While researching this she came under the spell of the Statistical Account and was fascinated by the richness of the material and the sheer human interest.

Maisie Steven is married to Campbell Steven, author of many books about outdoor Scotland, and her son Kenneth is a poet and novelist. She is a housewife and lives in Aberfeldy, Perthshire.

ACKNOWLEDGEMENTS

Sincere thanks are due to both the Russell Trust and the Scottish Arts Council for generous grants towards the first printing of this book.

For their support of this publication and for permission to reproduce Sir John Sinclair's original questionnaire in full, thanks are also due to the Special Collections staff at Edinburgh University Library; and to EDINA (Edinburgh University Data Library) and the Joint Board for the Statistical Accounts of Scotland.

To my husband Campbell I owe an immense debt for his meticulous proof-reading and constant encouragement; both he and our son Ken deserve warm commendation for their tolerance during the seven-year long incubation period. I am extremely grateful too to Alasdair Steven (no relative, but a family friend of long standing) for much early information about the parish accounts, as well as for the Foreword; and to my friend Brenda Muir for checking the lengthy list of references. Warm thanks, too, to Angus and Irene Howat for their careful reading and encouraging evaluation of the MS. To Philip Cowan I owe special thanks for having been the first person to become excited over the potential of this book, at a time when the project might well have been abandoned.

INTRODUCTION

Ever since being introduced to the *Statistical Account of Scotland* (now generally referred to as the *Old Statistical Account*) I have been under its spell. Then, as now, it seemed scarcely credible that it should be so little known in Scotland or that, along with most of my friends, I could have passed through the educational system without ever having been aware of this fascinating document which is the envy of social historians elsewhere.

It was therefore in the hope of making these parochial accounts more accessible to ordinary people with a taste for social history that I conceived the idea of writing this book. Many times through the years of toil I have regretted it; more often than I can say, I could cheerfully have thrown the twenty fat volumes into the bin. But if eventually the initial hope is fulfilled, and if even a few of my fellow-Scots come to find in it as much enjoyment as I have done, then certainly the labour will have been worthwhile.

The book has been built around what is, inevitably, a personal selection of quotations. Other writers – especially perhaps 'real' historians, as opposed to one who is merely fascinated by the lifestyle, character and beliefs of an earlier generation – doubtless would have chosen differently. Here, choice has fallen on those excerpts which appealed to me as the most informative, vivid, moving, quaint, or at times flamboyant; some were chosen for the high quality of the writing; a few for pure entertainment value. Many more clamoured for inclusion, but a line had to be drawn somewhere, and the book is perhaps too long as it is.

Early on, I decided two things. First, this would be a purely sociological review; despite the undoubted interest of the material on archaeology, botany and geology, and especially the writers' fanciful speculations on the origin of place-names, I would confine myself strictly to those things which most closely affected the people of the time. Secondly, as far as possible I would allow these old accounts to speak for themselves. Not being a trained historian – and probably also with more than a touch of laziness – I thought it wiser not to become embroiled with other historical sources. And, indeed it was the chapters on food and health (of the history of which, as a nutritionist, I do have a certain knowledge) that I found most difficult to write, simply because of the temptation to cloud the issue by dredging up the researches and conclusions of other chroniclers of the time. Better, I decided, to compare parish with parish, opinion with opinion, thus building up under each heading some kind of composite picture of what was going on in the country as a whole.

But of course the *Old Statistical Account* is not true history any more than I am a true historian! At every turn (and to me this simply adds to the attraction) one is confronted with the personality, temperament and convictions of the 900+ writers who penned the reports. When it is a question of specific facts and figures – and, thankfully for one as unmathematical as I am, the 'statistical' in the title turns out to mean merely tables of such things as population, livestock, diseases – one can be reasonably sure of accuracy. Where opinion is called for, the human factor can never be left out. While the minister of one parish may soundly berate his parishioners, or at least find some serious flaws in their general character, a neighbour may well paint a glowing picture of his relatively saintly flock. This is only one of many possible examples.

The sheer diversity of the *Old Statistical Account* is nevertheless, to my mind, its most attractive feature. Whether in agriculture (about which there is so much that it must, at a guess, occupy at least a quarter of the space), or in industrial development; whether in the use of inoculation for smallpox or in the rate of emigration, what is happening in one parish is not necessarily happening even in the adjacent one. Nor is the standard of the accounts by any means uniform. Some ministers (or in a few cases, 'friends to statistical inquiries') have written with such erudition and at such length, taking infinite pains in their researches, that their reports could well stand as books in their own right; others have dashed off hasty replies reminiscent of the work of lazy schoolboys. (To be fair, these last are only a small minority; generally, the standard could be said to vary from good to excellent).

As to the subject matter, the claim could almost be made that whatever one's special interest or line of research, it is to be found in these old accounts. Some entries take one by surprise by their sheer modernity; who would have expected, for example, that 200 years ago the city of Perth would have boasted a nursery covering 30-40 acres, and containing 'all kinds of fruit and forest trees, evergreen and flowering shrubs, flower roots and plants', or that from that same city ship-loads of salmon would have been sent to London packed in ice? For those interested in linguistics, too, there is much to occupy the attention; most surprising to me, possibly, in view of frequent spelling reforms in certain countries today, is the minimal degree to which our own language has changed. A few words are to be noted – three common examples are 'chearful', 'chuse' and 'expence'; some words have altered in meaning, so that 'enthusiasm' refers, generally in a derogatory sense, to excessive zeal, while 'crazy' means simply of irregular shape.

Most importantly perhaps, one comes across situations which seem to lift these old accounts out of their parochial context on to the world stage. We see examples of a cottage industry which has sustained a rural people literally for centuries being ruined through industrial mass production; we find too the beginnings of friendly societies and of trade unionism. Very clearly too we see instances of exploitation of the poor, and of people being forced off their lands through the vested interests of the landlords (although occasionally also we find heartening exceptions, where the population flourishes under a local benevolent regime). All of these things have happened to the common folk elsewhere; they happen in many countries today.

While there is much which may seem quaintly amusing to modern minds, there is much more to touch the heart. At times one scarcely dares to allow the imagination full rein – to think perhaps what it must have been like to nurse a child with typhoid in a hovel with no water; to see whole families wiped out by smallpox; to suffer the oppression of the press-gangs; to be thrown off the land with no money and nowhere to go. All these harrowing events and many more are to be found in these pages.

There is much to warm the heart as well. While it is the frugality of the Scots which has become proverbial, it is rather their generosity which shines out in the reports; there is much evidence of the poor looking after the very poor. One outstanding example may suffice. The Dunkeld account states: 'Janet Macgregor was maid-servant to a respectable family. The parents died, and the children, then in infancy, were very destitute. The poor woman clung to them with a parent's affection, and in supporting and rearing the orphans, spent the hard-won earnings of a number of years.'[1] While, in a day of social services, one hardly expects such sacrifice, this example is a reminder to us not to adopt superior attitudes, nor to confuse civilisation with comforts and convenience.

What, finally, of the character of the eighteenth-century Scots as it appears from these parish reports? Certainly there is much to admire – the fortitude which so often triumphed over a harsh environment; the deep respect for, and determination at all costs to acquire, good education; the strong family life; the many instances of outstanding honesty; the depth of religious conviction, largely lost in modern times. Lost, too, in a far more materialistic and affluent age, is the art of simple celebration described in many accounts on the occasions such as marriages, baptisms and funerals, brightening a life of almost ceaseless toil and hardship. A strong people, undoubtedly; yet naturally the other side of the coin is also seen in a certain harshness and stubbornness at times. Let the Kinloch, Perthshire, writer – clearly striving for total objectivity – sum up: 'On the whole, the people are benevolent, humane, and charitable . . . but if we keep in view the great standard of perfection . . . which the Divine Author of it hath left for our imitation, I must say, that, upon a close examination, there are to be seen, on the face of this fair character, some specks.'[2]

Such, then, is something of the fascination of the *Statistical Account*. To have spent seven years of 'spare' time immersed in its pages, and to have reached the end even more enthusiastic than at the beginning, must surely say a great deal about the general interest and quality of a document of which Scotland should indeed be proud.

Maisie C. Steven
Aberfeldy
Perthshire

1. XII, 333
2. XII, 618

Henry Raeburn, *Sir John Sinclair*
(National Gallery of Scotland)

1 HOW THE ACCOUNTS CAME TO BE WRITTEN

Sir John Sinclair of Ulbster in Caithness, born in 1745, was the genius behind the *Statistical Account* (SA) of Scotland. Few would dispute the claim that this man – a land-owner with money, an agriculturist keenly interested in 'improving', a member of the Society of Antiquaries, and most importantly one with a parliamentary seat, having the privilege of sending out large numbers of letters under the parliamentary frank – was ideally placed for the onerous task of compiler and editor. It has often been said that his genius lay not so much in initiating this most significant document as in his sheer persistence in seeing the whole project through to the end. A man of many interests, and at all times with a deep concern for his native land, he studied at Edinburgh, Glasgow and Oxford, was admitted to both the Scottish and English Bars, and founded the Board of Agriculture, whose first president he became.

The Edinburgh bookseller William Creech, a popular wit and story teller, also played an important part as co-ordinator, in charge of publishing; the often difficult job of production and distribution also fell to his lot.

The great project began on 25 May 1790, when Sir John wrote this first circular to the clergy of the Church of Scotland:

Sir,

I take the liberty of transmitting the inclosed Queries to you, in hopes that a plan, which has been fortunate enough to meet with the approbation of some of the most respectable and distinguished characters in these kingdoms, will be favoured with your assistance.

To procure information with regard to the real political situation of a country, is what wise Statesmen in every age have thought desirable, but which in these enlightened times is justly held of the most essential public importance.

In many parts of the Continent, more particularly in Germany, Statistical Inquiries, as they are called, have been carried to a very great extent, but in no country, it is believed, can they be brought to such perfection as in Scotland, which boasts of an ecclesiastical establishment, whose members will yield to no description of men, for public zeal, as well as for private virtue, for intelligence, or for ability.

I flatter myself, that upon this occasion, they will not be backward in contributing their aid, to promote an attempt, which may prove of considerable service to the country at large, and cannot fail to add to the reputation and character, which the Church of Scotland has already so deservedly acquired for public utility.

I have the honour to be,
Sir, your very obedient,
And faithful, humble servant,
John Sinclair.

There followed a truly daunting list of 160 questions, to which six others were subsequently added (for a reproduction of these, *see* Appendix), with an addendum which perhaps helped to cheer some faint hearts: 'It is not expected, that all the inclosed Queries should be answered by any individual; nor is minute exactness looked for'. Later, Sinclair attempted to ensure replies to those questions he considered most important, viz. 'population, agriculture, stipend, poor, school, boats, fishermen etc.'; and in January 1791, as a guide to other respondents, he sent out as a sample four of the best early replies he had received. Another kind of encouragement was offered by his intimation that he intended to donate profits to the Society for the Benefit of the Sons of the Clergy.

It was to be nine long years before Sir John would, by a great deal of cajolery and much use of psychology, extract the last of the parish accounts. (It should be said in the ministers' defence, all the same, that indolence or negligence were not necessarily the reason for the tardy response of some; on the contrary, some of the very best accounts arrived late, due to extensive research and careful deliberation.) Only a few of the stepping-stones in the journey need be mentioned here. During this time Sir John was to send many more circulars, in a persuasive, but always gentlemanly, tone which became noticeably more importunate as time went on; the last, sent out as late as July 1797 – by which time the number of recalcitrant ministers was down to six – was written in red ink! But in December 1796, the boot had been on the other foot, when Sir John wrote to twelve unfortunate respondents to confess that he had lost their accounts, and to request that copies be sent. One can only guess at the dismay his missive must have caused to those affected, who may well have gone to great lengths in conscientious research, and possibly kept no copies.

Eager to publish the accounts, Sir John did so exactly as they were received; the sheer exasperation these 21 higgledy-piggledy volumes must have caused to users through the years, however, can well be imagined. A great debt is thus owed today to E P Publishing, with their two general editors Ian R Grant and Donald J Withrington, who in the 1970s brought out the modern version – twenty well organised volumes in alphabetical order, in which parishes are grouped by county, each edited by a scholar who contributes an introduction explaining the regional significance of the SA. Doubtless this is how Sir John himself would have liked to produce the work, had this been possible.

Exactly nine years from the date of his initial appeal, his long time of waiting was triumphantly over, and on 3 June 1799 he was able to present to the General Assembly of the Church of Scotland a complete set of the printed *Statistical Account*, 'handsomely bound in 21 volumes octavo'. The Moderator thanked him warmly 'for the many instances of his polite attention to the ministers of this Church; for his zeal in setting on foot, and his unwearied perseverance in bringing to an accomplishment, this great work of the *Statistical Account of Scotland*.'

If Sir John was the ideal compiler and editor, then this closing decade of the eighteenth century seems to have been an ideal time for such an undertaking – an era of maximum change in agriculture, with rising wages, and improvements in both housing and health, and with the Industrial Revolution well under way; indeed, in the face of rapid economic change, these reports may be said to record a way of life which was soon to disappear. That the production of no fewer than 938 parish accounts dealing with every aspect of life in Scotland was in itself 'an accomplishment' it would be hard to deny. But what exactly was accomplished by these painstaking researches?

Sir John's stated aim had been to employ them for positive benefit to Scotland, showing up any strengths and weaknesses and, by demonstrating to the government areas in which specific action was required, to 'add to the quantum of happiness' in the country. While at no time claiming that his initiative was entirely new, he did emphasise that basically it should be of practical use in building a foundation for a wide range of social and political responses. Always he was at pains to keep the whole project under the eye of Parliament. And certainly some developments following publication – for example the repeal of the hated tax on coals carried by coast, and improvements in the abysmal conditions of the country's dominies – could justly be claimed to have been based on its findings.

Much honour must go to Sir John Sinclair for his outstanding leadership; much too to a body of men, educated, astute and for the most part with unrivalled knowledge of their parishes, who generally come across as having undertaken their onerous task with the altruistic aim of improving the lot of their fellow-countrymen.

2 DRESS

With the exception of tea and whisky drinking, few things seem to have occasioned greater disapproval among the writers of the parish accounts than did changes in the people's mode of dress. In the last decade of the eighteenth century, the humbler folk of Scotland were clearly at last beginning to find a little extra cash to spend on clothes. In some cases this may have amounted to no more than a few pence, and indeed in the Crieff account even the wearing of ribbons earns a mention: 'About the year 1780, female servants and others of that rank began first to wear ribbons . . . Now, instead of the grave and solid productions of the country, the gay cloths, silks, muslins, and printed cottons of England, adorn on Sundays almost every individual.'[1]

It was of course mainly on Sundays that the drab working garb tended to be replaced by something more becoming – a change frequently condemned as inordinate 'love of luxury'. In account after account, the writers make unfavourable comparisons between modern frivolous tastes and the sobriety of the old days. To be fair, some are concerned about the decreasing use of local materials. According to the writer for Aithsting and Sansting, Shetland: 'The people, in general, have too great a turn for fine clothes'. Sensibly, however, he goes on to suggest that a prize be offered to counteract the trend: 'A great deal of money is laid out in a year for Scotch and English cloths, stuffs, cottons, lawns etc., while their own wool is neglected or destroyed. Perhaps a premium offered to the man who had the best suit of clothes spun in his house, and manufactured in the country, if not in the parish; and to the woman who had the best plaid, gown and petticoat of her own spinning, might prevent this, and give the people, in general, a turn for manufacturing their own wool.'[2]

Other ministers were concerned at the level of expenditure on clothes to the detriment of other necessities. The writer for Kirknewton in the Lothians enlarges on the potentially dire consequences: 'About 50 years ago, it was usual for the most substantial farmers to appear at church in home-spun cloth and plaiden hose. Now their menial servants and cottagers are equipped in English broad cloth, silk and satin. This turn for finery is a great loss to them, as they live up to their wages, notwithstanding their being so high. Thus they enter into a married state, with their whole substance upon their back, especially women; and when sickness, or any other misfortune prevents their daily labour, they immediately sink into the depths of poverty.'[3] The Dunoon writer takes a similar view: 'The young woman, who 50 years ago, thought of endeavouring to make 100 or 200 merks for her portion, now sinks all the money she makes, in dress and ornament. The scarlet cloak, that only covered the shoulders of our ladies 50 years ago, now falls down to the heels of our servant maids; and many of them purchase a silk gown to be married in.'[4] And in the account for Wattin, Caithness, the people are 'fond of dress, rather to excess; too much of their earnings, particularly of the younger part of both sexes, goes to gratify their fancy in that respect; and it is not always with the best or most substantial articles of any kind, that they are supplied. Being naturally of a sprightly turn, what appears the most showy gains their choice.'[5]

In Coldingham, refreshingly, the writer of the account does not share the generally disapproving view: 'The generality of the people in this parish are sober, frugal, and industrious, plain and decent in their dress and deportment; and very few of them discover any desire for fineries, or expensive amusements.'[6] As always with the SA, one is left wondering just how subjective the content is – were the folk of Coldingham really different, or was it simply that the recorder, in this case not a minister, merely looked at them through more tolerant eyes?

Headgear receives considerable comment. Some of the writers bewail the passing of the bonnet – in some places, specifically the familiar blue Kilmarnock bonnet – and its replacement (at least on Sundays) by the more modish hat. An intriguing anecdote is included in the report for Laurencekirk: 'As a specimen of the change, that has taken place within these 20 years, with regard to dress, it may be worth mentioning, that about 18 or 19 years ago, a hatter came from Edinburgh to settle in the village, and having arrived upon a Saturday, but seeing only three hats in the whole church beside his own, he was discouraged, so that he dropped his scheme, and left the place on Monday.'[7] His business prospects would have been considerably brighter in other areas, for example in Lilliesleaf in the Borders, where 'the dress both of the men and the women has undergone a most surprising change . . . Thirty-two years ago, there were only seven hats in the church; but at present there are not as many bonnets.'[8] And in Forglen, Banffshire: 'Hats are as common as bonnets now; and the bar plaid is changed for a scarlet one. On Sundays, there is no distinguishing the country clown from the town beau; the farmer's goodman from the merchant's clerk; and the lasses have their ribbands and muslins to match them.'[9]

A more sombre note, in a reference to the proscription of tartan following the Jacobite Rising, comes from Kincardine, Inverness-shire: 'The Act of 1746, discharging the Highland Dress, had the worst of consequences. Prior to that period, the Highland women were remarked for their skill and success in spinning and dyeing wool, and clothing themselves and their households, each according to her fancy, in tartans, fine, beautiful, and durable. Deprived of the pleasure of seeing their husbands, sons, and favourites, in that elegant drapery, emulation died, and they became contented with manufacturing the wool in the coarsest and clumsiest manner; perhaps thinking, that since they *must* appear like the neighbouring Lowlanders, the less they shone, in the ornaments of Lowland dress, they would be the more in character.'[10]

One of the most intriguing aspects of the SA is that for every opinion expressed, a totally different one can usually be found – in this case, the account for the Small Isles would seem to suggest that some of the Highland women were more likely to be keeping up with their Lowland neighbours in abandoning their former fashions: 'The kerchief, formerly worn by married women, and the "tonnac", or short plaid, worn by females in general, are now almost wholly out of use. Instead of these, caps of various fashions, short and long cloaks, great coats, and ribbands, have been substituted . . . The change in the dress of the women may be thus accounted for. Most of our young women go to the low country for some weeks in harvest; this time they spend in shearing; and with the money thus earned, they endeavour to dress themselves after the low country fashion; the fashion, thus introduced, raises an emulation among the women in general, and, of course, merchants are encouraged to import like articles. The periodical migration of our young women to the low country in harvest, is entirely with a view to dress.'[11]

The description of the male Highland dress in the Portree account is also of interest: 'A sort of coarse woollen cloth called "cloa", or "caddoes", the manufacture of their wives, made into short jackets and trousers, is the common dress of the men. The philibeg is rarely wore, except in summer and on Sundays, on which days, and some other occasions, those in better circumstances, appear in tartans, a bonnet, and short hose, and some in a hat, short coat, and breeches of Scotch or English manufacture. The women are in general very cleanly, and so excessively fond of dress, that many maid-servants are known to lay out their whole wages that way.'[12]

A few of the writers show concern that the people do not sufficiently regard the weather or the temperature in their dress habits – for example in Wamphray, Dumfriesshire: 'It would be well if we were as attentive to the constitution and temperament of the body as to the produce of the earth; but all the seasons find us in the use of the same dress; and hence it is easy to account for the frequency of rheumatisms. The dress which is warm enough in winter, is certainly too warm for summer.'[13] An even gloomier view comes from Kirkconnel in the Borders: 'It would seem to be unnatural to suppose, that to the modern passion for this light, flimsy, airy dress, so prevalent among all ranks, so unsuitable to the constitution of all, and to the occupations and the funds of most, particularly of the poorer sort, may be ascribed no small share of the equally common prevalence of colds, fevers, rheumatisms, asthmas, and consumptions.'[14]

Montquhitter, Aberdeenshire, offers a useful comprehensive description of past and present sartorial fashions followed by the entire country hierarchy: 'Gentlemen always wore good linen of home manufacture; on extraordinary occasions they were adorned with Holland shirts, and with English cloth embroidered with gold and silver. Ladies, when at home were neatly plain; when abroad, abundantly showy. The poorer class of farmers, tradesmen and day labourers, some of whom did not aspire to the luxury of a shirt, commonly wore sarges, either grey, or tinged with a hasty blue. The richer class of farmers, a few in opulent circumstances excepted, contented themselves with a harden shirt; the collar and wrists of which were concealed at kirk and market by two pieces of linen, called "neck and sleeves". On working days their cloaths were coarse enough; on Sundays and holidays they dressed in best sarge or sey, double blue, shorn from their own flocks, and manufactured in their own families. The blue bonnet adorned every head. Whenever a hat appeared, an idea of opulence, literature, or rank immediately excited profound obeisance. I am sorry to add, that cleanliness was little attended to . . . But now, hats, broad cloth, good linen adorned with ruffles, are occasionally worn by all ranks of men. Duffle and silk cloaks, printed and muslin gowns, by all ranks of women. And the gentry can only be distinguished from plebeians by their superior manner, and by that elegant simplicity in dress which they now admire.'[15]

For the sheer flamboyance of the writing, it is hard to deny the last word on the subject of changing dress fashions to the minister of Symington in Ayrshire: 'They have a taste for dress, and young women of the middle, and even of the lower ranks, would now blush to be seen in the blue cloaks, red plaids, and plain caps, which only 20 years ago, adorned their sex. Nay, even the scarlet mantle, which lately was a badge of distinction among the daughters of farmers, is now despised; and, *O tempora! O mores!* the silk-worms of the East must be pillaged, to deck the heads and shoulders of our milk-maids.'[16]

1. XII, 296	5. XVIII, 236	9. XVI, 177	13. IV, 527
2. XIX, 388	6. III, 105	10. XVII, 512	14. IV, 273
3. II, 338	7. XIV, 169	11. XX, 251	15. XV, 341
4. VIII, 93	8. III, 547	12. XX, 203	16. VI, 642

Sir David Wilkie, *Distraining for Rent*, 1815 (National Gallery of Scotland)

3   LIFESTYLE

The late eighteenth century was an era of profound change in many respects, not least in the way of life of the common folk of Scotland. After the 1745 Rising the people, in the Highlands especially, were left in a wretched state, many of them living in hovels, with the prospect of starvation never far away. Now, some 50 years later, things were at last showing signs of real improvement, largely due to those benefits which followed the agricultural advances. As always, however, it is unwise to risk generalisations. These accounts make it very clear that the situation around the country was far from uniform.

While affording few glimpses into the lifestyle of the upper classes of society, the SA represents a reasonable picture of daily life in the average labourer's cottage in the final decade of the eighteenth century. Here and there are to be found minute details of domestic economy, of working attire and finery for special occasions, of houses and building materials, of wages, prices and working conditions. An especially interesting study is to note those articles taken for granted today which were then regarded as the height of luxury. On the whole, it is clear that the writers tended to look on 'foreign' items of food and dress with suspicion, the fear often being expressed that departure from the simpler habits of their forefathers might lead the people into excesses harmful both to their purses and their morals. A good example comes from Kippen, Stirlingshire, in which the minister makes a plea for some kind of happy medium between the wretched poverty of the past and the greater affluence, with its attendant dangers, being experienced in his area at the time: 'In a country where improvements are altogether unknown, much happiness cannot be enjoyed; for there the necessaries of life are procured with difficulty, or, if they are easily procured, little scope is afforded for active exertion. On the other hand, where improvements in agriculture and the arts have been brought to a high degree of perfection, luxury and other evils accompany them, which are no less unfriendly than poverty and indolence to the happiness of man. It is in some intermediate state, where improvements have begun, and are still advancing, that the circumstances of society appear most calculated to promote the comfort of human life.'[1]

Arguably the best barometer of improvement seen from the accounts is the state of housing, and predictably the writers' descriptions (or perhaps more accurately their viewpoints) show a wide divergence, varying from such terms as 'miserable hovels' to 'most excellent dwellings'; and indeed, such wide variations may very well have existed throughout the country. The writers' perceptions of the probable consequences for health are perhaps less readily acceptable, as the following excerpts will show. In the report for the Borders parish of Polwarth, the writer appears to see little wrong with the dampness of the houses in his district: 'The village of Polwarth is situated on very wet, even swampy ground, so that almost in any house they have a hole dug to collect the under water, which requires to be often emptied in wet weather; and yet the inhabitants are very healthy, being neither subject to rheumatic or aguish complaints.'[2]

A somewhat different picture emerges in the report of the parish of Cleish, Kinross-shire: 'The people are not peculiarly liable to any disease except the rheumatism . . . this distemper seems to be owing principally to the dampness of the air and the houses. The dampness of the houses is occasioned, in a great measure, by the water which soaks through the ground, in its passage from the hills to the valley. This inconvenience might be remedied, by chusing proper situations for houses, and cutting drains to intercept the water from above.'[3]

The accounts describing the general improvement in housing standards are so numerous that it has been necessary to select just a few to illustrate something of the situation across the country. In Stornoway, it is perhaps the variety which is of special interest: 'The number of inhabited slate houses in this town is 67. They are all made of the best materials; some of them large, commodious, and well furnished; they are generally two stories and a garret . . . On the NW side of the town there are upwards of 20 thatched houses, which have strong walls and gables, with glass windows, all in a line, fronting the sides and the bay. On the N side of the town there is a great number of miserable thatched huts, occupied by sailors, fishers, and other people, with their families.'[4]

The scene in another Highland town, Inverness, sounds similar: 'Houses built in the last 14 years: in the town and parish, upwards of 60 of from two to three stories high, and about 70 thatched houses in the country and suburbs; some of the thatched houses are two stories high.'[5] In Central Scotland, the minister of Little Dunkeld says: 'Many new houses have been built, and old houses allowed to go to ruin, for six or seven years past. Five farm houses are two stories high, with slate roofs . . . A taste for cleanliness, and even some degree of elegance, is beginning to display itself. Instead of mean dirty hovels, built with stones without cement, dwellinghouses are now built by good masons with mortar, cast on the outside with lime, and neatly finished within.'[6]

The East Coast town of Montrose illustrates what was probably a common situation – good housing within the town, but much more primitive conditions in the outlying parts: 'The houses, if not elegant, are, on the whole, well built and regular; but, like those of Flanders, their gabel ends are often turned towards the street. With one or two exceptions, they are now all of stone, and many of them covered with blue slates. In the principal part of the town, every family possesses a separate house. But beyond the port, and at the shore, the case is otherwise.'[7]

A good summary is offered in the account for Old Luce, Galloway: 'The arable farms are all enclosed, and the improvement of farm houses is going hand in hand with the improvement of land. So late as 1780, they were, almost without exception, miserable hovels. Since that time, above 20 have been built, all of them good, and many of them very good; having not only the farm house, but the offices, with slated roofs, and many have been enlarged, repaired, and rendered more comfortable habitations for men.'[8]

Sadly there are, in contrast, many accounts which paint an altogether less rosy picture. The minister of Heriot in the Lothians, for example, takes a gloomy view of the accommodation of all classes of the population: 'The people are rather badly accommodated for houses, which are shabby, dirty huts. Although the parish is within two or three miles of lime at Middleton, they are still built of turf and stone in regular succession. The seats of our lairds are very little better.'[9] Similarly, the minister of Clunie, Perthshire, deplores the low standards, at the same time pin-pointing the root of the problem: 'The materials for building good houses abound in the parish; many of the people live in miserable smoky cribs, more like sties for hogs than habitations for men. Several of the farmers have too short leases, and some of them no leases at all. Consequently, they are discouraged from carrying on improvements to any extent.'[10] The disincentive of short or non-existent leases is cited, indeed, in a number of reports.

The Wattin, Caithness, account illustrates the poor conditions prevailing in many Highland parishes: 'They themselves, as well as their cattle, are poorly accommodated. The walls of their dwelling-houses consist of two or three feet of stone, coarsely huddled together with three or four feet of feal laid above them. Their roofs very thinly wooded, and covered with the lightest of divots (or turfs) they can procure, tied down with ropes made of heather, to prevent blowing off by the wind.'[11]

Things seem to have been little better in Kilmarnock, Ayrshire: 'In general, a stranger still views with concern the poor and mean-looking huts, in which the farmers are condemned to dwell, throughout all this country. Their habitation, and that of their cattle, are generally under one roof, and only separated from one another by partitions. Scarcely any of them have an upper story, so that the whole family are obliged to sleep upon the ground, on a damp soil, where the floor is not so much as paved with stone or flags, and where there is not even a fireplace to draw off the moist and stagnant air.'[12]

Finally, the Libberton, Lanarkshire, writer offers his opinion that 'the best way to meliorate the people's condition, is to give them better houses: for at present, the cottages, and many even of the farm houses, are fitter for the habitation of beasts, than of human beings.'[13]

His injunction was in fact being followed in a number of places through the building of model villages, most frequently for workers in a variety of industries, as explained in the Cromdale, Morayshire, account: 'Grantown is a village erected under the influence of the Grant family, it being little more than 20 years since the place where it stands was a poor rugged piece of heath. It now contains from 300 to 400 inhabitants, some of whom are as good tradesmen as any in the kingdom. Shoemakers, tailors, weavers of wool, linen and stockings, blacksmiths, wrights, masons, and twelve merchants keep regular shops in it. There are two established schools.'[14]

Another village equally well known to tourists in Scotland today had its beginnings at this time too. The Lochbroom account states: 'The British Society have fixed one of their villages here, at a place called Ullapool . . . in this village there are now about 72 houses, of which 35 are slated; the rest are thatched with turf, fern roots, and heather. The principal inducement to settle in this village is its advantageous situation for the herring fishing, which indeed is very great.'[15]

Several accounts describe villages specially built for miners. The account for Westerkirk, Dumfriesshire, states: 'There are 40 people, exclusive of an overseer, employed at present in the mines, and in preparing the antimony. A miner's wages are from £23 to £26 a year, and, as such, he enjoys many other advantages. The company has built a village . . . in which every miner is provided with a comfortable lodging for himself and his family, at a moderate rent: he has grass for a cow, during the summer, for which he pays no more than 20s., and 10s. for coarse hay for her provision in the winter; and may have as much land as he has occasion for, at the rate of 10s. per acre, for cultivating cabbage and potatoes.'[16] Various other advantages enjoyed by the workers are then described – a library amounting to 120 volumes; a schoolhouse, with a teacher, for their children's education; a storehouse in which grain will be stored when prices are low and later, in times of scarcity, sold to the people at the rate for which it was purchased. Similarly, in the latter years of the settlers on the Great Moss, the Kincardine account tells of the provision of a school, schoolhouse, kailyard and fuel for a teacher 'well acquainted with the Gaelic and the English languages', who officiated during the week as a schoolmaster, and on Sundays gave all the people religious instruction.

Villages for craft workers, miners or fishermen are to be expected; one built specifically for ex-soldiers seems more surprising. The Cargill, Perthshire, account states: 'There are several villages in this parish, but none of them deserve particular notice, excepting the village of Strelitz, so named in honour of Her Majesty. It was built in 1763, by the Commissioners for managing the annexed estates, and was intended as a place of residence for the discharged soldiery at the conclusion of the German war. It consists of about 80 dwelling-houses, with necessary office-houses, built in a commodious manner, after a regular plan, forming a spacious street, 90 feet broad, watered by a small stream, which runs along the side of the street. To every house is annexed a good garden, with about three acres of land properly inclosed with hedge and ditch, and sheltered with strips of planting. As these houses and lands were intended as an encouragement to industry, and a reward for laborious services, they were given to the soldiers at a mere quit-rent, and are still possessed by such of them as survive, at the same rate.'[17] An unusual bonus, surely, for those times!

Here and there are to be found references to planned villages built by local landlords or benefactors, one being the village of Dalgairn in Ayrshire, mentioned in the parish account for Sorn. A certain Dr Stevenson, who was a physician in Glasgow, chose a 'beautiful holm' and divided this into small lots; a village was established, laid out in a single row of 24 houses in which, at the time of writing, 43 families lived. 'Most of these families are provided with gardens of various dimensions, behind their houses, which they cultivate with great care, and raise in them not only the common kinds of esculent plants, but also strawberries, gooseberries, and currants, and occasionally flax and barley. Some of them, too, are very successful in the management of bees.'[18]

Cardross, on the Firth of Clyde, is another place where the village housing seems a far cry from the conditions under which the vast majority of poorer folk were living at the time: 'Sir Archibald Edmonston . . . has furnished an example which, it is hoped, will be generally followed. His tenants are all well lodged, and, comparatively speaking, elegantly. Instead of the old low-built and confined houses, which their fathers inhabited, Sir Archibald has given them houses and offices suited to their respective farms, upon a plan, which conveys an idea of neatness and improvement that is highly pleasing.'[19]

Comparing these glowing descriptions with some of the other reports of miserable, damp, crowded and comfortless dwellings, one cannot help wondering whether reports of these 'ideal homes' spread around the country, and whether ordinary people throughout Scotland perhaps began to be a shade more materialistic, longing for a house with a slated roof, or a garden, possibly even a window with glass? Or were most of them, as their parish ministers frequently maintained, remarkably contented with their lot?

That many of the writers selected housing as the most significant indication of living standards is in no way surprising; stranger perhaps to modern minds are some of the other items mentioned – often very simple things, which are today taken for granted. The possession of a clock or watch, for instance, or a pair of hand-bellows; a spinning-wheel in place of the ancient spindle; ownership of a tea-kettle, and the use of tea. Tea-drinking, which had become fashionable in Scotland around 1720, had had to make its way against fierce opposition; from many of the reports it is clear that all the writers are by no means reconciled to its use, even in this final decade of the eighteenth century.

Two extracts from the county of Angus are particularly descriptive; from Forfar: 'About 50 or 60 years ago, there were not above seven tea-kettles, as many hand-bellows, and as many watches in Forfar; now tea-kettles and hand-bellows are the necessary furniture of the poorest house in the parish, and almost the meanest menial servant must have his watch . . . Formerly a man who had bought a shillings worth of beef or an ounce of tea, would have concealed it from his neighbour like murder.'[20] And at Lethnot: 'Within these last 50 years, a great alteration has taken place in the manners, dress, and way of living of the people of this place. About 50 or 60 years ago, there was neither a spinning wheel nor a reel within the parishes . . . About 50 years ago, neither buckles were used for shoes, nor metal buttons for clothes. There were very few carts within the parishes. Loads were then carried on horseback. Prior to the 1745, there was not a tea-kettle within the parishes, except the minister's, now there is not a farmhouse without one, and several of the tenants use the same article of furniture.'[21]

The minister of Montquhitter, Aberdeenshire, in an outstanding report, provided an interesting summary of parish life: 'A very great change, as to diet and dress, has taken place during the 40 years last past. Prior to that era, neither tea-kettle nor tea could be found but in two families. Two hats only appeared at church. A lady adorned herself with the plaid, and a gentleman was not ashamed of home spun cloth. But now, most families drink tea once, and many twice a day. The farmer, merchant, and tradesman, enjoy in moderate degree the comforts of life. The ploughman turns out to church and market, with his hat, good linen, and broad-cloth; and it may be taken for granted, that the country belles will exert themselves to outshine the country beaus.'[22]

A great many of the ministers' complaints about their parishioners' extravagance, and their irresponsibility in budgeting their meagre funds, centre upon their love of finery in dress (*see* Dress); allusions to changes in food habits (which, as in numerous areas of the world today, identify meat as the single item most likely to show increased intake as affluence advances) are quoted in the chapter on Food. One example here, from Eccles, will suffice: 'The writer of this article is old enough to remember, that butcher meat was seldom seen on a farmer's table, except on a Sunday. But how is the scene changed! No person now entertains better than the farmer, nor is there more neatness or elegance any where to be found, than in their houses.'[23] (It should be added, all the same, that the menu in the cottars' houses still relied almost exclusively upon dairy foods, oatmeal, potatoes, and kail.)

Another thing commented on by some is wheeled transport. Until the early part of the eighteenth century, the almost total lack of suitable transport had been a very great obstacle to any kind of marketing in Scotland – even between one farm and another. Difficulties in the transport of fuel, especially of coal and peats, are referred to again and again in these accounts. But once more the scene was changing, and predictably, in some areas more than in others. Principally it was the cart which was becoming much more common. The report for East Kilbride, Lanarkshire, describes how, in 1723, when a cart was used to carry a load of coals from there to Cambuslang, a large crowd went out to view the strange new contraption; in the same county, we have this from the parish of Cadder: 'It appears that there is a dog, a clock, or a watch for every house in the parish; that there is a cart, or a plough, for every house; and that there is nearly one horse, and more than three cows, for every house in it.'[24] Certainly this sounds a great deal more prosperous than most, although in some of the county towns there are signs of some kind of public transport becoming available; in Inverness, for example: 'About 30 years ago, there was only one chaise, a four-wheeled one; but at this time, there are two coaches, twelve four-wheeled chaises, and one two-wheeled; six of the four-wheeled chaises are let for hire by inn-keepers.' Reflecting on the quality of inns, too, as a measure of advancing prosperity, this writer continues: 'The principal inns in town were indifferent until of late; they are now commodious and comfortable, and, in attendance, entertainment and beds, emulate the best inns in the southern part of the kingdom.'[25] (If note is taken of reports by some of the early travellers in Scotland, this last statement is, to say the least, somewhat doubtful!)

What is striking is the absence of any mention of recreation, at least in the great majority of the reports. Life appears to have been taken up with the grim struggle for survival, leaving little time for such frivolity (*see also* Games and Amusements).

Much of the foregoing, however, deals in generalisations. Obviously wide variations existed – between town and country, between the old-style housing and the modern villages, between farmers and cottars. Of immense interest, therefore, are the detailed budgets of poor families which some of the writers took great pains to incorporate in their accounts. A representative selection is reproduced here, in order to demonstrate not only the extreme frugality of the poor, but also the amazing way in which they contrived, somehow, to feed and clothe their families and even find the means to afford some kind of education for them as well.

Auchterderran, Fife [26]

Annual earnings of a day-labourer, wife, and three children, deduction four weeks' earnings of the man on account of holidays, bad health, attendance at funerals, &c., and excessive bad weather; and four weeks' earnings of the woman, on account of holidays, bad health, and lying-in.

To 48 weeks' labour of a man at 1s. a day	14	8	0
To 48 weeks' labour of a woman, in spinning, besides taking care of her house and children	3	12	0
To the earnings of three children at the age of six, seven, and eight years	0	0	0
	£18	0	0

ANNUAL EXPENSES

By 2 pecks oatmeal a week, at 1½d. per week	4	19	8
By 2 pecks barley or pease meal a week at 7½d.	3	5	0
By 6 bolls potatoes, at 5s. the boll	1	10	0
By barley for kail, at 3lb a week	0	16	3
By a kail-yard, and a wretched house		13	0
By milk, at 4d. a week		17	4
By salt, cheese and butter		12	6
By soap for washing clothes		2	6
By coals in a year, and carriage	1	0	0
By shoes to the whole family	1	0	0
By body clothes to the man	1	10	0
By ditto to the woman and children	1	5	0
By worsted thread for mendings		7	0
	£17	18	3

The writer points out that this family 'manages' because of the small number of children, and the woman's ability to work. 'The greatest evils of their situation,' he adds, 'arise from the lowness of their diet, and the wretchedness of their lodging, which is cold, dark, and dirty.'

Moulin, Perthshire [27]

The following is an estimate of the expenses and earnings of a labouring man, his wife, and four children, the eldest under eight years, the youngest an infant:

SUBSISTENCE PER WEEK

3 pecks potatoes, at 4d.; 2 pecks of oatmeal, at 11d.; 2 pecks of bear meal at 7½d.; salt, milk, eggs, beer &c. 6d. Total 4s.7d., or £11.18.4 the year, from which, deducting 4 weeks subsistence of the man in harvest, at 1s.10d. the week, or 7s.7d., there remains £11.11s.

Rent of house and garden may be estimated at 15s., fuel at 20s., 12 carts of peats at 1s., 8 carts of turf at 8d., heath or wood 2s.8d., soap and blue for washing at 4s.6d., and oil for light at 2s. Total £2.1.6d.

The ashes will dung the garden, and pay the expense of digging and planting it with greens or potatoes.

Man's clothing: coat at 5s.9d., vest at 2s.4d., the lining of the coat and vest, and back of the latter, made out of the wife's old clothes; breeches and hose 4s., 2 pairs shoes 7s., 2 shirts 6s.9½d., also a great coat at 10s., and a bonnet at 1s., and handkerchief at 1s.6d.; these three last articles only once in two years, hence 6s.3d. Total £1.12.1½d. the year.

Wife's clothing: gown and petticoats at 16s.10½d., 2 shifts 5s.7½d., hose 8d., 1 pair shoes 4s., neck handkerchief 2s., apron 1s.6d., bodice 2s.3d., this last article once in two years; hence 1s.1½d. Total £1.11.9½d.

Children: 3 pairs shoes, 5s., jackets 13s.2d., shirts 4s.11d. Total £1.3.1d.

Bed clothes and household furniture are supposed to be provided either before marriage, or soon after it. It is also supposed, that the wife has provided so much body clothes, as will reduce the yearly expense of her own and the children's clothing one third.

Hence the annual expense of clothing the family will be:	3	8	9
Subsistence	11	11	0
House rent, fuel, &c.	2	1	6
	£17	1	3

The man earns, in 26 weeks, during spring and summer, at the rate of 6s. the week £7.16.0d. Four weeks in harvest (beside victuals) £1.6.0d. 22 weeks in autumn and winter, at 3s.6d., £3.17.0d. Total £12.19.0d.

The wife earns, by spinning or otherwise, 1s. the week, £2.12.0d. Man's earnings brought over, Total £15.11.0. Deficiency: £1.10.3d.

Although there appears to be a deficiency of earnings, after the charges have been estimated in the most frugal, and even scanty manner, and no allowance made for casual expenses, it is certain, that, in this country, people, who seem to have no livelihood but the fruits of their daily labour, do, by some means or another, bring up families, and even give their children such education as the nearest school affords.'

Kirkpatrick-Juxta, Dumfriesshire [28]

LABOURER'S BUDGET	EARNINGS		
The man earns, with victuals, 8d. a day for 265 days	8	16	8
Children's wages	1	0	0
Charity or presents		10	0
	£10	6	8

		EXPENSES	
Oat-meal, 40 stone, at 1s.8d. the stone	3	6	8
Butcher-meat	1	0	0
Wool, 2 stone, spun for clothes		12	0
Milk and butter	1	5	0
Salt		4	0
House rent		16	0
Barley, 4 stone		6	8
Shoes		15	0
Potatoes for seed, and bought		10	0
Linen, aprons etc		10	0
Lying-in and burials, etc		10	0
Peat		7	0
Tools, repairs of house and furniture		4	4
	£10	6	8

'I have omitted several articles of dress and finery, watch, pocket money at weddings, fairs, &c., education of children at school &c. How these can be defrayed by the earnings of the wife from harvest work or spinning beyond what is necessary for the family, 'tis difficult to conceive.'

The three budgets quoted above are all for agricultural workers – obviously by far the commonest type of labourer at the time.

The following is for a weaver and his family:

Caputh, Perthshire [29]

A weaver, his wife, and 3 small children, the eldest under 5 years of age, the youngest an infant.

EARNINGS PER WEEK

The earnings of the man and woman cannot be separated, as they are both employed in manufacturing the same piece of cloth.

Their earnings at a medium	0	9	0
Amount in the year	23	8	0

EXPENSES PER WEEK

Three pecks of oat-meal, & two of barley-meal	0	3	8
Milk, salt, onions, and potatoes	0	1	0
Butter, cheese, bacon, or other meat	0	0	8
Soap, starch, blue, and oil	0	0	6
Thread, thrum, and worsted	0	0	1
	£0	5	11
Amount in the year	£15	7	8
Excess of earnings	£8	0	4

ANNUAL EXPENSES

The man's wear of a suit, 4s.6d.; of a working jacket and breeches, 4s.; of a hat and handkerchief, 2s.	0	10	6
Of 2 shirts, 8s.; of a pair of shoes and a pair of stockings, 9s.	0	17	0
The woman's wear of gown and petticoats, 5s.; of 2 shifts, 6s.6d.; a pair of shoes, 4s.; of 2 aprons, 3s.	0	18	6
Of a pair of stockings, 1s.6d.; of handkerchiefs, caps, etc., 7s.	0	8	6
The children's wear	1	2	0
Fuel	0	12	0
Lying in, sickness and loss of time thereby, and burials, one year with another	1	5	0
Total	**£5**	**13**	**6**
Balance	**£2**	**6**	**10**

Rent of a house and garden, £1. The garden, dressed by the man in the mornings and evenings, affords them cabbages, greens, and potatoes, to the amount of the rent.'

With an annual balance of £2.6s.10d., this weaving family was in an enviable situation – although this was to change drastically in later years, after the advent of the power loom. At this time they were faring much better than the agricultural labourers, whose budgets were also shown above; more strikingly, their lot was infinitely better than that of the schoolmasters, some of whom (*see* Education) were paid as little as £5 per year, and had to eke out this pittance by working as session clerks, precentors, or even gravediggers.

The writer of the Doune, Perthshire, report mentions the wages of the highest earners in the cotton industry there as being two guineas a week; this was for piece work, judged by both quality and quantity. The Kincardine report points out that these wages are equal to the earnings of most ministers: 'A cotton spinner, in the second year after leaving the plough, gains annually a sum equal to the average of the stipends of the Church of Scotland, which are the recompence held forth for an expensive education of 15 years at least, and for many more perhaps of expectation.'[30] But the ministers themselves did not fare badly when compared with the schoolmasters; their salaries normally amounted to between £75 and £150 a year, some of which was paid in grain.

A final quotation, which is fairly typical of the whole country as regards wages, comes from Aberlemno, Angus: 'A male labouring servant's wages are from £5 to £8 a year; a female's £3; a good labouring married servant receives as wages about £6 sterling in money, a house and yard, the value of which is between 20s. and 30s., he gets a cow maintained through the year, and his fuel brought home; all which generally enable him to bring up a family.'[31]

Although the wage increases over the preceding years are mentioned frequently in the accounts, the period was in fact one of inflation, and most food items had risen in price. A comparative selection from around the country may therefore be of interest here:

Golspy (Golspie), Sutherland [32]

beef – 2½d.per lb
mutton – 2d. per lb
geese – 1s.6d.
ducks – 6d.
pork – 2½d. per lb
cheese – 4d. per lb

Kilmalie (inc. Fort William) [33]

beef and mutton – 2½d./3d. per lb
a goose – 2s.6d./3s.6d.
a duck – 1s.
a hen – 6d./8d.
butter – 8d. per lb
cheese – 6d. per lb
salmon – 3d/–4d.
eggs – 2d./3d. dozen
potatoes – 7d./9d.
pork – 3d.

Newburn, Fife [34]

beef – 3½d. per lb
mutton – 3½d. per lb
veal – 3½d. per lb
a hen – 1s.
a duck – 9d.
butter – 8d. per lb

Muirkirk, Ayrshire [35]

beef – 5d.–5½d. per lb
mutton – 4½d.–5d. per lb
veal – 6d.
pork – 5d.–6d.
cheese – 4s.–7s.6d. per stone
fowls – 9d.–1s. each
eggs – 3d.–5d. dozen

Kirkcudbright, Borders [36]

beef – 3d. per lb
mutton – 3½d. per lb
pork – 3½d. per lb
hens – 1s. each
eggs – 3d. dozen
butter – 7d. English lb
cheese – 5s.4d. stone

It will be seen that these prices are fairly constant throughout the country. Some writers point out, however, that prices could not be quoted for grain, which was very variable.

A useful summary comes from Halkirk, Caithness: 'The usual hire of a day-labourer is almost double what it was about twenty years ago. This is both natural and reasonable, because, as has been already observed, the expense of living has greatly increased in that period. It is various, according to the various jobs in which they are employed. The average here, per day, I would estimate at 9d.; and the sum necessary to support a family, consisting of man, wife, and four children, per week, at 3s.6d.'[37]

Something worthy of special note is that, following the severe scarcity of 1782, some of the poor people fell into penury, a fact brought out in the report for the North-East parish of Grange: 'Formerly every householder could command a draught of small-beer and killed a sheep out of his own little flock; but now the case is different; few of the poorer sort of householders can kill any sheep . . . Among the poor, the want of a nourishing diet, nay, the frequent want of even the very necessaries of life, which their industry is often not sufficient to procure for them, to which may be added, their wretched damp miserable uncomfortable houses, to which they enter through the dunghill, the putrid effluvia of which they breathe continually; and among the middling ranks, dejection of mind, consequent upon a change of circumstances from affluence and independence to struggling with debt and want, appear to be the principal causes of the prevailing distempers, and mortality in this parish.'[38] This picture of abject misery, it should be added, is not reflected in the vast majority of the reports.

One more aspect that should be mentioned, although again it appears in few parish accounts, is the very real advance in civil administration and rule of law which had taken place over the previous few decades. It is highlighted by the writer for Kildrummy, Aberdeenshire, when he describes life in an earlier era: 'The fortunes, persons, and lives of the people, were at the uncontrolled disposal of their petty, yet arbitrary chiefs; and the people were continually harassed by robberies, murders, and predatory wars, among their rapacious and capricious landlords . . . But the civil liberty and the equal distribution of justice which they now enjoy, costly as these blessings are, by affording some degree of security, both to their persons and their substance, hath produced among them a satisfaction and elevation of mind, unfelt in former times.'[39] The minister of Rannoch, Perthshire, noting that, previously, the parish was 'in an uncivilized barbarous state, under no check, or restraint of law,' added that, 'now the people know the security and protection which the law affords them.'[40] Perhaps, after all, the greatest advance in the mode of living towards the end of the eighteenth century was this – not simply the fact that many people possessed tea-kettles or clocks or watches, not that they could afford some fancy clothes for church or a piece of beef for their Sunday dinner, not even that they had a bed to lie on instead of heather or bracken, but that they could lie in their beds in relative peace and safety.

1. XII, 655	11. XVIII, 231	21. XIII, 387	31. XIII, 3
2. III, 281	12. VI, 306	22. XV, 325	32. XVIII, 421
3. XI, 632	13. VII, 502	23. III, 52	33. XVII, 144
4. XX, 34	14. XVI, 41	24. VII, 79	34. X, 689
5. XVII, 102	15. XVII, 556	25. XVII, 109	35. VI, 476
6. XII, 423	16. IV, 562	26. X, 46	36. V, 209
7. XIII, 562	17. XI, 60	27. XII, 757	37. XVIII, 81
8. V, 455	18. VI, 532	28. IV, 346	38. XVI, 214
9. II, 276	19. IX, 356	29. XII, 208	39. XIV, 545, 546
10. XII, 266	20. XIII, 255-56	30. XII, 551	40. XII, 433

4   FOOD

The SA, being concerned almost exclusively with the conditions of the ordinary folk of Scotland, has little to say of the food of the wealthier classes, although exceptionally the account for Montquhitter, Aberdeenshire, states that 'in summer and autumn a gentleman's table was fully supplied with lamb and mutton.' Although times were now beginning to change, it had been the custom in winter, even for the gentry, to have only salted meat (and heavily salted at that, so that strong spices were required to disguise the flavour) because of the necessity to slaughter most of the cattle at Martinmas. 'In winter and spring,' the Montquhitter chronicler continues, 'except poultry, whereof great numbers were extracted from the tenants, no fresh provisions can be procured but at the time when the mart, i.e. the fatted ox or cow, was killed, which, even in genteel families was an era of luxury and consequence. As tea was seldom drunk, breakfast consisted of pottage and strong beer, cold meat, fish, eggs etc.'[1]

In contrast to the above picture, meat appeared rarely on cottage menus throughout most of Scotland, the diet – wholesome but undeniably monotonous – being based predominantly upon cereals (oats and barley, and occasionally rye) and dairy foods, with the addition of eggs and cheese, fish in some areas, and potatoes. The only other vegetables mentioned to any extent are kail, carrots, onions and turnips; wild plants receive an occasional reference.

Probably the most useful and comprehensive summary comes from Speymouth: 'The diet of the labouring people here, and in general, all through the Lowlands of the North of Scotland, is porridge, made of oatmeal, with milk or beer, to breakfast; sowens (a kind of flummery, made of oatmeal, somewhat soured) with milk or beer, to dinner; and kail, i.e. greens or cabbage, boiled with oatmeal, to supper. With all these, they use bread of oatmeal, or what is called *household meal*, i.e. some mixture of barley, rye and pease. On Sundays they have generally barley broth, with some meat in summer and butter in winter. In places near the coast, they have sometimes fish. Turnips are sometimes used in place of cabbage or greens; and potatoes, dressed in different ways, with butter, milk, onions etc., is commonly a third of their food from the beginning of September to the end of March.'[2]

Here the lack of meat – except on Sundays and special occasions – is apparent. In contrast, however, the workers in the burghs (or at least the more prosperous of these) were becoming accustomed by this time to a more varied diet. Kelso provides a good example: 'Although the mechanics in town generally eat meat for dinner, the labourers in town and country seldom do so; but one and all of them live much upon hasty pudding, and boiled potatoes with milk;

without deviation, they all breakfast and sup upon the one or the other. Most of the adults eat of this food, at a meal, from 6 to 8 pounds weight, including milk; children eat in proportion.'[3]

Although in some areas there was a definite aversion to pork, it is mentioned as a common article of diet in a few of the accounts – for example in that for Kirkpatrick-Irongray in the Borders: 'When the corns are got in, they buy a pig, which they ring, and get liberty from their landlords to let it run about. This they feed upon offals and potatoes, which they get planted somewhere for work in harvest, and the animal becomes a good morsel at the end of March, and affords a mouthful now and then throughout the summer.'[4] Not surprisingly, in the villages around Crieff, where at the time of the great trysts many thousands of cattle were gathered, meat is fairly prominent. One such village is Foulis Wester: 'Such a farmer's family as that now described [cottars] feed chiefly on oatmeal, barley meal, potatoes, milk and cheese. What animal food they use is from Michaelmas to Whitsunday, and consists of one bullock fattened for winter beef, one hog in spring, and between 20 and 24 quarters of mutton purchased occasionally throughout the year.'[5] To most cottars in other parts of Scotland, particularly in the Highlands, this would have seemed high living indeed; for them, meat was reserved for the 'high days' – marriages, baptisms and funerals.

One item which was finding its way on to the tables of all who could afford it (and causing controversy in many places) was the still new-fangled tea. The writers of the accounts often use it as a barometer of the generally rising standard of living; some condemn its use outright, lamenting the loss of the more nourishing ale which was formerly drunk by all. For instance, the report from Mid-Calder, Lothians, states: 'Oatmeal made into porridge, and a thin, hard bread, made also of oatmeal, together with milk, butter and cheese, constitute a considerable part of the food, which is common to the inferior, as well as the middle classes of the people. Butcher meat is more in use than of late, and the practice of drinking tea is every day becoming more common.'[6] And from Dalmeny in the same county comes this observation: 'The food consists of oatmeal porridge, oatcakes and pease bannocks, barley-broth, with greens, potatoes, butter-milk and water. Some begin to use wheaten bread and small-beer, but seldom any eat butcher meat. The luxuries in which they indulge are tea, and what is worse, whisky.'[7] To some ministers, it almost seems at times that tea ranked far worse than whisky.

The extent to which ordinary folk had already become too dependent on potatoes – something which would lead to a disastrous situation with the failure of the crop in 50 years' time – is apparent in many of the accounts, notably in the Highland area. In that for Sleat, Skye: 'There is hardly any barley, the sea-ware growing on the shore being almost entirely laid out in manuring potatoes. That useful root is much, and indeed necessarily cultivated here, the inhabitants living great part of the year on potatoes, and various sorts of fish, chiefly herrings.'[8] And again in the Highlands, the Creich account has this to say: 'The people here are come into the practice of cultivating potatoes to a considerable amount, and find their account in it; they raise as many potatoes as, at an average, may be sufficient to supply the place of bread for four or five months of the year.'[9] This, it should be said, was only about half of the amount used in some other places. In Glenorchay and Inishail, Argyll, the account states: 'Nowhere are potatoes cultivated with more ease, or thrive better . . . For nine months of the year, potatoes make a great part of the food of the middling and lower ranks of people.'[10] This writer goes on to emphasise the immense improvements which the potato had brought: 'It may be said, with truth, that, till the general introduction of potatoes into this country, so little adapted, from soil and climate, to the growth of grain, the poor and lower classes pined away, nearly the half of their time, in want and hunger.' The number of other eulogies of 'this most valuable root' to be found throughout the whole account is far too great to mention.

To anyone with an interest in the history of nutrition, it is intriguing to look for mention of the dreaded disease scurvy, and to see whether, for example, a connection seems to be made between its incidence and vegetable consumption. As always with the SA, there is diversity in the replies, and a definite answer would certainly be difficult. The minister for St Fergus in the North-East writes: 'The scurvy, with which many here were affected, is not so general, owing perhaps to the more liberal use of vegetables . . . Every cottager now has his turnips, cabbages, and potatoes.'[11] And from Walls and Sandness, Shetland, comes this observation: 'Cabbages are produced in great plenty, and form a great part of the food of the lower people. They are considered a good corrective of scorbutic habits.'[12] There would seem to be less awareness in the report for Kinloss: 'The most prevalent distempers are cutaneous diseases, scurvy, rheumatism; owing, perhaps, to hard labour, the sharpness of the air, a spare or fish diet, and want of cleanliness.'[13] Again, scurvy is mentioned in the Blackford, Perthshire, account as being a common disease: 'The soil in this parish is not good; the effects of the cold are sensibly felt in retarding and marring the growth of vegetables. Most of the diseases, which take their rise from a cold damp air, prevail here, such as rheums and pulmonary complaints; but the scurvy is the most prevalent disease.'[14] In some places at least it is likely that wild fruits and plants gave protection against scurvy, which must certainly have been a hazard in the period before the potato crop was ready. The minister chronicler for Clunie, Perthshire, clearly no mean botanist, not only mentions hipthorns, hazel-nuts, brambles, wild raspberries, crowberries and cloudberries, but describes the use of various plants of which infusions were made for medical purposes – all with their Latin names.[15]

Scarcity of salt is a very real grievance which is stressed again and again; the 'iniquitous' salt laws are clearly seen as the cause of much hardship. The lack of this valuable commodity causes great resentment in the Western Isles especially, the reports making it clear that fish catches cannot be cured because of the scarcity. The Portree minister pleads: 'It would insure to the inhabitants a certain provision to their families for the year, and prevent a vast consumption of meal imported into the country, if a report was annually given in of the number of the small class of tenants, to whom a barrel of salt might be distributed upon oath, for the purpose of curing the relative quantity of herrings to be eat with their potatoes; even one barrel would totally change the face of affairs, where subsistence is so scanty, and population so overbearing. This trifling indulgence would contribute to the necessities of many thousands.'[16]

The Small Isles report contains a similar plea: 'The salt laws are an object of great complaint in this parish, as well as in its neighbourhood. The late alterations in these laws have facilitated the getting, at a moderate rate, salt for curing fish; but still the custom-house forms, to which every purchaser of salt must submit, may be considered as a real grievance. If a person wishes to procure two or three barrels of such salt, to cure fish for use of his family, he must enter it in a custom-house, if it should be 50 miles distant; there he must unship and re-pack it; and all this trouble and expense for a few barrels for his own family use. Such a grievance evidently needs a remedy.'[17] In the South of Scotland, too, ministers were speaking out against this particular form of injustice; in the Whithorn account, the writer claims that 'the salt-laws have a most unfriendly operation upon this parish and neighbour-hood; and need only to be read, to be condemned by every wise and patriotic statesman.'[18]

In addressing Sir John's questions on food, a great many of the writers make reference to – or frequently, enlarge upon – the years of scarcity, 1782-83, making it poignantly clear that this was a season in which the crops failed in large areas of the country, causing exceptional hardship.

In Cobrach, Banff, an explanation of the disastrous harvest is offered: 'So early as 15th September 1782, there was a great fall of snow, which laid all the corns, then hardly begun to fill, in most places. The frosts were often intense, and vegetation was stopt here. The corns which had milky juices in the ear were totally ruined; those which had only watery juices wanted season; there were none of them perfectly full or ripe. They were therefore given mostly unthreshed to the cattle. It was after Christmas before they were all cut. The meal made of what was threshed was bad.'[19] In the county of Banff, the minister of Grange paints a sad picture of the reduction of large numbers of agricultural workers to a state of abject penury which in many cases led to emigration – an instance in which the landowners are shown in a particularly unfavourable light. 'A succession of bad seasons and crops . . . greatly reduced the tenants,' he writes. 'This broke their spirit for industry and exertion, as they then laboured only for, and held their all at the discretion of the landowners, who from time to time seized and confiscated their whole effects for payment of their arrears, and left the poor families no resource, but to go to service, to begging, or to emigrate to the south country, or elsewhere in search of employment.'[20]

Further north, too, a tragic picture emerges from the accounts. Here is the description by the minister of the parish of Tarbat, East Ross-shire: 'The spring of the year 1782 falls to be noticed for a scarcity of provender, and the ruin of many families, both in the Highlands and low country, by the loss of their cattle, as the consequence of that scarcity . . . But those losses were forgotten in the miseries which followed them in the year 1783, from the failure of the crop of the previous year, and a real want of bread for the use of man. The want commenced early in the Highland parts of the country, and in January of that year (1783) many came down to this and other parishes of the low country, in search of provisions for their families; as the season advanced, their wants and numbers increased, and multitudes from the heights of both Ross and Sutherland might be daily seen traversing the different parishes, supplicating supplies of meal or corn, in any quantity, for their money; and a pitiable case it was, to see persons young and otherwise vigorous, in this condition, having hunger and distress of mind painted on their countenances.'[21]

The harsh attitude of the landowners recorded in the account for Grange above is not, it should be said, repeated in all the accounts; some indeed record acts of generosity, as in that for Gamrie, Banff: 'He [the landowner] was not like many others, who, when they saw a tenant thriving, thought he had too good a bargain, and would demand a very high rent at the next letting. It was his joy to see his tenants carrying on their improvements, and prospering by their honest industry . . . there are few tenants in the North of Scotland more thriving than in the parish of Gamrie.'[22] In similar vein, there are instances of heritors who, at the time of the scarcity, rendered invaluable service to the hard-hit people, for example in this heartening anecdote from Creich, Ross-shire: 'This parish, like others in the neighbourhood, was in great distress in summer 1783 and 1784, but especially in 1783. None however died for want. On several estates, the heritors procured victual to their tenants from time to time; the victual, sent by government, was distributed among most of the families of the parish. The poor were singularly indebted to a gentleman in Glasgow, of uncommon benevolence, who had lived in the parish when a boy, and who sent money, and five bolls of white pease, which were distributed among upwards of 80 persons, in proportion to their necessities. Some few removed with their families to the shores abounding with cockles etc., which were uncommonly plentiful that season, and supported them for some time. By these means the lives of the people were providentially preserved.'[23]

This is a striking feature of many of the accounts, as writer after writer affirms his belief that the survival of the people has been providentially assured in spite of the famine. In the report for Tain, East Ross-shire, it is again cockles which receive special mention: 'It is remarkable,' writes the minister, 'though cockles be not usually found on this bank, that, in 1783, when there was great scarcity of bread, it afforded, in April, May, June, immense quantities of them, of an excellent quality, which contributed to the support of multitudes, not only in this parish, but in the neighbourhood.'[24] In Kintail, it is herring: 'The dearth and scarcity of 1782, was not perceptible to the inhabitants. Since 1740, famine did not shew its face so much as in summer 1791, when 440 bolls of meal were imported, and sold in the parish at 18s.6d. the boll. The wound, however, was soon healed by the uncommon take of herring in Lochduich, the ensuing season.'[25] In Cabrach, Banffshire, it was livestock that saved the day: 'To some it may appear trivial, to others worthy to be remarked, that, in spring 1783, cows had calves much earlier, and in greater numbers than was ever remembered; a fortunate circumstance, in a year when the victual of home produce was excessively bad, and in a place where milk is a constituent part of ordinary fare. It was observed, too, very truly, that there was less sickness that year than usual.'[26]

Some writers go so far as to claim actual benefits from the scarcity. The recorder for Rosemarkie has this to say: 'In this country, the crops in a great measure failed in 1782 and 1783, which were remarkable hard for the farmers. Yet none here, at that time, were supposed to have died of real famine. The white pease and other grain from England, on the event of the peace, afforded a most seasonable supply to many poor families. One thing remarkable was, that in these years, severe as they were, fewer were sick among parishioners, than have been observed before or since . . . Another good effect proceeded also from this temporary scarcity – that various kinds of grain having been then imported, from England and other countries, they were sown in various soils, and on different farms; and according to the goodness of the produce, they were preserved and continued in the country. The early potatoes were particularly distinguished.'[27]

By far the most eloquent description of scarcity comes from the pen of the minister of Montquhitter, Aberdeenshire: 'When the era of industry and improvement commenced, it was fondly hoped that the wants known to our fathers would never be known among us. Our fields and gardens, said we, provide a variety of provision, which will infallibly preserve us from starving, even though our corn should fail. Thus the people reasoned, but to their reasoning the year 1782 gave the lie direct. The coldness and storminess of summer 1782 excited fears in the minds of the discerning; but none suspected the magnitude of the impending evil. On 5th of October, when oats and barley were generally green, a frost, armed with almost the rigour of a Greenland climate, desolated in one night the hope of the husbandman. The grain, immediately attracting a hoary whiteness, ripened no more . . . Complete and hopeless ruin stared us in the face; and all ranks indulged the views of gloomy despondence. If, at this critical period, the American war had not ceased; if the copious magazines, particularly of pease, provided for the navy, had not been brought to sale, what a dire scene of desolation and horror would have been exhibited in the country! From these magazines, the exertion of heritors and people received regular supplies. Cattle sold extremely well. By the divine blessing, health in an eminent degree prevailed. The efforts of industry were redoubled. Many a precious hoard of gold and silver was unlocked; and temperance, stern but friendly, established her reign on the solid base of necessity.'[28]

With the obvious exception of this period of extreme hardship, it is still apparent that by this final decade of the eighteenth century the living standards of many of the poor people of Scotland were at last beginning to rise. That the improvement included food is apparent from many of the accounts. 'Tradesmen do not live nearly so much on oatmeal as they did 50 years ago,' writes the chronicler from Kilwinning, Ayrshire. 'There is scarcely one of their families in which tea, with wheaten bread, is not used for breakfast; and very few that do not drink it in the afternoon. Farmers, tradesmen, and day-labourers live a good deal on butcher meat, with potatoes.'[29] And in Mains, Angus: 'The children at school have wheaten bread, sweet milk, butter, cheese, eggs, and sometimes roast meat.'[30] An amusing dictum from the account for Keith-Hall and Kinkell, Aberdeenshire, makes a fitting conclusion for this section: 'It has been said, that the people of Kintore and Inverury put all their money in their bellies, and those of Keith-Hall and Kinkell on their backs.'[31]

It would be hard to deny the sheer monotony of Scotland's diet – at least that of the bulk of the working people – with its heavy reliance on oatmeal, barley and potatoes, along with dairy foods and fish, and its extremely limited selection of vegetables and virtual absence of fruit. What is equally undeniable, however, is the highly favourable assessment of the general health of the people which comes across in the vast majority of the reports in reply to Sir John's questions on this subject. It is hard to escape the conclusion that their frugal but nourishing diet was at least to some extent responsible, and that those who had escaped the many hazards of childhood were indeed a people of outstanding physique, capable of quite astonishing feats of strength and endurance (*see* Health).

1. XV, 340	9. XVIII, 338	17. XX, 249	25. XVII, 529
2. XVI, 675	10. VIII, 112	18. V, 548	26. XVI, 120
3. V, 256	11. XVI, 415	19. XVI, 120	27. XVII, 614
4. V, 256	12. XIX, 527	20. XVI, 215	28. XV, 332
5. XII, 447	13. XVI, 620	21. XVII, 649	29. VI, 352
6. II, 96	14. XII, 87	22. XVI, 191	30. XIII, 490
7. II, 729	15. XII, 231	23. XVIII, 338	31. XV, 236
8. XX, 207	16. XX, 205	24. XVII, 626	

5 FUEL

It is probably unlikely that most readers of the first SA, if asked to list the important factors determining the happiness and comfort of the poorer Scots folk in the late eighteenth century, would even think of including fuel. Yet even the most superficial reading of these parish accounts will soon reveal that the availability of cheap fuel was indeed considered an immense advantage, while its lack caused almost unbelievable hardship.

Two excerpts from accounts from the Western Isles will immediately make this clear. The Small Isles account states: 'Isle Muck, within itself, is ill provided in fuel . . . In winter 1790 and 1791, there was a general scarcity of firing throughout this parish, which Isle Muck most severely felt. They were reduced to the necessity of burning different kinds of furniture, such as beds, dressers, stools, barrels; and also house timber, divots, tangles, straw etc., to dress their victuals.'[1] Contrast this picture of misery with the comfortable state of a parish in which fuel was abundant, as in Kilchoman, Islay: 'No country is better supplied with fire and water. Almost every farm has peat moss within itself, of an excellent kind, affording charcoal for the smith, as we have no coals. These peats, and the fish oil they burn in lamps, make the habitation of the meanest cottages warm and cheery.'[2] It is perhaps no coincidence that the writer goes on to say that in this parish 'they are as contented with their lot as most people, as they have the comforts and conveniences of life in a reasonable degree,' and proceeds to list – an almost unique feature in the Hebridean accounts – the games and amusements which are common among them.

Peat was still the principal fuel in most parishes of the Highlands and Islands. The trouble was that the labour involved took up a disproportionate amount of time – a complaint voiced in a great many accounts. That for Kilfinan, Argyll, sums up the position succinctly: 'The making, preparing, and leading of peats consumes the greatest part of the people's time in summer,' – a statement which could doubtless be echoed by many peat-users today. The people of the eighteenth century, however, faced an additional deterrent. 'Too often,' the Kilfinan writer goes on, 'in spite of all their labour and attention, they lose most of them, from the wetness of the climate, and the softness of the roads.'[3]

In some parishes which lacked the benefit of peat, the poor often resorted to other substances; for instance the account for Kinnoull, Perthshire, states that 'some of the poor use brushwood, and some of them make a kind of peat of culm, or dross of coals, mixed with cow-dung.'[4] It is interesting too to note the widespread use of broom in certain areas, as in Abernyte, Perthshire: 'In summer the peasantry burn only broom and furze, which they frequently have for the cutting, at all times for a small price. The light lands in the hills, after being a year or two out of tillage, are over-run with broom. Indeed, about 40 years ago, when the excessive badness of the roads rendered the transportation of fuel difficult, it was reckoned no inconsiderable improvement to sow out light lands with broom for fuel.'[5]

But wherever coal was to be had, the people wanted it. In some places, where it was accessible and relatively cheap, this is invariably marked out as a cause for gratitude; whereas in other parishes, particularly those in Perthshire, distance from coal is a strongly-felt grievance. Out of many possible examples, the account for Trinity Gask offers this useful summary: 'One great disadvantage, under which the inhabitants of this parish labour, is their distance from fuel. The works from which coals is generally procured, are distant about 20 miles, and the roads far from being good. Half the summer is spent in bringing home as much coal as is necessary for the winter's supply. Peats are procured from the moss of the higher grounds, but not without great labour and waste of time. And it is obvious, that the time and labour which the necessary provision of fuel requires, must be equally unfavourable to the industry of the mechanic and of the farmer. These disadvantages, however, are common to many places in the neighbourhood.'[6] The people of Caputh, Perthshire, had even further to go for their coal. 'Peat and turf, broom and furze were formerly the only fuel used in this district. To these, coal is now added . . . They justly reckon it cheaper, as it is more easily procured, than any other kind of fuel. In summer, the farmers sometimes go 30 or 40 miles to the coal pits in Fife, where it is purchased at a comparatively low price.'[7]

Two other factors emerge from the accounts. One is the health hazard posed by fuel scarcity. For example the Dornoch account states: 'The diseases most prevalent here, among females, seem to be stomach and hysteric complaints. All these seem to arise from cold, poor diet, comfortless lodgings, and scarcity of fuel. The common mode of providing for winter firing here, is peculiarly injurious to health. During the season, in which the poor people are employed in carrying it out of the hills, they go to the moss, or so far in their way toward it in the evening; lie out in the open air all night, and load their horses in the morning. The great distance, badness of the roads, weakness of their horses, and scantiness of pasture, impose this cruel necessity.'[8] One group of poor people who, although they suffered many deprivations, certainly did not lack the benefit of ready fuel, were those who had settled on the great mosses of the central belt. (*see* Mosses)

Another feature of many of the accounts, arising from discussion of the difficulties involved in transport of coal, is a repeated plea for the construction of canals – sometimes with elaborate details on how best these may be achieved. One such is the Aberfoyle account, which includes the suggestion that the upper Forth be rendered navigable for small vessels.

If the universal complaint in the Perthshire reports is distance from coals, that of many of the Argyll ones is the sheer iniquity of the coal tax. This is summed up in the account for Inveraray: 'The heavy duty, laid on coals carried coastwise, appears to be as unreasonable as it is impolitic, and is universally complained of, as an intolerable burden; and, with respect of the whole of Argyleshire, so

45

unproductive that it is not equal to the expense of the officers employed in collecting it . . . A change of the laws in that respect, would, therefore, be very desirable, for, until that takes place, an insuperable bar lies in the way of every improvement in agriculture, and of every establishment in manufacture.'[9]

Nor were these grievances felt only on the West Coast. In Cummertrees, Dumfriesshire, a more nationalistic note appears: 'The duty on water-borne coal appears the more grievous and partial to the people on the Scotch side of the Frith, because their neighbours on the English side are exempted from it, although it is difficult to determine upon what principle such exemption was founded. Many applications have been made to government upon this subject, but the duty remains unrepealed, to the great obstruction of the improvement and cultivation of the country.'[10] Some recorders have no hesitation in linking the coal tax with high rates of emigration. 'There is not one sensible man in Galloway,' the writer for the parish of Urr claims boldly, 'who will or can deny, that if the tax on coals had been suppressed ten years ago the king would have had 10,000 subjects more in the maritime part of the country.' Later on he adds: 'If to what has already been observed, we add this unquestionable truth, that nine tenths of the diseases, which afflict the poorer part of the people, are those of debility, and chiefly arise from cold, it can hardly be wondered at, that the above tax has been productive of considerable discontent, and much emigration.'[11]

All of the above quotations come from reports received by Sir John before 1793. During that year the hated tax was at last repealed. Interestingly, the writer for Borgue, Galloway, begins by complaining bitterly of the tax, asserting that local farmers are being forced to spend much of their summer getting peats. Having heard the glad news, he then writes: 'It is with no small pleasure, that the author of this report has just received intelligence, that the duty on coals is taken off. The advantages of this will soon be felt by all ranks; and it will scarcely admit of a doubt, that in a short time it will prove equally advantageous to the State.'[12]

The writer of another Galloway account, that for Kirkinner, sums up vividly the misery endured by large numbers of poor people in Scotland at that time: 'A human being pinched with cold, when confined within doors, is always an inactive being. The day-light, during the winter, is spent by many of the women and children in gathering *elding*, as they call it, that is, sticks, furze, or broom, for fuel, and the evening in warming their shivering limbs before the scanty fire which this produces.'[13] It is perhaps salutary for those who read these words today to have their imaginations stirred – to conceive the sheer misery of a cold winter in a damp house with little or no fire; but much more difficult to picture a starving family with possibly no food other than potatoes, yet lacking the fuel with which to cook them.

1. XX, 244	5. XI, 26	9. VIII, 139	13. V, 424
2. XX, 391	6. XI, 612	10. IV, 70	
3. VIII, 230	7. XII, 207	11. V, 376	
4. XI, 311	8. XVIII, 361	12. V, 44	

6   CUSTOMS

Marriage

The modern reader probably approaches this section of the SA expecting some unusual features – the irregularities of Gretna, for example, or the much maligned Penny Bridals – although it is perhaps some of the less well-known aspects which may cause more surprise. For instance it was common for young men to marry very much older women so as to enjoy the 'comforts of life' which their savings made possible, and for men to marry very young so as to escape being drafted into the navy. Immediate re-marriage of widowed persons was not unusual. As always with the SA, it is the variety which makes for much of the interest; while in some areas early marriage was discouraged through the scarcity of accommodation for married farm servants, in others it is clearly the norm.

In the entry for Graitney (Gretna) the minister, not altogether surprisingly, inveighs strongly against the local irregular marriage ceremonies: 'This parish has long been famous in the annals of matrimonial adventure, for the marriages of fugitive lovers from England, which have been celebrated here. People living at a distance erroneously suppose, that the regular and established clergyman of this parish is the celebrator of those marriages: whereas the persons who follow this illicit practice, are mere impostors, who have no right whatever, either to marry, or to exercise any part of that clerical function. There are, at present, more than one of this description in this place. But the greatest part of the trade is monopolised by a man who was originally a tobacconist, and not a blacksmith, as is generally believed. He is a fellow without literature, without principles, without morals, and without manners. His life is a continued scene of drunkenness . . . The following is a copy of one of the certificates of marriage: "This is to sartsay all persons that may be consernid, that AB from the parish of C and in county of D, and EF from the parish of G and in county of H, and both comes before me and declayred themselfs both to be single persons, and now mayried by the form of the Kirk of Scotland, and agreiable to the Church of England, and givine ondre my hand, this 18th day of March, 1793."

'Is it not a disgrace to the police of a civilised country, to permit such irregularities to be practised with impunity? And is it not a reflection on the good sense and discernment of the Nobility and Gentry of England (for some of the English Nobility have been married here), to suffer themselves, to be imposed upon, and their pockets to be picked, by such miscreants?'[1] This practice being confined to a single place, it is not possible to compare the views of different ministers on such an intriguing subject!

Many writers disapproved of or roundly condemned the common Penny Bridals (*see* Games and Amusements). In contrast, the writer for Avoch in the Black Isle offers the following account without comment: 'Marriages, in this place, are generally conducted in the style of penny weddings. Little other fare is provided, except bread, ale, and whisky. The relatives, who assemble in the morning, are entertained to a dram and a drink *gratis*. But, after the ceremony is performed, every man pays for his drink. The neighbours then convene in great numbers. A fiddler or two, with perhaps a boy to scrape on an old violoncello, are engaged. A barn is allotted for the dancing; and the house for drinking. And thus, they make merry for two or three days, till Saturday night. On Sabbath, after returning from church, the married couple give a sort of dinner to the present friends on both sides. So that those weddings, on the whole, bring little gain or loss to the parties.'[2]

While it is easy to see from some of the reports that these bridal feasts could and did lead to disorder, drunkenness and quarrelling – the Montquhitter, Aberdeen-shire, report describes the Penny Bridal as 'this scene of feasting, drinking, dancing, wooing, fighting' – it is also, surely, easy to understand how it was that the three principal domestic events of marriages, births, and deaths provided rare holidays, and opportunities for social gatherings in a life which, for most, consisted of an unceasing round of toil. These were at the same time occasions on which generosity and hospitality – strongly present in the Scottish character alongside the more commonly recognised frugality – were allowed free rein. The account for Methlick, Aberdeenshire, reflects this aspect: 'They are a social people; as one evidence of their being so, there may be sometimes 60, 70, and sometimes 100 at a wedding, to the expense of which the guests contribute, by sending some milk, butter, cheese, poultry etc., and some send stone plates and stone jugs.'[3] The use of stoneware was perhaps only prudent under the circumstances?

It is in Ayrshire that we come across the intriguing custom in which the local innkeeper is employed as go-between in the betrothal arrangements. Thus in the account for Galston: 'A singular custom prevails here. When a young man wishes to pay his addresses to his sweetheart, instead of going to her father's, and professing his passion, he goes to a public-house; and, having let the landlady into the secret of his attachment, the object of his wishes is immediately sent for, who almost never refuses to come. She is entertained with ale and whisky, or brandy; and the marriage is concluded on. The second day after the marriage, a *creeling*, as it is called, takes place. The young wedded pair, with their friends, assemble in a convenient spot. A small *creel*, or basket, is prepared for the occasion, into which they put some stones. The young men carry it alternately, and allow themselves to be caught by the maidens, who have a kiss when they succeed. After a great deal of innocent mirth and pleasantry, the creel falls at length to the young husband's share, who is obliged to carry it generally for a long time, none of the young women having compassion on him. At last, his fair mate kindly relieves him from his burden; and her complaisance, in this particular, is considered as a proof of her satisfaction with the choice she has made. The creel goes round again; more merriment succeeds, and all the company dines together, and talk over the feats of the field.'[4]

The bearing which late marriages could have on the size of the population, as well as on the vigour of the children produced, is one aspect which a few accounts mention; for example the Elgyn (Elgin) account states: 'The most favourable size of farms, to make a country populous, is from 15 to 40 acres of arable land. The occupiers of such farms marry early . . . But when the farms are over-grown, they are mostly inhabited by servants and day-labourers; and every measure is tried to keep wages and the price of labour low, by which marriage is discouraged.' And later: 'Luxury and its certain attendant, an exorbitant expense of living, most materially affects population. It discourages marriage, until persons acquire an income, adequate in their estimation, to that state; or, in other words, until they are advanced in years, and then a puny helpless race of children is produced. Hence, how many men of every description remain single? And how many young women of every rank are never married?'[5]

Nearby, in the parish of Liff and Bervie, Angus, it seemed that at least some of the young men had found a short-cut to the desired material standards, through marriage with older women whose years of thrift had paid off. Yet here again the writer of the report saw the practice as adversely affecting population increase: 'In cases of marriage here, it often happens, that the man is far less advanced in years than the woman he marries. The former depends very much on the experience of the latter, and generally too on the savings of her industry, to enable him to begin with some comfort a married life. The disparity of years happening on the side of the woman, must needs be a hindrance to population.'[6] In some areas marriages appear to be strongly discouraged, generally because of a bias against married farm workers on the part of farmers. One such example comes from Kinnettles, again in Angus: 'Since the inclosing and labouring of ground with attention have taken place, that accommodation for married servants is withdrawn, and other servants are thereby discouraged from marrying. The servant finds, too, that when married, he cannot so easily find a place with a farmer, whom, perhaps, he would be most willing to serve; nor are masters, in general, fond of retaining married servants. In fact there is no class among whom marriages are so infrequent, as farmers' servants.'[7]

The frequency and speed of re-marriage forms the substance of the Stornoway report on this theme: 'The common people of this island marry very early, and when death separates them, if the surviving party, whether male or female, finds it convenient to engage a second or third time in that state, some of them remain a few weeks, and some only a few days, in widowhood; so that grief for the loss of husband or wife is an affliction little known among the lower class of people here. A woman in this country, whose husband shot himself accidentally, by an unguarded management of a firelock, settled her contract of marriage, *in the way she thought fit*, before the body of her late husband was interred, and was married the next day after she performed that last duty to the deceased.'[8] Marriage would seem to have been equally popular in the Northern Isles, although the reason given by one of the writers there is somewhat different; the minister of Walls and Sandness, Shetland, writes that 'one reason why few young men remain unmarried is, because, if not married, they are sure to be fixed upon by the landmasters, for the service of the navy, when a draft for that service is required from the country; and rather than be forced from their native soil, and the society of their friends, they will submit to many inconveniences.'[9] One wonders whether the humour was intentional?

Many curious superstitions were associated with marriage; for example taboos concerning certain days or months of the year considered inauspicious. (These are looked at more closely in the chapter on Character.)

Burials

Funerals in the eighteenth century were great occasions in which the entire community generally played a part, often accompanied by much feasting and even revelry. Considering the unceasing round of toil which was the lot of most of the common folk at the time, this is more easily understood. But more than this comes through in the various accounts. A notable feature is the very great attention paid to the bereaved family from the moment, it seems, that the death occurred. Visits of condolence, presents of food, taking turns to watch the corpse (some areas held a 'lyke-wake', or watching of the dead) were the order of the day. And while those who penned the reports are obviously aware of the benefits of such neighbourly offices, they are also clearly concerned about their negative consequences: there was inevitably a great deal of eating and drinking, leading not only at times to riotous excesses but often to the impoverishment of the bereaved family. Some of the comments are very similar to those made about the ubiquitous Penny Bridals.

From Carmunnock, near Glasgow, comes a comment in which inordinate expense is the main concern: 'It is usual in this parish, as in many other parts of Scotland, to invite on such occasions, the greater part of the country around; and though called to attend at an early hour in the forenoon, yet it is generally towards evening, before they think of carrying forth the corpse to the church-yard for the interment. While, on these occasions, the good folk are assembled, though they never run into excess, yet no small expense is incurred by the family; who often vie with those around them, in giving, as they call it, an honourable burial to their deceased friend. Such a custom is attended with many evils, and frequently involves in debt, or reduces to poverty, many families otherwise frugal and industrious, by this piece of useless parade, and ill-judged expense.'[10]

The minister of Kilmaurs, Ayrshire, in similar vein but with a somewhat more acid pen, also deplores this custom: 'No unusual customs prevail among the inhabitants of this parish. There is one indeed common to the whole country, that of gathering many people together, and entertaining them at considerable expense when they bury their dead. However ill it may be afforded, nothing must be spared that custom has sanctioned. By exploding this in a great measure, many would have it in their power to do more essential acts of kindness to their friends and relations when living. There is little merit in burying those whom we help to starve. Nor do the deceased feel or enjoy any of the gratifications of vanity or misplaced veneration, which prompt to this custom.'[11]

In milder vein, the account for Tongue, Sutherland, informs us that 'burials in this parish are conducted with great decorum. None, even of the common people, attend without a particular invitation. After some entertainment (for at the burial of the poorest here, there is a refreshment given, consisting of whisquy beath, or some foreign liquor, butter and cheese, with oat bread), the friends of the deceased, and neighbours of the village, who come to witness the interment, are drawn up in rank and file, by an old serjeant, or some veteran who has been in the army, and who attends to maintain order, and give, as they term it here, the word of relief. Upon his crying Relief! the four under the bier prepare to leave their stations, and make room for [an] other four, that instantly succeed. This progression is observed, at the interval of every five minutes, till the whole attendants come in regularly; and if the distance requires it, there is a second, a third, or a fourth round of such evolutions gone through. When the persons present are not inflamed with liquor, which is now seldom the case, there is a profound silence generally observed, from the time the corpse has been taken up, till the interment is over.'[12]

The ringing of bells at funerals seems to have been fairly common, a hand bell – perhaps a less ceremonious form of tolling – being customary. Thus in the Lothians parish of Borrowstowness: 'At the burials of the poor people . . . the beadle perambulates the streets with a bell, and intimates the death of the individual in the following language: "All brethren and sisters, I let ye to wit, there is a brother (or sister) departed, at the pleasure of the Almighty, (here he lifts his hat) called —. All those that come to the burial, come at — o'clock. The corpse is at —." He also walks before the corpse to the churchyard, ringing his bell.'[13] (There were certain lingering superstitions in some districts, one being the belief that the ghost of the person buried kept the gate of the churchyard till relieved by the next.)

A sad note which enters into several of the accounts when addressing Sir John's question on burials is the high proportion of child deaths (*see* Health and Welfare). One minister states that 'it is generally allowed that more than half die before the age of 10 years.' And in the account for Collington, Edinburgh, the writer, quoting from the register of burials over the previous 49 years, states that 'of the 944 persons buried, 452, or nearly one half, were children under 14 years of age.'[14]

Use of the parish mort-cloth (or pall) was one of the main ways of raising funds for the support of the poor. Consternation was caused, therefore, when the local body of colliers in Newton, Lothians, decided to provide their own: 'They purchased a set of mort-cloths, the use of which was given, gratis, to the contributors. The body of carters, who have a fund of the same kind, followed their example. As the great body of the parish consists of these two descriptions of people, the kirk session foresaw, that this practice, if allowed to continue, would soon go nearly to extinguish altogether the funds arising from the use of the parish mort-cloths.'[15] Another reference to the poor is found in which the Campsie report states that 'when a pauper dies, it is customary for the session to provide the coffin and winding-sheet, and mort-cloth, gratis. And if there shall be no relation of the deceased in the parish, to contribute for the little entertainment necessary at the funeral, which seldom happens, 5 shillings is allowed for such expense.'[16]

Several writers mention the complications arising from the common practice of having burials in the place of birth rather than that of residence. 'According to a prejudice of a very ancient date,' writes the recorder for Borthwick, Lothians, 'the common wish is to be buried with our fathers; and from the change of residence, which ever must take place among the great body of the people, and the fluctuating state of all human affairs, there are not above two farmers in these bounds who bury in this place. They carry their deceased friends elsewhere; and, in return, the dead are brought here from neighbouring parishes, and sometimes from a very considerable distance.'[17]

As a final illustration, the description of a traditional Scottish funeral, from Campsie, Stirlingshire, makes interesting reading: 'It was customary, till within these few years, when any head of a family died, to invite the whole parish. They were served on boards in the barn, where a prayer was pronounced before and after the service, which duty was most religiously observed. The entertainment consisted of the following parts: first, there was a drink of ale, then a dram, then a piece of shortbread, then another dram of some other species of liquor, then a piece of currant-bread, and a third dram either of spirits or wine, which was followed by loaves and cheese, pipes and tobacco . . . A funeral cost, at least, a hundred pounds Scots, to any family who followed the old course.'[18]

1. IV, 191	6. XIII, 395	11. VI, 334	16. IX, 254
2. XVII, 324	7. XIII, 329	12. XVIII, 481	17. II, 78
3. XV, 318	8. XX, 38	13. II, 712	18. IX, 254
4. VI, 224	9. XIX, 526	14. II, 139	
5. XVI, 608	10. VII, 173	15. II, 365	

7 GAMES AND AMUSEMENTS

Undoubtedly the most noticeable thing about the recreational habits of the Scots of the late eighteenth century is the sheer lack of them. In the vast majority of accounts, no amusements are recorded whatsoever. It may well be that, as in many poor countries today, most people were far too busy scraping a meagre living to have time or energy for any recreation; indeed, many writers give a distinct impression that life is far too serious for such frivolity. Yet, as always with the SA, it is unwise – even impossible – to generalise; the state of affairs in one parish bears remarkably little relation to that in a neighbouring one. An example of this diversity comes from Drainy, Morayshire: 'Their general character is that of a sober, honest, peaceable people . . . rather grave than lively, seldom indulging themselves in any relaxation or diversion, excepting the young people, who sometimes take a dance at Christmas, or at a penny-wedding.'[1] In contrast, the Birnie account states that 'music is the people's favourite diversion. Some of them can play on the bagpipe, and others on the violin.'[2]

The contrast is particularly marked, too, among the reports for the Western Isles. What comes across all too vividly in the great majority is the grim, unending struggle for survival. Here and there we do find brief mention of the people's fondness for singing and dancing; a Tiry (Tiree) report recounts that they 'frequently entertain themselves by composing and singing songs, by repeating Fingalian and other tales, and by dancing assemblies at different farms by turns.'[3] Of all the island accounts, however, a single one stands out in almost total contrast. From Kilchoman, Islay, it is very clear throughout that the tenants there enjoy the advantages of an unusually benevolent regime, which allows time and opportunity for recreation: 'They are in general, as contented with their situation as most people, as they have the comforts and conveniences of life in a reasonable degree . . . The dance and the song, with shinty and putting the stone, are their chief amusements. Numbers of them play well on the violin and bagpipe. They have a natural ease and gracefulness of motion in the dance, which is peculiar to themselves.'[4]

Surprisingly, Christmas festivities receive fairly prominent mention. The account for Duffus, Morayshire, contains this reference: 'That horror of the name of *holidays* (holy days), which was once a characteristic of the Puritans, and true blue Presbyterians, never took possession of our common people here; and they still celebrate (perhaps without ever thinking of the origin of the practice), St John's day, St Stephen's day, Christmas day etc., by assembling in large companies to play at foot-ball, and to dance and make merry.'[5] In Kirkden, Angus, the writer singles out Christmas thus: 'Christmas is held as a great festival in this neighbourhood. On that day "the servant is free from his master", and goes about visiting his friends and acquaintances. The poorest must have beef and mutton on the table . . . Many amuse themselves with various diversions, and particularly with shooting for prizes, called here *wad-shooting*. And many do little business all the Christmas week; the evening of almost every day being spent in amusement.'[6]

In a significant number of accounts, however, it is the Penny Bridals – vilified by some, grudgingly allowed by others, approved by almost none – which feature as the principal, if not the only, occasions of real revelry (*see* Customs). The writer for Montquhitter, Aberdeenshire, offers, more than a little contemptuously, one of the most detailed descriptions: 'People who are not regularly and profitably employed rejoice in a holiday, as the means of throwing off that languor which oppresses the mind, and of exerting their active powers. So it was with our fathers . . . The market-place was to the peasant, what the drawing-room is to the peer, the theatre of shew and of consequence. The scene, however, which involved every amusement and every joy of an idle and illiterate age, was the *penny bridal*. When a pair were contracted, they, for a stipulated consideration, bespoke their wedding dinner at a certain tavern, and then ranged the country in every direction to solicit guests. One, two, or even three hundred would have convened on these occasions, to make merry at their own expense for two or more days.'[7] (It may be added that, although this writer appears to consign these celebrations to a past age, others do not.)

One cannot help noting that other writers record the seriousness and sobriety of the people with as much contempt as the one quoted above deplores their dissipation. Here is the picture painted by the writer for St Andrew's, Llanbryd, Morayshire: 'Funerals are conducted without expense; there is no company or dancing on the occasion of a wedding; nor at baptisms, in general, is there any kind of entertainment. Almost the only pleasure they indulge in is meeting occasionally, to the number of 15 or 25, for the purpose of conversing about some of the abstrusest doctrines of Calvinism, in which they display their eloquence in the only kind of spouting in which they have any notion.'[8]

The account for Old Kilpatrick, Dunbartonshire, displays a tolerant attitude on local revelry: 'They meet together occasionally, and make merry. Their chief amusement is dancing, and upon these occasions there is a pleasing cheerfulness and innocence among them.'[9] Not so, it would seem, in the village of Tammtoul (Tomintoul) described by the reporter for Kirkmichael, Banffshire: 'All of them sell whisky, and all of them drink it. When disengaged from this business, the women spin yarn, kiss their inamoratos, or dance to the discordant notes of an old fiddle.'[10] Much more genteel, one imagines, is the scene in the county town of Banff where the town house has two drawing rooms, 19ft wide and 33ft long, and where 'during the winter season, there are dancing assemblies once a fortnight.'[11] Most genteel of all, perhaps, and with the longest list of amusements to be found anywhere, is Montrose. After mentioning 'social visits at all seasons', a monthly club for gentlemen, visits to the wells or the countryside in summer, 'exhibitions to gratify curiosity and increase knowledge', golf, bowls, billiards, cards, shooting, winter assemblies 'conducted with the greatest decorum,' and plays, the writer continues: 'At Christmas and the New Year, the opulent burghers begin to feast with their friends, and go on a round of visits, which takes up the space of many weeks. Upon these occasions, the gravest is supposed to be merry, and to join in a chearful song.'[12]

There are brief mentions of a few sports – sometimes only in a single reference. In Kilwinning, Ayrshire, it is archery: 'After the invention of firearms, archery was laid aside, as no longer useful and necessary in war. Though for this reason it was disused in most other places in Scotland, it has been practised here, as an elegant and manly amusement, almost without any interruption, to the present day.'[13] In Kirkmichael, Perthshire, it is football: 'a common amusement with the schoolboys.'[14] Here too we find the custom of holding cock-fighting contests on Shrove Tuesday. Cock-fighting receives prominent mention also in the Applecross account, where the dues form part of the schoolmaster's salary (as they also did elsewhere): 'The schoolmaster's salary is 200 merks Scotch; he hath no perquisites, but the quarter payments, of 1s. 6d. for English scholars, and 2s. 6d. for Latin and arithmetic, and the cock-fight dues, which are equal to one quarter's payment for each scholar.'[15]

From Stevenston on the Ayrshire coast: 'Saltcoats is the principal watering place in Ayrshire. From 300 to 500 people usually resort there, during the Summer months, for sea-bathing, from the inland country, especially from the towns of Paisley, Glasgow, and Hamilton.'[16]

From Scone, Perthshire, an intriguing description is offered of a game nowhere else mentioned, played each Shrove Tuesday between bachelors and married men. The teams having been drawn up at the Cross of Scone, a ball was thrown up, and the game proceeded from 2pm until sunset. 'The object of the married men was to hang the ball, i.e. to put it three times into a small hole in the moor; that of the bachelors was to drown it, i.e. to dip it three times into a deep place in the river. The party who could effect either of these objects, won the game.'[17]

It need scarcely be said that it is for references to the two ancient games of curling and golf that one looks most eagerly in the pages of the SA. Several mentions are made of curling, although considerably fewer than might have been expected. In Drysdale, Dumfriesshire, 'sometimes scores of people assemble on the waters, and in the most keen, yet friendly manner, engage against one another, and usually conclude the game and day with a good dinner, drink, and songs.'[18] The convivial nature of the game is also underlined in the most detailed description, which comes from the Muirkirk, Ayrshire, report: 'The chief amusement in winter is *curling*, or playing stones on smooth ice; they eagerly vie with one another who shall come nearest the mark, and one part of the parish against another – one trade or occupation against another – and often one whole parish against another – earnestly contend for the *palm*, which is generally all the prize, except perhaps the victors claim from the vanquished, the dinner and bowl of toddy, which, to do them justice, *both* commonly take together with great cordiality, and, generally, without any grudge on the fortune of the day.' This writer, on a magnanimous note, adds: 'The amusement is healthful; it is innocent; it does no body harm; let them enjoy it.'[19] From Wamphray, Dumfriesshire: 'We have but one general amusement, that of curling on the ice; and the parishioners take much credit for their superior skill in this engaging exercise. After the play is over, it is usual to make a hearty meal upon beef and greens, in the nearest public house.'[20]

The references to the royal and ancient game of golf are, to say the least, disappointing. After turning with some eagerness to the St Andrews account, one reads merely that there is a large tract of 'downs or bents' which, besides providing pasture for sheep, forms the links well known to golfers. Fortunately other less renowned links are given slightly more coverage. Not surprisingly, the courses mentioned are in coastal areas. Returning to the recreation-oriented Montrose: 'Playing at the golf is a favourite and wholesome amusement. There is excellent ground for this purpose, and also for walking; as a large part of the links is level, and dry at all seasons.'[21] The report for Ayr also refers to the use of flat, sandy fields for golf (as well as for racing)[22], as does that for Rosemarkie in the Black Isle.

By far the fullest and most interesting comments, however, come from the pen of Dr Alexander Carlyle, minister of Inveresk in the Lothians, a man noted for his benevolent views, and the author of a masterly report. After having stated his belief that golf owed its origin to a Dutch game called *kolf*, he goes on: 'The golf, so long a favourite and peculiar exercise of the Scots, is much in use here. Children are trained to it in their early days, being enticed by the beauty of the links, and excited by the example of their parents. To preserve the taste for this ancient diversion, a company of gentlemen, about 18 years ago, purchased a silver cup, which is played for annually in the month of April, and is for a year the possession of the victor, who is obliged to append a medal to it, when he returns it to the company.'[23] He finishes on a warning note with a strangely modern ring: 'The inhabitants of Musselburgh had better watch over this precious field for health and exercise, lest in some unlucky period the magistrates and council should be induced to feu it out, on pretence of increasing the revenue of the town.'

Gardens

While for the most part the writers of the SA confine themselves to observations on the daily life and work of ordinary folk, this chapter presents an interesting contrast. Mention is made not only of the beginnings of gardening skills among the poorer people but also of the more ambitious productions of the wealthy and learned. There are some records of early commercial ventures in horticulture, of experiments in growing exotica, and also of allotment holdings. There is also fascinating diversity. While in many areas it emerges clearly that the poorer people had no gardens worthy of the name (nor would they have had the means to obtain expensive plants or fruit trees), in some others, particularly in the planned villages, cultivation of a modest range of vegetables, and even of some fruits, appears to have been more advanced.

Some reports are unclear, as the writer fails to specify whose garden he is describing; for example, in the account for the parish of Birsay and Harray, Orkney: 'The gardens will produce early cabbage and colliflower; as also onions, leeks, garlick, parsnips, carrots, turnips, and small sallad herbs; very fine flowers will in some years likewise blow, which I have tried.'[24] This minister is probably writing about his own garden. Certainly many of the writers come across as very knowledgeable indeed, not only in botany, but in horticulture and agriculture as well. Glebes were in many cases like mini-farms.

The Rev. David Moncrieff of Redgorton, Perthshire, follows a plea that landowners would allow ministers much larger glebes with a strong exhortation to his fellow clergy to beautify their gardens: 'Would it not be an inducement that the present incumbents would pay a little more attention to what land they already possess, and join with the *utile* some degree of elegance; as enlarging their gardens, and bestowing some pains on their cultivation, and, where the situation of the manse permits, have a small lawn and shrubbery round the house?' He is not unaware of the commercial potential either. 'It would be no great expense to plant an hundred fruit trees or more, which in a few years would become profitable. I speak not from theory, but from my own experience. I know a neighbour, who, by enlarging his garden, has got a plot of onions which yields him from five to ten pounds yearly, and that without the aid of the spade. Another sells apples to the amount of ten pounds and upwards; a third, garden roots and gooseberries to the same amount. Why should not the practice be general?'[25]

In the case of the Wick report, it is more difficult to tell whose gardens the minister has in mind. 'In regard to gardens, Caithness is no fruit country, at least for apricots, peaches, or the finer sorts of fruit.' Nor indeed would one have expected it to be! 'Common apples and pears, however, together with cherries, strawberries, and currants, answer well when properly attended to; cucumbers are raised in hot beds; artichokes are found here in highest perfection; collyflowers, cabbages, coleworts, savoys, spinage, beet, turnips, carrots, parsnips, onions, and all sorts of kitchen stuff may be reared in abundance, as also pot, aromatic, and medicinal herbs, by due attention.'[26] In this and many other reports, it is more than likely that the reference is to the gardens of the local landowners.

It has to be said that the list of produce is astonishingly sophisticated. One such example comes from Carstairs, Lanarkshire: 'In the gardens of Carstairs House, which are extensive, not only the fruits which are common, but grapes, pineapples, melons, and everything which the country can produce in that way, are raised in great abundance. The tea, coffee, and other foreign plants have been tried, and thrive beyond expectation.'[27] Much further north, in the account for Kiltarlity near Inverness, there is a highly unusual garden: 'Lord Lovat's principal garden measures about 7 Scotch acres. It is fenced with a wall 18 feet high lined with brick. The wall is contrived to have a great variety of curves, so as to catch the sun in every direction . . . The wall of the garden, from its various curvatures, measures upwards of 800 yards, so that with favourable seasons, a considerable quantity of fine fruit is produced on wall-trees.'[28] Another nobleman's garden, again in the Highland area, is also noteworthy: 'There is a large old house, called Castlestuart, belonging to the Earl of Moray . . . around this house there is a large garden and orchard, surrounded and sheltered by large forest trees. The garden is remarkable for different kinds of excellent straw-berries; and the orchard for a great number of large old trees, bearing the species of small cherry, called black and red geens. These geen-trees were sent there from Kent, about a century ago, by Alexander Earl of Moray.'[29]

The Dunkeld account includes a reference to an interesting (and lucrative) experiment carried out in the Duke of Atholl's garden, on the growing of rhubarb – later to be found in every cottage garden, but at the time of the SA a rare plant, much prized for its aperient qualities. 'In 1770, some seeds of the true rheum palmatum were sent from Petersburgh, by Dr Mounsey, to His Grace. They were planted, and considerable attention was paid to the culture of that root. Rhubarb, to the value of £160 Sterling, was sold in one season, to a London druggist, at the rate of 8s. the pound. In short, full proof was afforded, that rhubarb may be raised and dressed in Britain, equal, in all its qualities, to what is now, at so high a price, imported from the East Indies, and from Russia and Turky.'[30]

A somewhat surprising description is found in another of the Perthshire accounts; from Longforgan: 'The only gardens in this parish worthy of notice are at Castle Huntly. There are above 300 feet of glass; a melon-pit, of 20 feet by 12, worked by steam alone, without dung; and plenty of peaches, nectarins, apricots, figs, almonds, and other fruits, which ripen on the open wall.'[31] There follows a highly complex description of the melon-pit and its steam furnace.

In contrast to all this abundance, the general poverty of the common people's gardens is summed up well by the writer from Abernyte, Perthshire: 'While the improvement of land in general has been pretty well attended to, one branch of it, of importance both to the pleasure and healthy subsistence of the artisan, has been almost entirely neglected, viz. gardening. In the gardens even of the farmers, the only vegetables raised are kail and potatoes, and sometimes a few cabbages. In the cottager's yard, the last is entirely omitted; though they are all fond of, and consume great quantities of the onion tribe, they never think of cultivating a single plant of them.'[32]

Predictably, reports from other areas tend to paint a different picture; there are even some mentions of plants being grown for aesthetic reasons – for example the writer for Forgandenny, Perthshire, states that 'in most of the gardens of the common people, are raised coleworts, cabbages, onions, leeks, turnips and carrots. Some of them have likewise introduced gooseberry bushes, chiefly for shelter to their hives of bees, of which there is no inconsiderable number. And others, in the low part of the parish, have of late begun to plant in their little gardens, thyme, southern-wood, balm, mint, camomile, and some flowers, which serve both for ornament and use.'[33] It has to be said that this list is unusual. Much more representative is the report from Lamington, Lanarkshire: 'There is scarcely a garden which deserves the name, as being almost without flowers, and having little or no fruit excepting gooseberries, currants, and black-berries . . . but also every cottager has his kail-yard.'[34] This last, of immense importance to poor families in winter especially, receives prominent mention in many of the accounts.

A surprising addition comes from the parish of Orphir, Orkney: 'Cabbages and garden roots grow in great perfection; and perhaps the finest and largest artichokes in the world are to be found in this country, in the common kail-yards, springing up amongst the grass without any cultivation.'[35] While from

Unst, Shetland, the report states that 'artichokes of a delicate taste are produced here, with some small fruit, and most of the garden flowers that grow in the north of Scotland.'[36]

Gardens were obviously an important feature of the planned villages which were to be found in a number of places by this final decade of the eighteenth century, and these were to lead to a new advance in horticultural skills. One such village was Dalgairn, which is described in the report for the parish of Sorn, Ayrshire. Here a certain Dr Stevenson, physician in Glasgow, had 'parcelled out a beautiful holm'; the village now comprised 24 houses and 43 families: 'Most of these families are provided with gardens, which are of various dimensions, behind the houses, which they cultivate with great care, and raise in them not only the common kinds of succulent plants, but also straw-berries, gooseberries, and currants, and occasionally flax and barley.'[37]

From Banff comes evidence of another new initiative, in what sounds like an early kind of allotment system: 'A few fields adjoining the town are rented as high as £5 and £6 the acre. These are chiefly occupied by gardeners, who raise pot-herbs and other vegetables, for the supply of the inhabitants.'[38] Obviously this was merely a small-scale commercial venture; in other areas, however – predictably near the larger population centres – commercial gardening was already a flourishing business, the dung from city streets being used as fertiliser. 'Gardening is carried on here to a considerable extent,' runs the account for Lasswade near Edinburgh. 'The attention of the gardener is chiefly directed to the cultivation of strawberries, than which he has not a surer or more profitable crop . . . and when properly cultivated, this fruit will yield at an average 18lbs from an acre.'[39] Modern growers take note!

The report for Prestonpans states that 'considerable quantities of cabbage plants are raised. The season of sowing them is at Lammas. Besides the sale in the neighbourhood, 150,000 at a medium are sent annually to Glasgow, and about 70,000 to Falkirk and Carron. The severer the winter, the demand for them is greater.'[40] Again from the Edinburgh area, market gardens are mentioned in the account for Inveresk: 'The demand for vegetables has increased tenfold within these 50 years, and horticulture has been so much encouraged in richer soils near the capital, that all the superiority that the gardens here can now pretend to, is to furnish the earliest crops of pease and beans etc., for a week or two, as the markets are soon filled from the more luxuriant gardens near the city.'[41]

Several of the Lanarkshire accounts make it clear that the growing of hard fruits was already established in the area, although some of the deterrents are also mentioned. The Hamilton account states that 'there are a good many little orchards in the lower parts, producing apples, pears, plumbs, and cherries. In good seasons, they bear very good and well-flavoured fruit; but, upon the whole, this is a very precarious article of produce, subject to many injuries from spring-frosts, the depredations of caterpillars, summer's blights etc., so that there is scarcely one year in three, in which the orchards turn to good account.'[42] The account for Carluke includes a lengthy and fascinating description of the fruit industry and of the names of some of the 47 species of apples and 32 of pears (whistleberry, lady's finger, purse-mouth, lady's hemmon, summer strawberry, and bloodheart being a few of the apples mentioned; and grey honey, farrow cow, green pear of Pinkie, brier bush, and muirfowl egg of the pears). 'Fruit abound in this parish more than any other upon the Clyde. The orchards in this district extend about 5 miles, and are the property of many different proprietors. They comprehend, in all, upwards of 80 acres of land.'[43] Some of the Stirlingshire accounts also indicate the existence of a hard fruit industry, as in the parish of Bothkennar: 'There are 12 orchards in this parish, the largest of which is about 3 acres in extent. They produce chiefly apples and pears, and, in good fruit seasons, bring the proprietors a plentiful return.'[44]

From several districts come reports of early nurseries, employing a number of workers; for example from Hawick: 'In this parish there is a considerable nursery carried on by the Messrs. Dicksons . . . These two nurseries contain all kind of fruit and forest trees, flower plants and roots, and flowering shrubs, that are naturalized to this country; besides a great collection of exotic plants . . . At some seasons, there are 50 people employed in the nursery grounds.'[45] And from Kinnoull, Perth, a surprisingly extensive nursery: 'About the year 1767, a nursery was begun in this parish . . . this contains between 30 and 40 acres of ground, on the east bank of the Tay, directly opposite to Perth; for the cultivation of which the number of hands varies, according to the exigencies of the season; but at an average, more than 40 find constant employment. The soil and exposure of these grounds, are both remarkably fitted for rearing plants of such a vigorous and hardy nature, as are suitable not only to the sheltered, but to the exposed situations, with which the varied face of the country abounds. This nursery contains all kinds of fruit and forest trees, evergreen and flowering shrubs, flower roots and plants, which are naturalized to the climate. The proprietors have always been particularly careful in the selection and proof of the various kinds of fruit-trees, and in consequence of this, the demand has always been very extensive. On the nursery grounds, they have lately erected a large well constructed greenhouse, in which there is not only a numerous, but a rich collection of exotic plants. And at their shop in Perth, they keep a complete assortment of all kinds of garden, grass, tree, and flower seeds. These various articles, find a ready market, not only in the rich adjacent country, but in the more remote parts of Scotland. They are even frequently sent to England and Ireland.'[46]

From the neighbouring parish of Scone comes an altogether optimistic prognosis for the future of the gardening scene in Scotland: 'Several of the gentlemen's gardens are elegant, particularly the Earl of Mansefield's; and most of them are well stocked with vegetables, and fruit trees, and bushes. And not only the handicraftsmen, at their leisure hours, but the farmers, begin to pay more attention to their gardens than formerly; a certain indication of the thriving state of this country, men commonly attending, first, to what is necessary, and then to what is commodious and ornamental. Indeed, the appearance both of the country and the people, compared to what it was 20 years ago, plainly shows, that they are growing richer and happier; an evident proof of the excellence of that constitution of government, under which we have the good fortune to live.'[47]

 1. XVI, 484
 2. XVI, 467
 3. XX, 395
 4. XX, 395
 5. XVI, 502
 6. XIII, 347
 7. XV, 343
 8. XVI, 642
 9. IX, 71
10. XVI, 279
11. XVI, 65
12. XIII, 560

13. VI, 369
14. XII, 678
15. XVII, 293
16. VI, 585
17. XI, 585
18. IV, 112
19. VI, 482
20. IV, 539
21. XIII, 560
22. VI, 560
23. II, 306
24. XIX, 10

25. XI, 537
26. XVIII, 258
27. VII, 197
28. XVII, 186
29. XVII, 245
30. XII, 343
31. XI, 321
32. XI, 23
33. XI, 184
34. VII, 419
35. XIX, 169
36. XIX, 500

37. VI, 532
38. XVI, 22
39. II, 342
40. II, 577
41. II, 294
42. VII, 386
43. VII, 129
44. IX, 134
45. II, 455
46. XI, 294
47. XI, 573

8 CHARACTER

When one comes to consider the character of the late-eighteenth-century Scots as seen through the eyes of the writers of these accounts it is, ironically, their own characters which at first seem to come under scrutiny. Just how seriously are we to take this assessment of their parishioners? When, for example, one of them writes harshly or critically, are we to conclude that he was perhaps cantankerous, judgmental or at the least, unsympathetic by nature; or was it perhaps that he knew his flock better than did the more tolerant-sounding minister?

Consider for instance the following excerpts from two neighbouring parishes, both in the Carse country of Central Scotland. According to the writer of the Kilspindie, Perthshire, account: 'Common people in the Carse are in general rather tall, strong and clumsy in person; dull, obstinate, rude and unmannerly; live well. The better sort of farmers, luxurious and expensive in their way of living, without the least claim to neatness and elegance.'[1] Yet in nearby Errol: '2445 belong to the Established Church, who, for numbers and genteel appearance, will not be excelled or equalled by many country districts in the kingdom. Their stature is considerably above the common size, and their proportions otherwise well adjusted. In temper and manners, they are gay, cheerful and active. The higher ranks are opulent, and the lower have it in their power, from the great wages they can earn, to purchase the conveniences of life. They are far removed from sordidness, and are not unsusceptible of generosity, of which they have given proof on several occasions. As the people equal their neighbours in useful, and far surpass them in elegant accomplishments, it is expected that they will be exemplary also in that devout and religious demeanour, which gives every embellishment its true lustre and dignity.'[2] Do these represent very different types of people or simply very different views of humanity?

Two totally divergent accounts of the character of farm servants also make interesting reading. In Kirkmichael, Banffshire: 'Male servants receive £3 sterling, in the half year . . . The advanced price of labour is one of the grievances of which farmers chiefly complain. They feel, from experience, that in point of ease, comfort, and independence, the condition of servants is more eligible than that of their masters. The short term of engagement, wages immoderately high, inspire them with a pride, insolence, and indifference, that would frequently require a meek and patient spirit to brook. Nice in the choice of their food to squeamishness, it must neither fall short, nor exceed the exact proportion of cookery, which their appetites can relish. Care too must be taken, that no offence be offered them. They must sleep in the morning as long, and go to bed at night as soon, as their pleasure dictates. Expostulations are opposed by rudeness.'[3] While, on the other hand, from Livingstone in the Lothians: 'The degrading servility of the feudal system is·here totally eradicated; they approach their superiors with abundance of discretion, but without cringing; for a good deed they are not ashamed to be grateful to their inferiors; and they would forgive an injury from a beggar, which they would resent from a peer.'[4]

These very different writings make interesting reading. What one minister sees as pride and insolence, the other attributes to an independent spirit. Such variety is of course to be found in every aspect of the SA, and is one of its main attractions; but subjectivity comes through more obviously in such topics as character and mode of living than, for example, in accounts of agricultural practices or industry. Always the human factor has to be taken into account!

It is at least arguable that the fact that the reports were by no means secret may have influenced some of the writers. This very real dilemma is set out most frankly in the account for the parish of Mortlach, Banff: 'It here obviously occurs, that a minister may be induced, from various motives, to go to the extreme of truth, on the favourable side for his flock. His regard for them may blind and mislead him; or, by condemning them, he may think that he obliquely condemns himself; at least, if another did it, he might perhaps be led too readily to think so. Few chuse to depreciate their own importance; few to diminish the happy effects of their pastoral care; and fewer still are inclined to render themselves ungracious. Thus it may often place a clergyman in a delicate situation to be obliged to characterise his parishioners.'[5]

By far the greater number of reports, it has to be said, take the favourable view; very typical, for instance, is that for the parish of Blairgowrie, Perthshire: 'The inhabitants of this parish are, in general, sober, industrious, attentive to their respective callings, and exemplarily regular in their attendance on divine ordinances. They are charitably disposed, and seem contented with their condition.'[6] Some are seen to be striving hard for objectivity. The report for Kingussie, Inverness-shire, after describing the miserable poverty of the people states that: 'Should a people thus obnoxious to poverty and all its train of concomitant evils, be found less scrupulous in other particulars, than others who enjoy a happier lot; perhaps the liberal mind would find some alleviation of their errors in the necessity of their situation. But even this excuse is unnecessary on the present occasion. Instances of theft are very uncommon; more flagrant crimes in a great measure unknown. Like most of the natives of the Highlands, they are brave, hospitable, and polite. Their vices may be said to be grafted on to their virtues. They are quarrelsome, addicted to drunkenness, and little to be depended on for the sincerity of their professions.'[7]

'The character of the people is various,' writes the minister of the parish of Callander, Perthshire, 'but in general, both here, and along the eastern side of the Grampians, they are divested of the sullenness of those, who inhabit the champaign country farther east and south, and of the idleness of those, farther north and west. They have not perhaps arrived at the plodding industry of the former, while they have relinquished much of the pride of the latter. They are fast acquiring the diligence and attention necessary in the agricultural state of society, and are in a great measure free from the vices of great towns. The people are humane, affectionate, and polite. But if the enlargement of farms is introduced, and the country depopulated to make room for sheep, the inhabitants must emigrate, or crowd to villages. And if villages are increased, without due regard to their police, their employment, and their manners, it were much better for the people, and their country, that they had never seen a village, but had remained in the simplicity of rural life, wrapped in their plaids all day long, as their fathers were, on the brow of a hill, attending their cattle, and composing sonnets.'[8]

To round off the issue of impartiality, an amusing comment by the minister of Kilsyth parish shows that he had rather more reasons than most for pursuing this aim: 'The characters of the inhabitants of this parish are as varied as their countenances; as in any mixed society, the good and the bad are blended together,' adding, revealingly: ' . . . upwards of 500 of them are my blood relations.'[9]

Many of the reports go into great detail on the subject of character, often bringing in totally unexpected facets – for example, the Kilmaconnell and Kilberry, Argyllshire, account reads: 'The most unaccountable part of the conduct of the lower classes in this and other parishes, and that which can be least easily reconciled to the hardships of their situation, is their fondness for dogs. Almost every family has one; and in some families, there are two or three. Even paupers were found to have so unwarrantable an attachment to these animals, that threats to strike them off the poor's roll were obliged to be used before they could be prevailed upon to part with them . . . It appears there are 400 dogs in the parish. The food devoured by these animals would feed 400 pigs, which, when a year old, would sell at £400.'[10]

Some answer the question on character in a brief comment reminiscent of a school report; this from the parish account of Drumblade, Aberdeenshire: 'They are not remarkably indolent; but with regard to industry, there is room for improvement.'[11] This reference to idleness highlights one of the vices most frequently mentioned; the Rogart, Sutherland, account runs: 'The people seem to be inclined much more to idleness than to industry. They are extremely frugal of the little they have; but as to earning anything more, it is a melancholy fact, that a poor tenant, who rents land only to the value of 20s. or 30s., and whose labour could well be spared from his little farm many days in the year, will rather saunter, or sit idle at home, than work for 6d. a day, which would be a considerable addition to his own and his family's scanty meal.'[12] And the minister of Halkirk, Caithness, writes in a similar vein: 'We have rather too many who are idly disposed, and who will not work, unless compelled to it by the extremity of the last necessity; for if they happen to have what will enable them to hold out until night, or any prospect of any other shift, though at the expense of their more industrious neighbours, to whom they are no small burden, they have no concern about their debts, or any provision for tomorrow.'[13]

Along with idleness, apparently, went a great deal of curiosity; mention is made of this particular character trait from the Highland parish of Canisbay (which is typical of many): 'During their hours of idleness, which are many, languor and lassitude are never observable about them. The mind, having no interests of its own to fasten upon, exerts its power, for the sake of employment, in making investigations into the condition and character of others. Hence that solicitude after news, that spirit for prying into the most hidden concerns of their neighbours, with the view of gratifying curiosity rather than malevolence . . . their discernment of the purposes of others, and dexterity in concealing their own, are no less remarkable.'[14]

In a few reports, smuggling comes up for censure, as for example in Orphir in the Orkney Islands, where the minister deplored 'the low spirit for smuggling which has been the bane of Orkney for half a century past.'[15] (In answer to Sir John's question as to what are the principal advantages of the parish, this writer cites 'fire, water and fine women.')

By far the greatest number of adverse comments, however – not to say at times passionate condemnation – concern the immoderate drinking of whisky. The subject is dealt with in so many reports that a number of examples must be used in an attempt to illustrate the complete picture. In account after account the writers attack what they clearly see as the outstanding social evil of the day; many, too, bewail the loss of the greatly preferable home-brewed ale which whisky had universally replaced since the Malt Tax was introduced in 1725 (6d. on every bushel of malt). This is highlighted in the account for the Lothians parish of Borrowstowness: 'Here, as in many other places specified in the *Statistical Account of Scotland*, tippling houses are too numerous. It may be seriously regretted, by the friends of religion and virtue, that so many people are licensed to vend ardent spirits in every town and village. Such places ensnare the innocent, become the haunts of the idle and dissipated, and ruin annually the health and morals of thousands of mankind. Perhaps, if the malt-tax were abolished, and an adequate additional tax laid upon British spirits, as in the days of our fathers, malt-liquor would be produced, to nourish and strengthen, instead of whisky, which wastes and enfeebles the constitution.'[16]

In the Ayrshire reports particularly, where the numbers of whisky houses seem to have been staggeringly high (Kilmarnock for example had 50), the ministers write nostalgically about the goodness of the old ale. 'Fifty years ago,' writes the minister of the parish of Mauchline, 'good two-penny, strong-ale, and home-spirits were in vogue: but now even people in the middle and lower stations in life, deal much in foreign spirits, rum-punch, and wine. In former times, the gentlemen of the county entered into a resolution to encourage the consumption of their own grain, and, for that purpose, to drink no foreign spirits; but, in consequence of the prevalence of smuggling, and the heavy taxes laid on home-made liquors, this particular resolution was either forgotten or abandoned.'[17] The only Ayrshire parish which seems to have survived the onslaught of whisky is Kirkmichael: 'Whisky, so prevalent in many places, is not esteemed a genteel drink in this corner. The general beverage, of late, among the better sort of farmers, is good porter, which they find to afford nourishment as well as chearfulness, when moderately used.'[18]

The writer of the account for Sorbie, Galloway, lashes out at the owners of public-houses as bearing much of the responsibility for the decline in moral standards: 'The effects of public houses, are most injurious to the morals and industry of the people, especially when little else than whisky is sold in them. A few pence procures as much of this base spirit as is sufficient to make any man mad. The landlords of superfluous petty public-houses generally waste their time, and ruin their constitutions, by acting like decoys on their silly half-resolved neighbours. In their shameless business they are flattered with the notion of promoting trade.'[19] In the Callander account, the writer deplores the ease with which it is possible to sell whisky: 'The number of dram houses is out of all bounds too great. These haunts of the idle, the prodigal and profane, contaminate the morals of the lower classes of the people beyond description. A poor widow must pay a tax, before she can obtain a candle to give her light, in spinning for the support of her fatherless children; and yet a dram-seller, it seems, can get a licence, under the sanction of law, for little more than one shilling, to corrupt the morals of the lieges for a whole year.'[20]

On whisky stills there is surprisingly little written apart from a few references, mainly in the Western Isles. The account for Gigha and Cara states how the condition of the people has improved since these were removed: 'They are, upon the whole, in a thriving condition, content with their situation, and greatly attached to their native country. The suppression of private stills, (which are as unfriendly to the industry and morals of a people, as they are pernicious to their health), has been attended with happy effects. They are now less addicted to *dram-drinking*, and more attentive to their business; though still they are not as industrious as could be wished.'[21] In Kilninian, Islay, things were not so happy: 'This island hath a liberty of brewing whisky, without being under the necessity of paying the usual excise duty . . . We have not an excise officer in the whole island. The quantity of whisky made here is therefore very great; and the evil, which follows drinking to excess of this liquor, is very visible in this island. This is one chief cause of our poverty; for the barley, that should support the family of the poor tenant, is sold to the brewer for 17s. the boll; and the same farmer is often obliged to buy meal at £1. 3s. sterling, in order to keep his family from starving.'[22]

Not all the comments on drinking habits are adverse, however; honourable mention in this regard is given to the Borders village of Traquair: 'Within less than 30 years, the people of the parish have changed their character very much to the better. They were then much addicted to drinking to excess. There were at that time more than six ale-houses; at present there is only one public house, which is seldom, if at all, frequented, but by those who are transacting business, or by travellers, and is on these accounts necessary.'[23] At the opposite end of Scotland, receiving a similar accolade, is Cross, Burness, and North Ronaldsay, Orkney: 'There is one happy change among the poor people within these last 30 or 40 years, which is, that there is not one fourth part of the spirituous liquors used now as formerly. The proprietors, sensible that it wasted the means, and corrupted the morals of the people, have endeavoured to check it, by suppressing the retail of it. True, the poorer sort are moderate from necessity; those of the higher rank are so from choice.'[24]

As a final comment on the theme of drinking, the Banff minister offers an amusing addendum in his report:

> 1748 – a joyous company, after dinner, have been seen quaffing the wine of a dozen bottles from a single glass.

1798 – a sober party sometimes meet, whose libation consists of a solitary bottle, with a dozen glasses.[25]

The above sentiments are both familiar and predictable; what does cause genuine surprise is the amount of spleen vented on what seems to modern minds a fairly innocuous beverage: 'Above 20 times more tea is used now than 20 years ago,' writes the Crieff minister in a typical comment. 'Bewitched by the mollifying influence of an enfeebling potion, the very poorest classes begin to regard it as one of the necessaries of life, and for its sake resign the cheaper and more invigorating nourishment which the productions of their country afford.'[26] The Gargunnock, Stirlingshire, account sheds interesting light on the prevailing attitude: 'Tea is universally used. Even the poorest families have it occasionally, and the last cup is qualified with a little whisky, which is supposed to correct all the bad effects of the tea.'[27] Tea was of course a very expensive beverage in the late eighteenth century. For a much cheaper intoxicant, an intriguing recommendation is made in the account from Stronsay and Eday, Orkney: 'A mineral spring is to be found among the rocks on the east coast of the island of Stronsay. The water, clear as chrystal, not unpleasant, is full of fixed air, as may be easily discovered by any who drink some glasses of it; for they will soon find themselves affected in the same way, as if they drank some fine brisk bottled small beer.'[28]

Another aspect of the character of the people – although mentioned in relatively few accounts – is their various superstitions and occult practices. One or two of the ministers are strongly of the opinion that all such things belong to a past age, as illustrated in the Clunie, Perthshire, report: 'They are not, as formerly, the dupes of superstitious credulity. Many old useless rites and ceremonies are laid aside. Little attention is paid to bug-bear tales; superstitions, charms, and incantations have lost their power. Cats, hares, magpies, and old women, cease to assume any other appearance than what nature has given them; and ghosts, goblins, witches, and fairies have relinquished the land.'[29] And in a different area of the country, the minister for Mid-Calder in the Lothians voices very similar sentiments: 'It behoves us to rejoice, that we live in happier times, when the darkness of error is fast giving way to the light of reason, truth, and science. As this darkness is removed, so will those opinions, prejudices and spectres die, to which ignorance and folly gave birth. I cannot say, that the belief in witchcraft, has entirely left the people in this parish; but it appears to have little influence on their lives or their conduct. May the human mind daily increase in wisdom, and assert more and more its native dignity, till it rise superior to folly, superstition, and vice!'[30]

The belief that a new age of enlightenment had dawned is not, however, borne out in all of the accounts; for example, the minister for Kilfinan, Argyll, after asserting that 'superstition is losing ground in this parish pretty fast,' goes on to tell of one superstitious belief which obliged the people to 'carry their children out to baptism' on the second day after their birth, a custom which led to the deaths of a considerable number, as they were frequently carried for many miles in bad weather.[31] Many of the practices cited are centred on events such as marriages and baptisms. The account from Logierait, Perthshire, includes by far the longest descriptions of these: 'A variety of superstitious practices still prevail among the vulgar, which may be in part the remains of ancient idolatry . . . Lucky and unlucky days are by many anxiously observed. That day of the week upon which the 14th of May happens to fall, for instance, is esteemed unlucky through all the remainder of the year; none marry, or begin any serious business upon it. None chuse to marry in January or May; or to have their banns proclaimed in the end of one quarter of the year, and to marry in the beginning of the next. Some things are to be done before the full moon, others after . . . When a child was baptised privately, it was not long since customary, to put the child upon a clean basket, having a cloth previously spread over it, with bread and cheese put into the cloth; and thus to move the basket three times successively round the iron *crook*, which hangs over the fire, from the roof of the house, for the purpose of supporting the pots when water is boiled, or victuals are prepared.'[32] Although this type of superstition could be said to be fairly typical of those mentioned in the reports, others refer to more bizarre customs; from Kilfinichen and Kilviceuen, Western Isles: 'It is believed . . . that the spirit of the last person that was buried watches round the churchyard till another is buried, to whom he delivers his charge.'[33] Other superstitions centred around livestock; from Killearn, Stirlingshire: 'Superstition yet continues to operate so strongly in some people, that they put a small quantity of salt into the first milk of a cow after calving, that is given any person to drink. This is done with a view to prevent *skaith*, if it should happen that the person is not *canny*. A certain amount of cow dung is forced into the mouth of a calf immediately after it is calved, or at least before it receives any meat; owing to this, the vulgar believe that witches and fairies can have no power ever after to injure the calf.'[34]

A much larger number of beliefs concerned curative or magical qualities of wells; from Avoch in the Black Isle: 'A well, called Craiguck, issuing from a rock near the shore of Bennetsfield, is resorted to in the month of May, by whimsical or superstitious persons, who, after drinking, commonly leave some threads or rags tied to a bush in the neighbourhood. But if they derive benefit from this, it would seem to be more owing to their own credulity, than to any effect of the water, which differs nothing in taste or appearance from common.'[35]

Greater powers seem to have been attributed, in the Gigha and Cara account, to a well on the island of Gigha:'It would be unpardonable not to mention the well of Tarbat, a well famous for having command of the wind . . . Six feet above where the water gushes out, there is a heap of stones, which forms a cover to the sacred fount. When a person wished for a fair wind, either to leave the island, or to bring home his absent friends, this part was opened with great solemnity, the stones carefully removed, and the well cleaned with a wooden dish or clam shell. This being done, the water was several times thrown in the direction from which the wished-for wind was to blow, and this action accompanied with a certain form of words, which the person repeated every time he threw the water . . . This ceremony of *cleaning the well*, as it is called, is now seldom or never performed; though still there are two old women, who are said to have the secret, but who have cause to lament *the infidelity of the age*, as they derive little emolument from their profession.'[36]

There appears to have been a considerable number of wells with reputedly therapeutic effects; none, however, is described with greater enthusiasm than the one at Peterhead. This was a chalybeate spring (i.e. impregnated with iron salts); so popular was it that 'by six or seven o'clock in the morning, the spring is often literally dry,' great crowds apparently coming from distances of 40 or 50 miles. In one respect it seems to have been lacking – it did not cure kidney stones. The account cites the case of one sufferer from 'gravel' who, strangely, 'is thinking of trying the Peterhead water, because his father thought he derived benefit from it, who, after having tried it for nearly 30 years, was cut for the stone.'[37]

Not surprisingly we also find superstitions connected with the heavenly bodies, often, for example, in relation to matrimonial customs. The Kirkmichael, Banffshire, report runs: 'It may be easily imagined, that this country has its due proportion of that superstition which generally prevails over the Highlands . . . Poor Martinus Scriblerus never more anxiously watched the blowing of the west wind to secure an heir to his genius, than the love-sick swain and his nymph for the coming of the new moon, to be noosed together in matrimony. Should the planet happen to be at the height of her splendour when the ceremony is performed, their future life will be a scene of festivity, and all its paths strewed over with rosebuds of delight. But when her tapering horns are turned towards the North, passion becomes frost-bound, and seldom thaws till the genial season again approaches.'[38] Superstition takes a different form in another Banffshire parish, that of Forglen: 'The superstition of former times is now much worn out. There remains, however, still a little. Some charms are secretly used to prevent evil, and some omens looked to by the older people. There are happy and unhappy days for beginning any undertaking. Thus, few would choose to be married here on Friday, though it is the ordinary day in other quarters of the church. There are also happy and unhappy feet. Thus, they wish bridegrooms and brides a happy foot; and to prevent any bad effect, they salute those they meet on the road with a kiss. It is hard, however, if any misfortune happens when you are passing, that you should be blamed, when neither you nor your feet ever thought of the matter.'[39]

Some of the writers clearly feared that the change to more rational views might tend to loss of religious belief. The outstanding report of the parish of Montquhitter, Aberdeenshire, seems appropriate in this respect to round off the section on the superstitious side of the Scots character at the time: 'In opinion, an amazing alteration has been produced by education and social intercourse. Few of the old being able to read, and fewer still to write, their minds were clouded by ignorance. The mind being uncultivated, the imagination readily admitted the terrors of superstition. The appearance of ghosts and demons too frequently engrossed the conversation of the young and the old. Elves by their arrows destroyed, and not seldom unmercifully, cows and oxen. Fairies held from time immemorial certain fields, which could not be taken away without gratifying these merry spirits by a piece of money. The old man's fold, where the druid sacrificed to the demon for his corn and cattle, could not be violated by the ploughshare. Lucky and unlucky days, dreams and omens, were most religiously attended to; and reputed witches, by their spells and their prayers, were artful enough to lay every parish under contribution.

'But now, ghosts and demons are no longer visible. The fye has withdrawn his warning, and the elf his arrows. Fairies, without requiring compensation, have renounced their possessions. The old man's fold is reduced to tillage. The sagacious old woman, who has survived her friends and means, is treated with humanity, in spite of the grisly bristles which adorn her mouth. And in the minds of the young, cultivated by education, a steady pursuit of the arts of life has banished the chimeras of fancy . . .

'From believing too much, many, particularly in the higher walks of life, have rushed to the opposite extreme of believing too little; so that, even in this remote corner, scepticism may justly boast of her votaries.'[40]

Despite the fears expressed by this writer, the accounts on the whole do not seem to indicate a move away from religious belief or practice; indeed, minister after minister enlarges upon the faithfulness of his flock. Fairly typical is this comment from the Dry'sdale report: 'The people are honest, sober, industrious in their respective occupations; well affected to the present government, both ecclesiastical and civil; peaceable and pious, regular in attending services on the Lord's day; are well acquainted with the principles of Christianity, are devoid of bigotry and hypocrisy, are moderate and humane, and delight to favour one another.'[41] All the same, some ministers tended to give an impression of being more concerned with outward appearance and decent, law-abiding behaviour, than religious zeal; the description in the report for West-Calder, the Lothians, is a notable exception: 'The great bulk of the inhabitants of this parish have a considerable share of religious knowledge, and a becoming fervency in their devotion. It is hoped that they will not be charged with singularity of manner, when we mention, that there are not perhaps six families in this parish, who do not daily, and in a family capacity, assemble together to acknowledge the Author of their mercies. Altogether detached from the capital, they are unacquainted with its vices.'[42]

The strong association between moral deterioration and industrial development comes across very clearly in several of the accounts, as in that just quoted. The West Kilbride minister writes: 'It may well be accounted a fortunate circumstance for the inhabitants of this place, that their sequestered situation has hitherto secured them from the incroaching influence of that corruption, which in other places of more business and resort, has produced so great a change in the morals of the people. They, on the other hand, have uniformly supported a character for industry, sobriety, and decent conduct . . . They are uncommonly regular in their attendance upon divine worship; and at church, exhibit a very decent appearance, from the neatness of their dress, and attention to the sacred service. In their behaviour, especially to their superiors, and to strangers, there is an affability and discretion, that distinguishes it remarkably from the morose and sullen rusticity of some of the more inland peasants. In fine, in their labours, their amusements, and the general tenor of their conversation, one may readily recognise the happiness, contentment, and comfortable independence, of an honest and peaceable people.'[43]

The traditional Scots respect for education is very apparent in a considerable number of reports, frequently giving rise to wonder at the sheer tenacity and determination of the desperately poor, who scrimped and saved in order to give their offspring the opportunities they themselves had been denied. A typical example is found in the account for Dalmeny, Lothians: 'In Scotland, many half-starve themselves, in order to make savings; not a few lay by several pounds sterling, which they reserve for old age, for putting their children to apprenticeships, or for otherwise bettering their own condition or that of their families.'[44] And after giving a detailed budget of a poor working family in the Moulin, Pitlochry, account, the minister adds this touching comment: 'Although there thus appears to be a deficiency of earnings, after the charges have been estimated in the most frugal, and even scanty manner, and no allowance made for casual expenses; yet it is certain, that, in this country, people, who seem to have no livelihood but the fruits of their daily labour, do, by some means or other, bring up families, and even give their children such education as the nearest school affords.'[45]

The pursuit of education is also amply illustrated by the many mentions of libraries and antiquarian and literary societies; one interesting example occurs in the report from Crawford, Lanarkshire, which tells of the setting up of a library for the workers in the lead industry there. There cannot have been many, however, who pursued education with such dedication as a certain shepherd in the Dollar area: 'There is living at present in this parish in a very advanced age, a man who was bred up, and lived merely as a shepherd, and who received only a common education; and yet possesses a valuable library of books, containing upwards of 370 volumes. They are upon many different subjects, as divinity, history, travels, voyages &c, besides magazines of different kinds, such as the Scots, the Universal, and the Christian magazines; a complete set of the Spectator, Guardian, Tatler, Rambler &c. They are all of them his own chusing and purchasing. They are neatly bound, and lettered on the back.'[46]

It seems a pity that it is the frugality – not to say meanness – of the Scots which has become proverbial, for in these accounts it is undeniably their kindness and generosity in the face of often abject poverty which is most strikingly apparent; some refer to individual acts of kindness, most to the customs of the people in general. In the former category, an outstanding instance comes from the Dunkeld report: 'Janet Macgregor was maid-servant to a respectable family. The parents died, and the children, then in infancy, were very destitute. The poor woman clung to them with a parent's affection, and in supporting and rearing the orphans, spent the hard-won earnings of a length of years. Pity on that cold heart which reckons this fact frivolous! To the eye of that Being, Who, in estimating charity, looks not to the rank of the giver, or the splendour of the gift, but to the principle of the deed, it will appear as of uncommon virtue.'[47]

The care of the poor by the poor is everywhere apparent in these reports of days long before social services of any kind, for instance in the account from Clatt, Aberdeenshire: 'Such poor as live in and about the more populous villages, are supplied, by their beneficent neighbours, with some little necessaries, which they could not otherwise procure; such as milk, whey, turnips, potatoes, fuel &c. When it is known, that any old or infirm person is in want, it is customary for the young lads of that corner, to go out in an evening through the parish, and to ask meal, or a little money, which the people very cheerfully give; and it proves a most seasonable supply to several who would be in hazard of suffering want.'[48]

From Tongue, Sutherland, comes this: 'The people of this country do not eat their morsel alone. They open their hospitable door to the traveller; they make the heart of the widow to rejoice; and they grant to the poor their desire. Generosity, indeed, is the principal trait of their character; to this they add devotion to the Supreme Being.'[49]

An impression not only of humanity but also of extraordinary honesty emerges from Kilfinichen and Kilviceuen, Western Isles: 'The people, in general, are sober, industrious, humane . . . The number of poor they support, shows their humanity; as also two shipwrecks that happened within these six years. In both instances, the poor sailors were treated with kindness and humanity. One of these vessels was wrecked in Ross; and it is very remarkable, that a quantity of cork, very useful, and much wanted in the country for their nets, scattered over a strand of upwards of a mile in extent, was not touched by the inhabitants, though many were too poor to buy it, even if they had the opportunity.'[50]

Another individual act of generosity is quoted in the account for Banchory Devenick, Kincardineshire: 'On the 19th of August 1710, seven boys, about 15 years of age each, sailed out of the harbour of St Andrews in a little boat, and losing one of their oars, were driven into the ocean. After six days and nights of continued fasting and labour, they got to shore alive, four miles south of Aberdeen, and 50 miles north of St Andrews. A humane country man, John Shepherd, kindly received them into his house, and sent information of so moving an accident to the magistrates of Aberdeen, who despatched their dean of guild, a physician, and a surgeon, to attend them. All of the boys were preserved in life except the two youngest, who died soon after they came ashore. John Shepherd was presented with a silver cup in the form of a boat, by Robert Bruce, goldsmith in Edinburgh, father of one of the boys, in testimony of his gratitude for the active part he took in recovering his son.'[51]

The SA is generally devoted to chronicling the life and times of the common people; however, from time to time, comments were made on the part played by those gentry who tended to exploit the people. There are, though, a few references to those of altruistic character, for instance in Kincardine, Ross: 'Having mentioned the distress incurred in the year 1782, the author considers himself called on to record an action of the late gallant Sir John Lockhart Ross, which does him the highest credit. Understanding the distress of the poor people on his estate, he sent a seasonable and bountiful supply of large quantities of pease, barley, flour and potatoes, to which God-like beneficence many owed their lives. Let it be added, that he ordered his factor or steward to give his Highland tenants, who did not save as much as would sow their grounds, seed from his farms in the low country . . . And at the conclusion of the war, upon his return to his native country, he discounted one third of the arrears of rent, over the whole of his estate.'[52]

The clearing of the great mosses of Central Scotland (*see* Mosses, p. 145) earned the poorest of workers the reputation of being competent and reliable throughout their years of hard labour, which the Kincardine, Perthshire, account notes: 'Of the whole inhabitants full nine tenths are Highlanders, from the neighbouring parishes of Callander, Balquhidder, &c., a sober, frugal and industrious people, who, inured to hardships in their own country, are peculiarly qualified to encounter so arduous an undertaking . . . Neither ought it to be forgotten, that, from their first settlement to the present day, not a single instance has occurred among them of theft, bad neighbourhood, or of any other misdemeanour, that required the interposition of the civil magistrate. Nor, however poor in circumstances, has any one of them ever stooped to solicit assistance from the funds of the parish appropriated to that purpose.'[53]

To sum up this chapter, the balanced list of good and bad characteristics offered in the Kinloch, Perthshire, account seems fitting: 'On the whole, they are benevolent, respectful to superiors, obedient to those who have the rule over them, quiet in their behaviour, and, from the religious principle, thankful and loyal subjects of the British Government.

'But if we keep in view the great standard of perfection . . . which the Divine Author of it hath left for our imitation, I must say, that, upon a close examination, there are to be seen, on the face of this fair character, some specks; and that there is good ground, and fair opportunity, for improving, purifying, ornamenting, and adorning it.'[54]

1. XI, 255	15. XIX, 178	29. XII, 244	43. VI, 282
2. XI, 173	16. II, 703	30. II, 106	44. II, 729
3. XVI, 277	17. VI, 449	31. VIII, 235	45. XII, 759
4. II, 787	18. VI, 383	32. XII, 712	46. IX, 766
5. XVI, 334	19. V, 512	33. XX, 321	47. XII, 333
6. XII, 136	20. XII, 188	34. IX, 398	48. XV, 62
7. XVII, 202	21. XX, 443	35. XVII, 301	49. XVIII, 486
8. XII, 181	22. XX, 325	36. XX, 428	50. XX, 320
9. IX, 766	23. III, 909	37. XV, 425	51. XIV, 14
10. VIII, 186	24. XIX, 63	38. XVI, 296	52. XVII, 509
11. XV, 124	25. XVI, 60	39. XVI, 179	53. XII, 596
12. XVIII, 472	26. XII, 290	40. XV, 346	54. XII, 618
13. XVIII, 81	27. IX, 373	41. IV, 113	
14. XVIII, 24	28. XIX, 325	42. II, 110	

9 EDUCATION

Considering the vital importance of the subject, it is surprising that some of the writers of the accounts do not address Sir John's questions on education at all. But among the many who do, there is a degree of unanimity unusual in the SA, with its fascinating diversity of views. One after another, the parish ministers, from Shetland to the Borders, take up their pens to pour out their indignation, or at times biting sarcasm, leaving the reader in no doubt about the precarious state of Scotland's education and above all, of the disgraceful exploitation of the schoolmasters.

Even ministers who might be thought to be concerned not to offend their landowning patrons take up the cudgels in this cause. Out of a large number of well-worded reports it is difficult to make a choice, but one or two may suffice as illustration. One who does not mince his words is the minister for Duffus, Morayshire: 'The school here, like those in many other parishes, is neglected; the salary only 7 bolls of barley; and the school fees so small, that nobody thinks it worth their while to accept of it, unless some young lad for a year or two. It seems the present generation of landlords wish to extirpate learning altogether, in order to introduce ignorance and slavery among the lower class of people, else they would give some encouragement to schoolmasters; and the opposition given to a late application to Parliament for augmenting the schoolmasters' salaries by the landed gentry, clearly marks their intentions.'[1]

In the parish of Craignish, Argyll, the writer's concern for the future of education in Scotland – formerly a just cause for pride – is evident: 'The school salary is only 100 merks, and 50s. arising out of a mortification, which, along with perquisites, may amount to about £20 per annum; a miserable allowance to a man of genius for employing his time and talents in qualifying the rising generation to fill up the vacant stations in society with honour. What a reproach to the people of Scotland, that this most useful class of citizens, in their late attempt for a small augmentation of salary, could not find, among all those who received the early benefit of their instruction, one to support their honest cause! At this rate, the ages of darkness will again commence; and Scotland will, ere long, be as remarkable for wealth and ignorance, as it was formerly for poverty and learning.'[2]

Describing the kind of learning for which Scotland had been renowned, the Campsie minister writes: 'Upon the whole, I would style the common education of Scotland, partly religious, and partly philosophical; it would not be in our interest to see it violently broken in upon; it is this mode of education which gives the Scotch nation such an attachment to speculation in religion.'[3] The

74

account for Auchterderran, Fife, in a somewhat patronising tone, underlines the generally high educational standards in comparison with some other European countries: 'In common with the rest of Scotland, the vulgar are, for their station, literate, perhaps, beyond all other nations. Puritanic and abstruse divinity come in for a sufficient share in their little stock of books; and it is perhaps peculiar to them, as a people, that they endeavour to form opinions, by reading, as well as by frequent conversation, on some very metaphysical points connected with religion, and on the deepest doctrines of Christianity. They likewise read, occasionally, a variety of other books unconnected with such subjects.'[4]

The reason behind the ministers' fears for the future and their anger at the present state of affairs thus seems plain – it is simply the abysmally poor livings offered to the schoolmasters. Around a century earlier, in the reign of William and Mary, an Act had been passed to ensure that each parish should have a school and schoolmaster. The minimum salary should be 100 merks Scotch, and the maximum 200, this sum to be paid by the heritors in the same way as the stipend of the parish minister. After a great increase in the cost of living, however, what had been a reasonable provision had become wholly inadequate; 100 merks was just £5.11s.1⅓d. sterling (in some cases augmented by local bequests); while the schoolmaster often held the offices of session clerk and precentor in the church – and even of gravedigger. Nevertheless it was estimated that more than half of Scotland's parish schoolmasters received less than £16 per annum. True, what was called a dwelling-house (but by many of the ministers 'a mere hovel') was usually provided, but some of these contained only a single room. A final demeaning touch was added in that in a large number of cases the legal salary was divided among the tenants, leaving the unfortunate dominie to collect it as best he could.

These injustices are well illustrated in many accounts, including Heriot, Lothians: 'He is also precentor, grave-digger, beadle, session-clerk, and yet his whole income does not exceed £8 sterling. This, with the paltry accommodation, holds out little encouragement to a teacher of any merit. Indeed, no man who possesses strength to lift a mattock, or to wield a flail, would accept of such a disgraceful pittance.'[5] Sarcasm is employed by the writer for Fala and Soutra, Lothians: 'The school-master's salary is not the largest in the country, being only £2.4s.4d. The school fees are in proportion. English is 1s.6d., writing 2s., and arithmetic 2s.6d. a quarter – very great encouragement, indeed, for a man of abilities to be schoolmaster of Fala!'[6] Again, after listing the various extra-mural earnings as registrar, session clerk and precentor (bringing the total salary to a princely £17.3s.5½d.), the Borthwick, Lothians, writer comments: 'This, by no means one of the worst livings of the kind, never can be an object to a man who has got anything like a liberal education. To one who is only tolerably well informed, or at all qualified to be useful, and who must dress, and is supposed to live, a little above the common lot, it is only a kind of genteel starving . . . But we shall cease to wonder, when it is observed, that although the wages of the very lowest of his employees have been doubled, and in many instances tripled, those of the schoolmaster have not been altered for a century.'[7]

In a few cases the accounts appeal to Sir John Sinclair – for example from Auchtermuchty: 'Upon the whole, if Sir John Sinclair wishes that his patriotic exertions should be effectually crowned with success, and the condition of the country meliorated, he must devise some means of increasing the salaries of country schoolmasters.'[8]

'Had not the present teacher been disabled for working as a common mason, he must have spurned at such a livelihood as this,' states the account for Kirkpatrick-Juxta, Dumfriesshire.[9] Interestingly, the earnings of masons would have been considerably more – their wages are given in several accounts as anything between 1s. and 1s.8d. per day. In a few other instances, too, it becomes clear that schools previously served by well-educated men have now been taken over by those with far lower qualifications. One extra perquisite of the schoolmaster, while it is believed to have been fairly common, is mentioned only once; this is the dues from cock-fighting, of which the Applecross, Wester Ross, account states: 'He hath no perquisites but the quarter's payment of 1s.6d. for English scholars, and 2s.6d. for Latin and arithmetic, and the cock-fight dues, which are equal to one quarter's payment for each scholar.'[10]

In considering comparative incomes, it is of interest to look in passing at that of the other educated men of the parishes, the ministers themselves. On the whole, their stipends were adequate – and in the light of the schoolmasters' poverty, positively affluent. The budget of the Campbeltown minister reads as follows: 'For the minister's clothes, linens, hat, stockings, boots and shoes, per annum, £10.'[11] On less than this, many dominies were expected to keep an entire family.

It would seem only sensible that, rather than starve, the schoolmaster might have been permitted to find as much supplementary employment as possible, but this was not at all popular with the people. The Glenholm, Borders, account relates the story of a schoolmaster who had become a shop-keeper, but 'this has created a prejudice against the school, and made several averse from sending their children to it, apprehending that the course of teaching will be much interrupted.'[12] Another Borders account suggested that the financial situation should be eased by allowing schoolmasters to carry out such duties as 'clerking to Trustees upon the public roads; to justices; to heritors; at parochial meetings,' – those duties not calculated to interfere with his calling. The account continues: 'Might not the schoolmasters keep the side post-offices, where only a runner is requisite; the opportunity of the scholars would be very useful in sending intimation of letters lying at the office to people who do not regularly send to the office for letters, etc.'[13]

For the whole unsatisfactory state of affairs, many writers have no hesitation in blaming the local landowners. One report is especially interesting since it was, unusually, written by the schoolmaster himself: 'When an attempt was made, some time ago, to have the condition of the schoolmasters of this country somewhat bettered, the argument, by which some lords and gentlemen opposed it, was, that "they wished parish schools were suppressed altogether, because their servants were corrupted, by being taught to read and write; that they would be more obedient and dutiful, were they more ignorant, and had no education." This, however, is not the opinion of any gentleman in this parish. They well know, that some of the first and most respectable characters in the nation, have been trained up at county schools.'[14] A Galloway account complains that the clergy's role in the management of parish schools has been entirely superseded by the landed interest: 'Heritors will not so much as allow a minister to vote in the choice of a schoolmaster. They will choose him from year to year; they will pull into fragments a salary of ten pounds; and the parish minister is neither able to dispute such proceedings in a law court, nor is it believed, that he would be well heard, if disposed to ask redress.'[15]

There are exceptions. In Ratho, Lothians, for instance, the dominie has fared well: 'About 10 years ago, the schoolmaster being rendered unfit, by age, for the duties of his office, most of the heritors voluntarily agreed to double the salary, and raised it to about £24, of which £10 with a free house, was allotted to the old schoolmaster for life, and £14 established as a salary for an efficient teacher, the choice of whom was left to the minister. Ever since there has been at Ratho a numerous and thriving school; and within these two years, the heritors have expended above £150 sterling in enlarging the schoolmaster's house and rebuilding the school; which is finished and furnished in so complete a manner, that it may be considered as a model for other parts of the country, there being few such in Scotland.'[16] Upon reading the SA, though, one would be forgiven for believing that not only were there 'few such', but none at all.

Yet all is not undiluted gloom. A minority of the reports are at pains to stress both the conscientiousness and the contentment of their schoolmasters. From Banchory-Devinick comes an account of quite extraordinary devotion: 'The parochial schoolmaster here is Mr Robert Cormack. He had his education at Marischal College; but never raised his views higher than his present situation. He is a most industrious and successful teacher, labouring in his vocation from Sunday to Sunday, and from morning to night. He has the merit of having established a Sunday School here as far back as 1782. Not fewer than 70, on an average, attend regularly in the course of a day, young men before public worship, and young women after it; and this indefatigable teacher attends them *gratis* from 6 o'clock in the morning till late in the evening. How inadequate is this man's salary, although amongst the highest enjoyed by country schoolmasters! It is £11.3s.10²/₃d. sterling.'[17] It may be added that a small garden was among the emoluments included in some areas – although in the case of an incumbent of this calibre it is difficult to imagine when he could ever have hoped to benefit from it.

Another account, not otherwise distinguished for a rosy view of the parish (for example the roads are described as being 'execrable') states: 'The encouragement for a schoolmaster here is very poor. The salary is only 4½ bolls of meal, and £1.13s.4d. Notwithstanding which, the present schoolmaster has remained in this office since the year 1745, and is perfectly satisfied and content with his lot.'[18]

From about 1750, most Lowland parishes at least had some kind of school. In some areas, however, especially in the more remote Highlands, the parishes were too large, and the population too scattered, for more than a small percentage of the children to be able to attend. A much-needed addition was provided in a large number of parishes by the Scottish branch of the Society for Propagating Christian Knowledge (SPCK). These schools are frequently given much credit in the accounts; for instance from Strathdon, Aberdeenshire: 'Excepting in a mild winter, the school is seldom throng, owing to the situation of the parish. It abounds in hills, and rivers and burns, so that children at a distance cannot attend in frost and snow . . . The parish has had the benefit of a schoolmaster, paid by the SPCK, for these years past. He has been generally stationed in the most distant parts of the parish from the parochial school; in all which places he has been highly useful.'[19] Often the people in sparsely populated districts had to resort to other arrangements; a young man who had just completed his university education might be engaged by several households, to live by turn in each, and instruct the children. There were even younger pedagogues than these − in Dunoon, for example: 'There are at least 8 schools in the district, for teaching to read and write; some of them are held only in winter, but 4 of them all the year round. The winter schools are taught by children from 12–15 years of age, who go from house to house, for about 20s. and their maintenance, to teach younger children than themselves; and it is surprising with what success they go through that business.'[20] Winter schools were by no means unusual. In summer, a great many children were employed in herding, their earnings, small as they were, making a significant contribution to the family budget.

Some of the educational projects highlighted in the SA make interesting reading − and have a surprisingly modern ring. Today we hear much of education orientated towards practical skills. This was being advocated in eighteenth-century Scotland! The account for Bothwell states that: 'This country is employed in agriculture, manufactures, and commerce. The education should be adapted to these objects. Academies, upon a similar plan established in towns, and endowed with proper salaries, would be much for the benefit of the public. The bulk of mankind have neither the time nor money to procure a liberal education; a scheme of this kind brings instruction within their reach, and tends to reconcile them to it; would produce genius and improvements in mechanics, manufactures, in all professions; and communicate to the generality of the people various branches of knowledge, of which they are at present destitute.'[21]

A very unusual teaching skill is highlighted in the account for Duplin and Aberdalgy, Perthshire, as part of a general eulogy of the local dominie: 'It will not be deemed improper to add, that he has acquired without any instructor, the rare talent of communicating knowledge to the deaf and dumb, and of teaching them to speak. A boy of this description, not 12 years of age, who never had another teacher, has made a very great proficiency under him. Already he articulates a great many words pretty distinctly, and his articulation appears to be fast improving . . . He can read, write, and solve any question in the common rules of arithmetic, as well as most boys of his age, who do not labour under his disadvantages . . . There are few better qualified to teach English, writing, arithmetic, book-keeping, and the first principles of mathematics.'[22]

Night-schools also flourished in some places − for example in Campsie, Stirling-shire: 'There being several works in the parish, the night-school is considerable, being wholly made up of grown persons, who attend for the purposes of writing, arithmetic, etc.'[23] Another interesting variation is provided in the report from Eckford in the Borders: 'As the school is not centrical, some infirm persons are employed to teach young children at a distance the English language, and the elementary principles of religion from the catechism. They are furnished with a house gratis from the farmers, and satisfied by their parents with what they can afford.'[24] And the Kirkmichael, Perthshire, report mentions voluntary teachers who taught English and writing in the remoter parts of the parish.[25]

Most remarkable of all, perhaps, is the teacher mentioned in the account for Aberdour, Aberdeenshire: 'There is a woman lives within ¼ of a mile of the church, who has taught young children to read English and knit stockings, upwards of 40 years with great success; and what is very extraordinary, has still a few scholars, who make a good progress under her instruction, though she is upwards of 90 years of age.'[26] Not least extraordinary was the fact of this venerable woman having become a teacher of English at all – girls were generally considered necessary to run a household. In Peterhead '9 women teach the younger children reading, and the girls knitting and sewing.'[27] On a more genteel note in Forres: 'There is a boarding school for young ladies, where the various branches of needlework, music, and other parts of female education, are taught with great success.'[28] And in Thurso, Sir John's home town, it is 'much to be regretted, that there is not in Thurso a boarding school for girls, where they might be taught needle-work, music, and the other branches of education suited to the sex.'[29]

Taking the country as a whole, it has to be said that for the time, the range of subjects taught is remarkable indeed. In addition to the elementary schools, grammar schools and academies existed, mainly in the large burghs but often also – principally through the bequests of local benefactors – in some of the smaller ones as well. From the accounts, the schools in Arbroath, Ayr, Banff, Brechin, Forres, Fortrose, Inverness, Kelso, Kirkwall, Nairn, Perth and Peterhead appear to have been outstanding; there are indeed so many, offering such a wide range of subjects, that one can only pick a few at random. Irvine, Ayrshire, for example, boasted two public and several private establishments. 'Before our connection with America was dissolved, many young men from that country and the West Indies were sent here for their education. Mr Cunningham, who was then rector, and had always a doctor under him, had frequently 20-26 boarders in his house.'[30] The subjects taught were arithmetic, writing, book-keeping, mathematics, French and geography. In Peterhead, there was an academy for teaching English, Latin, Greek, writing, arithmetic, book-keeping, mathematics and navigation, taught by two masters with 'very poor salaries'[31].

The 'magistrates and gentlemen' of Inverness went about the establishment of a 'seminary of learning' in the grand manner, subscriptions being opened eventually in Scotland, England, France, America, and the East and West Indies. An enclosure of about 3 acres was purchased and an elegant house built, consisting of a large hall and 6 spacious apartments in which a formidable array of subjects was taught: 'English, Latin, writing, arithmetic, Euclid's elements, book-keeping, geography, mensuration, trigonometry, navigation with lunar observations, architecture (naval, civil and military), practical gunnery, fortifications, perspective and drawing, civil and natural history, chymistry and astronomy.' The writer adds that 'at the desire of the Highland Society of London, there is a class opened for the teaching of the Gaelic language. There is likewise a dancing school, and a music school well attended.'[32] Several accounts mention classes in dancing; but few, if any, could hope to compete with the ambitious curriculum offered in the Highland capital.

Nevertheless, it is often the modest rural schools described in these accounts which attract the most attention because of their excellence. Perhaps the most notable example of all is the one which was set up by the SPCK to meet the needs of the displaced Highlanders who laboured to clear the great mosses (see Mosses) which now make up the rich farmland of the carse country of Central Scotland. This description comes from the Kincardine report. The Gaelic-speaking people, not at that time integrated with the rest of the population, clearly required their own school and teacher: the proprietor thus applied to the Society, with the plea that the children should have access not only to schooling but to religious instruction. 'For though,' writes the parish minister, 'by the rules of that Society, its benefactions are confined chiefly to the Highlands; they seemed to have a well-founded claim to the aid of the Society.'[33] At Martinmas in 1793 an experienced teacher was settled at the moss. Generously, the proprietor had added £5 per annum to the Society's £10 so as to procure an above-average teacher; he also agreed to the Society's requirements to provide a schoolhouse, dwelling-house, kail-yard, fuel, and the maintenance of a cow, and as a further bonus added one acre of carse land free of rent. 'This teacher, who is well acquainted with the Gaelic and the English languages, officiates through the week as a schoolmaster, and on Sundays convenes the people in the schoolhouse, where he instructs them in the principles of religion, and says prayers for them in their native tongue.' Surely a heartening story with which to end this brief survey of the educational scene in Scotland towards the end of the eighteenth century.

A summing-up comes from the Peebles account: 'The institution of parochial schools is to the honour, as well as the utility of Scotland. It shows the wisdom and patriotism of our ancestors in a high degree. At these necessary and useful little seminaries of literary knowledge, established by law in every parish, many have received the first principles of literature and religious knowledge, who have become ornaments to their country, and blessings to mankind.'[34]

1. XVI, 508	10. XVII, 293	19. XIV, 705	28. XVI, 614
2. VIII, 79	11. VIII, 52	20. VIII, 92	29. XVIII, 178
3. IX, 261	12. III, 758	21. VII, 66	30. VI, 250
4. X, 48	13. III, 861	22. XI, 162	31. XV, 414
5. II, 272	14. VII, 76	23. IX, 261	32. XVII, 98
6. II, 252	15. V, 385	24. III, 432	33. XII, 604
7. II, 74	16. II, 419	25. XII, 673	34. III, 875
8. X, 48	17. XIV, 20	26. XV, 6	
9. IV, 341	18. XV, 270	27. XV, 414	

10 POOR RELIEF

In much that is written about Scotland's past, it is often the extreme frugality – or at times the meanness – of the people which is highlighted. In the SA it is rather their generosity which is noticeable, as the account from Machlin (Mauchline), Ayrshire, states: 'There is, in general, ample ground for the common observation that "it is the poor in Scotland who maintain the poor".'[1] In a tribute to his parishioners, the Strachur and Stralachlan, Argyll, minister wrote: 'Many plans have been concerted by the Commissioners of Supply, and the Synod of Argyle, for preventing beggars from travelling about without the bounds of their respective parishes; but the prejudices of the people, in general, have been such a bar to these plans, that they have all proved ineffectual. No fine will prevent some people from giving alms to whoever asks it *for the love of God*. Though the master of a family should give strict orders against it, his orders will not be obeyed. The beggars take advantage of this prejudice; some from necessity, others from idle habits, will persist in going about. It is much to be wished for, that some criterion could be established, by which the truly necessitous could be known. But till that is clearly done, would it be proper to discourage giving alms? Giving daily to the poor, nourishes habits of benevolence.'[2]

In voicing his concern that 'some criterion could be established' by which genuine need might be recognised, this minister touches on the principal dilemma which faced those reponsible for relief of the poor in each parish; in some areas, large numbers were obviously involved. It is a question which arises in report after report, as the writers struggle to express their concern that a fair and just system might be evolved.

Two Acts of Parliament, passed in the late sixteenth century, had placed the onus of poor relief fairly and squarely on the 'indwellers' of the individual parishes. At the time of the SA being compiled, responsibility for allocation of the funds fell upon the Kirk Sessions. In an attempt to resolve the vexed question of eligibility, some had divided recipients into two categories. The first, the 'enrolled', or permanent, poor, comprised those infirm through age or disability, as well as widows and orphans; the second were those temporarily in need because of illness or unemployment, or those simply requiring to be tided over until harvest.

The funds distributed – in most cases, pitifully small sums – came principally from the collections at the church door, dues paid for use of the 'mort-cloth' to cover the coffin at funerals, and interest on charitable bequests.

Since there were many variations in the manner in which the problem of poor relief was dealt with around the country, it would seem helpful to offer some examples from the different areas. First, though, a snippet from the account for Newton, Lothians, has an intriguing note. As stated above, the rental of the parish mort-cloth at funerals was one of the main ways of raising funds for the poor. Imagine the consternation therefore when the local body of colliers had the temerity to purchase their own. Worse was to come, for the carters followed their example, and 'as the great body of the parish consists of these two descriptions of people, the kirk session foresaw that this practice, if allowed to continue, would soon go nearly to extinguish altogether the funds arising from the use of the parish mort-cloths.'[3] (*See* Burial Customs.) The matter eventually went to law, the Court of Session ruling that the use of any but parish mort-cloths was forbidden.

Some parishes were extremely generous. One such is Grange, Banffshire: 'The people in general are uncommonly humane and benevolent. When any poor person or family is afflicted with sickness, or any other unexpected calamity, the neighbours do not wait to be solicited, but carry meal, or whatever else the situation requires, or their circumstances afford; and they watch the sick, etc . . . Many of the poor also have bags in the mills, into which every one puts as much as he can spare, or as charity disposes him. And on the Christmas holidays, the young men go out in parties through the parish, a-begging for the greatest objects of charity; and several bolls of meal, and some pounds sterling of money, are collected every year, and committed to the care of members of session, for behoof of those for whom it is collected. This practice has an excellent effect upon the morals, both of young and old; it disposes the old to acts of liberality, and draws forth their sympathy towards the distressed; and it trains up the young to acts of benevolence and charity.'[4] It should perhaps be added that this parish was one which had suffered greatly during and after the severe dearth of the years 1782 and 1783.

In Montrose, charity was given particularly to widows, which included help with rents and purchase of coals. There was also a 'sailors' box', which according to the minister was generally 'not rich, as many of the mariners scruple to pay the dues.' Ship-wrecked sailors received help 'if their story is judged to be genuine.'[5]

The difficulty of deciding who was worthy to receive benefit repeatedly surfaces in the reports. Some made an attempt to discriminate on grounds of character, as this excerpt from Fearn, Ross-shire, reveals: 'Lady Ann Stewart, spouse to Baron David Ross of Balnagown, mortified 3,000 merks Scotch for the use of the religious poor . . . sometimes one parish will get more, sometimes another; but not disposed for beggars, but for aged and reduced people of good character. And the people on the list in each parish, get some 5, some 10, some 15 merks, as they are judged deserving, as far as it will go, for life.'[6] One cannot help wondering just how much heart-searching this caused among the recipients or envy among refused applicants, not to mention headaches to the clergy who were patrons of the fund.

The account for Kilsyth pays tribute to the sterling work of the elders of the Kirk in the administration, and especially the actual collection of the funds for the poor – work which he clearly feels the gentry would be unwilling themselves to undertake: 'With diligence and discretion they consider the case of the needy. By associating with every class of people, they become acquainted with the real wants and dispositions of the widow, the orphan, the fatherless, the feeble, the aged and infirm, and speedily administer relief. Upwards of £100,000 sterling at least, is entrusted to the elders of the Church of Scotland; and by them distributed with a degree of fidelity and public spirit, which reflects the highest honour upon their office. Yet though the landed interest are relieved of a burden, which they themselves could not submit to, it is seldom that they will allow a Session house, or even a shade [shelter] for collecting for the poor . . . and yet I suppose, that the greatest part of them would sooner erect such a shade, than submit to the drudgery of standing a whole hour, even one Sunday of the year, in a cold, bleak winter day in the open air, to collect the mite which every worshipper offers.'[7]

In the Western Isles, where the numbers on the poor roll were generally large, there seems to have been a fairly wide variation in the level of support given. According to the Harris account: 'Here the poor have many advantages, and, though numerous, are upon the whole well provided for. In the season of plenty they are liberally supplied by the people, who are very charitable.'[8] Unfortunately, it was in the lean seasons that things could be extremely serious for the poor. In Harris, too, matters were complicated by an abundance of 'vagrant sturdy beggars from other countries.' In this case, badges were given out to the local parish poor as a protection. According to the writer, however, they regarded these as 'an ignominious distinction', reflecting the general dislike of charity which undoubtedly characterised the vast majority of the Scots of the day.

The North Uist account reads: 'The number of poor to whom charity is given amounts to 50. The only fund for their support arises from the fines of delinquents, the collections made at the church-doors on Sundays, and at the time set apart for the celebration of the Lord's Supper. Lord Macdonald also orders a few pensions for the benefit of the most needy. But the poor are indebted for their personal support to the people at large, among whom they go about begging, and who are in general very charitable.'[9]

Very different views were being expressed on practically every subject, as well as the present one, by the writers of these reports, even in neighbouring parishes; from Oxnam in the Eastern Borders: 'It is much to be regretted, that a taste for finery, inconsistent with their station, prevents many from relieving their aged and indigent parents, and other near relations, and exposes them to want, upon the approach of sickness and old age; while, at the same time, it deprives them of a luxury, far superior to that of superfluous ornament, the *godlike pleasure* of dispelling grief, and *communicating happiness*.'[10] But it is not like this at all, according to the appendix to an account from the neighbouring parish of Jedburgh: 'The law which provides for the poor, instead of dissolving, tends to strengthen pastoral, and parental, and filial love. It is alleged, that the poor rate prevents the common people from laying up against the time of need. The desire of laying up is so strong, that the poor-rate has not yet, and probably never will extinguish it. A spirit of independence pervades the people; they feel the humiliation of receiving alms; they discern the difference betwixt having of their own, and trusting to what is given.'[11] (It should be added here that the writer refers to the poor's rate to which certain parishes had turned to supplement the normal funds. This will be discussed later.)

Two reports from mainland Highland parishes will serve to highlight the general position in that area; on the whole, the numbers of poor seem unusually high. 'Nowhere can the poor be on a worse footing than here,' the Dornoch account asserts. 'The principal heritors do not reside in the parish, and therefore contribute nothing towards their support.' And in neighbouring Golspie: 'The trustees of the poor's money sometimes find difficulty to give to each as much money as will purchase a pair of shoes, to enable them to beg about for their bread.'[12] In contrast, one cannot help noticing how much better things are for the ordinary folk in parishes which have the good fortune to be helped by a benevolent landlord. In Glen Urquhart near Inverness, for example, Sir James Grant, although not actually resident in that part of his estate (his principal seat was in Strathspey) gave the smaller tenants rye-grass and clover seed as well as lint seed for new ground, and built a lint mill. Most of the people had also 'the comforts of a milch-cow'. As a result 'industry has been encouraged among the females, and both sexes exhibit, on Sundays and holy-days, a much improved appearance, from what they were wont to do formerly, by being now dressed in linen of their own growth and manufacture.' Sir James also gave his tenants lime for new ground and, there being plentiful limestone in the district, even 'allowed quarry leave free'. Little wonder that there were no poor mentioned in this particular report.[13]

The heritors are blamed in many of the accounts, first for their lack of interest in the welfare of the poor, and, more frequently, for their failure to attend church and thus contribute to the poor fund. The sectarists, or dissenters, are also reproached because they too were, of course, absent from the established church, on which the burden of maintaining the poor fell. One can easily understand the ire of the ministers when, in some cases, the dissenters' own poor were left to the mercy of the parish.

This situation is addressed, in no uncertain terms, in the account for Libberton, Lanarkshire: 'Shall we call for an assessment upon the heritors, and by making the lazy depend upon the pockets of the rich, open wide the door for idleness and sloth? Or shall we continue the present unjust plan, by which our real poor are half-starved? I pretend not to be possessed of legislative powers; but I am sure I could contrive a plan for the support of the poor of this parish, by which our present evils would be corrected. And first, I would propose that tax should be laid upon the sectarists, equivalent to what people in the same circumstances, and who attend the established church, voluntarily give every Sabbath at the church door. This is no more than justice; and as the offering we receive every Lord's day from each individual who attends the established church is commonly a halfpenny, the tax laid upon each individual should be the same.' Nor would the writer of this account allow the rich to escape their responsibilities: 'The landholders should likewise be obliged to contribute their mite according to their respective possessions in the parish; as they never reside in the parish, we never see their faces on Sabbath, and are consequently deprived of their collections at the church door.'[14]

On the other hand, the accounts occasionally relate stories of individual generosity, as in this account from Gargunnock, Stirlingshire: 'George Moir, Esq of Leckie, now deceased, generously added 100 guineas to the poor's stock in 1788. Being of the Scotch Episcopal Communion, he seldom attended the parish church. He saw, however, and he had the humanity to acknowledge, that the poor of the parish suffered a loss by his absence; and when he gave the sum above mentioned, he said, "he was only paying what he owed them".'[15]

A heritors' tax, based on the value of the land owned, did exist in a relatively small number of parishes. From the accounts it seems clear that, generally speaking, the ministers were not in favour of this, believing that it would lead to a spirit of dependence, and a lessening of the sturdy self-reliance which was the hallmark of the people's character. The Neilston, Renfrewshire, account states: 'Assessments indeed, never fail to counteract charity; and were the people to be once assessed, they would probably with-hold their collections altogether.'[16] But the Inveresk account defends the practice: 'It cannot be denied, that where collections are sufficient for the purpose, there is no plan for the maintenance of the poor that can be compared to it . . . but where they are insufficient, recourse must be had to assessments or poor's-rates.'[17] As an example of the kind of levy made, in the parish of Kincardine, Perthshire, the landowners paid 11s. 6d. on each £100 of valued rent.

A recurrent theme throughout the reports is the nuisance caused by beggars from outwith their own parishes, often referred to as 'strolling vagrants', 'impostors' or 'vagabonds'. Parishes in Perthshire especially were visited by needy folk from the Highlands in times of particular hardship, and they are generally spoken of with compassion. Not so the Irish beggars who seem to have come over in large numbers, mainly to Galloway and Ayrshire. The account for Mochrum, Galloway, states, with some cynicism: 'The parish is continually infested with foreign beggars, and especially the Irish, who come over here in great numbers, as they say, to visit their friends, a duty to which, it must be allowed, they are exceedingly attentive.'[18] That these vagrants could cause a disturbance of the rural peace is not in doubt, as the Fortingal (Fortingall), Perthshire, account explains: 'There are a great many beggars from other places. The only grievance, in this respect, is from swarms of tinkers, sailors, and vagrants, from the great towns, who, by dreadful imprecations and threatenings, extort charity, and immediately waste it in drunkenness and riot.'[19]

A similar situation existed, it seems, in the Galloway area, where the minister of the parish of Tongland complained in the account: 'This parish is pestered with Irish vagrants and sturdy beggars, through all the seasons of the year. The charity given these is extremely detrimental to the native poor of the parish. The clamorous vagrants impose upon the humane and charitable spirit of the people, by their fictitious and tragical tales of misery; and spend the alms they receive, by getting themselves drunk with whisky.'[20]

Generally speaking the Ayrshire reports tend to give an impression of particular concern for the poor, individual parishes having their own preferred method of offering assistance. In Colmonell, for example, potatoes are the main prop: 'They [potatoes] are the chief means of subsistence to the poorer classes of people, for at least three quarters of the year. No one who has land in his possession, refuses a potatoe rigg to a poor person; and very often they have both land and dung given them, for nothing.'[21] And in Dailly: 'The wages of artificers and common labourers are in ordinary cases sufficient for rearing and maintaining a family; but do not always enable them to lay up a fund for old age or accidental disability. In such situations, they either receive occasional assistance, or are inrolled on the list of paupers for regular supply from the charitable funds of the parish. Idiots and furious persons, and the children of those who die in poverty, are also usually provided for from the same funds.'[22] In Ayr itself, the fund came from an interesting list of subscribers: 'The town gives £30, the sailors £10, the writers £5, the merchants £3; and other small corporations contribute to the extent of £14 or £15; besides which, there is a half-year's stent of £50.'[23] The town also supported what was called a 'Charity-house'. This had been built in 1756, and offered accommodation for 60 persons, but, as many pensioners preferred a small weekly allowance instead, it seldom housed more than 40.

Poor's houses are mentioned in a relatively small number of reports, mainly in the more prosperous towns. The Banff account states that 'the funds for the maintenance of the numerous poor in this parish are considerable' – a highly unusual statement – and also describes a 'small hospital or bede-house, which affords lodging to eight poor decayed women.'[24] The Falkirk account also tells of a 'hospital for the support of four aged and infirm people, endowed in 1640 by Lord Livingston of Almond and Callander.'[25]

Another feature of the Ayrshire accounts is the mention of the growth of Friendly Societies (although by no means exclusively in that area). The Galston account states: 'One [such society] is established in this parish. It consists of about 50 members, and is called the penny or halfpenny society. It has no funds, which are too apt to be embezzled; but, when a brother is confined to bed by sickness, every member pays him a penny weekly, and if able to go about, though not to work, a halfpenny. This institution is found to answer; and might be adopted in other places with advantage.'[26] Several Galloway parishes mention Friendly Societies also; the Kirkpatrick-Durham account states: 'Societies of this description are becoming frequent in different parts of the country, and they seem to deserve encouragement; because the delicacy of the human feeling will be less hurt, when supplies are received from a source of this kind, than when received from the ordinary sources of charity.'[27] It has to be said that such sensitivity when discussing the needs of the poor is rare in the accounts.

A final quotation on the subject of these self-help initiatives comes from Kirkcudbright, Galloway: 'In this town a society was constituted in the year 1783, by a few persons, under the designation of the United Society of Kirkcudbright. The sole object of this society was to relieve the distressed, by preventing their want of subsistence while in sickness, and, in case of death, to defray the expenses of their funerals. It extends also to the relief of the widows and orphans of deceased members.'[28]

From all that is written in these accounts, one does not require much imagination to picture the abject misery in which large numbers of people must have lived. This was especially true of some of the Highland areas, where the number of paupers was generally taken as being 5% of the population. Following the disastrous harvests of 1782 and 1783, however, the plight of the poor must have been abysmal. References to this time of extreme hardship are far too numerous to include here; a small number will serve adequately as an illustration. The Wattin, Caithness, account states: 'Since 1782, the number upon the poor's roll has been greater . . . And, were it not for the charity of their affluent fellow men, their wants would be insupportable. All that the funds will permit of, is the price of a pair of shoes to some; as much as will buy a coarse covering to others; and what may purchase a firlot or six pecks of meal, during the scarcest seasons, to the most indigent.'[29] Caithness was a county in which there was an unusually high proportion of poor.

Fortunately, at the time of scarcity, the Government did supply meal to relieve the people's want. The ministers of several parishes also emphasise the remarkable provision of other sources of sustenance. In the Contin, Ross-shire, account for example: 'The situation of the parish, in 1782 and 1783, was truly deplorable, and no doubt many of the poorer sort must have died from want, were it not for the timely supply of corn sent by government to this country. One remarkable circumstance to be observed was, that although these years produced little corn, they were particularly favourable for the growth of grass, which yielded immense quantities of milk, the principal support of the inhabitants; and the kind providence of God was very remarkably seen towards the poorer sort, in causing the sheep and goats, the only cattle they had, to yield greater quantities, and more fruitful milk, than they were ever known to do before, or ever since.'[30]

Further north, again in the county of Ross, the Fearn account stresses a miraculous supply of the needs of the poor: 'In the years 1782 and 1783, victual got up to an enormous height, hitherto unknown in this country . . . The poor were partly relieved by the wisdom and generosity of the Barons of Exchequer, who sent 300 bolls of victual . . . And Providence was kind in those days of scarcity, in providing plenty of fish from the sea, so that not only the ordinary fishermen caught abundance, and sold them to the poor until the next crop grew up, but many poor people joined, got different cobles, and caught a quantity of cuddies, red codlings, and flounders, near the shore; also an extraordinary quantity of fine cockles was had near Tain, on this side of the Dornoch Firth, which was almost a miraculous supply and support to this and all the neighbouring parishes; so that hundreds of men and women, with their horses, were seen daily coming home with great burdens and loads of the best cockles, in such abundance as they never appeared before or since.'[31]

It is heartening to note that individual heritors also offered practical help to the poor during the years of want. The Borders parish of Gordon, for example, had the good fortune to receive assistance both from the local landowners and farmers, as well as from the minister: 'In 1783, oat-meal was at 2s.6d. and upwards, the stone; bear and pease-meal were scarcely to be had. The heritors of the parish gave money to the kirk-session, to enable them to sell oat-meal to poor house-holders at a discount of 8d. and 6d. the stone, which was of great use to preserve them from want. White pease were imported at Leith and Fisherrow in spring and summer. The farmers and minister brought white pease from Leith, &c., carriage free, and then sold the meal at the prime cost of the pease at Leith, to all in the parish who had no horses of their own; this was continued for five months.'[32]

In some parishes, mainly in the North-East, it was the wife's earnings by stocking-making which saved them from penury. And in others, recourse was had to fund-raising in a manner generally disapproved of by the clergy – neighbours would rally round a particularly needy family and, each contributing a small sum, would hold a 'drinking' for them. As with the Penny Bridals, these often ended in undue revelry and drunkenness.

Commonly those registered as paupers were required to sign away all their belongings to be handed over to the parish on their death. The account for the parish of Kilmuir Wester and Suddy, Northern Highlands, states: 'The heritors and session would admit none, but such as would sign a bond, under certain limitations, to leave all they were possessed of at their death, as a fund for the poor of the parish; the session obliging themselves to see such as signed this bond as regularly supplied, as far as the funds would allow, and, in the end, have them decently buried . . . Many of the poor beg from house to house; it would be deemed impious to refuse alms, or a night's quarters to any.'[33]

The same rule applied much further south; from the Oxnam, Borders, account: 'In order of their enrolment [as necessitous poor] they must give inventories of their effects, which become the legal property of the heritors, and are exposed to sale at their death. The heritors, steadily and uniformly, insist upon having these inventories, both for enlivening their own industry, and for stimulating their children and near relations to give them aid.'[34]

An interesting point emerging from several accounts is that there existed in certain areas something like an early version of carer's benefit. Small grants were offered to those willing to foster orphans or nurse chronic invalids. Far more commonly, however, relations and friends undertook such duties with no remuneration whatever, no doubt on the most slender of means. The outstanding case of a servant maid who brought up the children of her employers on their death has been told fully in the chapter on character. An intriguing variation is described in the account for Aithsting and Sansting, Shetland: 'The number of poor on the roll are ten, all of them aged and infirm. Each of them has a particular district in the parish to which they are confined, and every household keeps them one night a week for every merk land he labours.'[35]

Other accounts also furnish intriguing variations; one such is the Benholme account: 'Besides the other charitable donations, under the management of the kirk-session, there is a fund for teaching poor scholars, and supplying them with books. An annual collection is likewise made at the church doors, for the Infirmary of Aberdeen, which entitles the poor to medical advice and assistance, when they labour under any bodily stress, and likewise to proper accommodation, while their cure is performing.'[36] And in Arbroath, a fund existed for seven poor widows of shipmasters in that area, of the names Carmichael, Pearson and Strachan; while in Dunbar the account asserts that, as in all sea-ports, the number of poor there is very great. 'The frequent misfortunes happening to seafaring people, often throw whole families of helpless children on the charitable funds.'[37]

A most interesting highlight from the Assynt, Sutherland, account shows such sensitivity in preserving the dignity of the older people that it might well have valuable lessons for the present day: 'When anyone becomes old and feeble, their nearest relatives build a little comfortable house for them, close to their own residence; and even there the distaff and spindle is well managed. These old matrons nurse the children of their relations; the songs and airs of Fingal, and ancient heroes, are sung in the Gaelic tongue, to which the little children dance. Old men are prudently engaged in some domestic affair, such as repairing the houses of the neighbouring tenants etc. In short, they share with their relatives all the viands of the family.'[38]

But then, as now, people could occasionally be mis-diagnosed as being poverty-stricken! A story of such a case comes from Gargunnock, Stirlingshire: 'An addition was made to the funds of the poor in 1784, by a very singular circumstance. Two old women, sisters, who lived in the village of Gargunnock, had for many years every appearance of extreme indigence; though without making application for assistance from the parish. One of them at last, applied to be received on the poor's list; and, as no doubt was entertained of her poverty, she received four shillings per month. She died about six months after commencement of her pension. On examining her bedclothes, one purse (of gold and silver) was found after another, till the sum amounted to upwards of forty pounds sterling. Some old chests and barrels were found stored with beef, meal, cheese, and various other kinds of provisions; and it was evident that the poor woman had lived in great affluence. The relations of the deceased, on hearing of the discovery, came from a distance, to lay claim to her effects. But according to the settled rule of the parish, she had bequeathed all her effects to the poor, at the time she was received on the poor's list. One half was allowed to be the property of her sister, who had received no pension from the parish. The other half became the property of the kirk-session, to the great mortification of the relations; who certainly deserved this disappointment, as they had taken no notice of the deceased, while she lived.'[39]

Finally, two short excerpts would seem to sum up prevailing attitudes of the time. First, from the parish of Oathlaw, Angus: 'I hinted to Mr H a reason why we have so few paupers here, viz. we have neither brewers, nor beggars, nor bastards, nor bankrupts; but a sober, frugal, and laborious people; no idlers nor drunkards; every family brew their own beer; no sectaries.'[40] And from Tibbermuir, Perthshire: 'Long may the lower classes of people in Scotland be distinguished by that laudable pride of independence, which makes them struggle, to the last, to maintain themselves on the fruit of their labour, rather than depend, unnecessarily, on the charity of others.'[41]

1. VI, 448	8. XX, 90	15. IX, 365	22. VI, 137
2. VIII, 412	9. XX, 115	16. VII, 818	23. VI, 22
3. II, 365	10. III, 601	17. II, 321	24. XVI, 33
4. XVI, 227	11. III, 603	18. V, 475	25. IX, 295
5. XIII, 558	12. XVIII, 438	19. XII, 431	26. VI, 226
6. XVII, 386	13. XVII, 260	20. V, 337	27. V, 245
7. IX, 448	14. VII, 510	21. VI, 87	28. V, 203

29. XVIII, 223
30. XVII, 334
31. XVII, 390
32. III, 191

33. XVII, 457
34. III, 601
35. XIX, 384
36. XIV, 37

37. II, 474
38. XVIII, 313
39. IX, 365
40. XIII, 583

41. XI, 597

11 DISEASES AND HEALTH

Even for those not particularly knowledgeable on the subject of medicine, there is a great deal of interest in the answers to Sir John's questions on health and diseases in the parishes. As always, the replies are nothing if not diverse; some writers hardly mention the subject at all, while others answer in such meticulous detail that one would almost suppose them to be doctors themselves.

Some of the prevailing attitudes to illness are highlighted in a drily humorous report from Saline, Fife: 'There is a practice here, only too common in most places, which, it were much to be wished, was abolished or less used. When any one is taken ill, the neighbours think it their duty, or a piece of civility, immediately to frequent the house, and even crowd the room where the patient lies ... On these occasions, they are all physicians; they feel the pulse, shake their heads, and have an unlucky turn to foreboding the worst. I have known a man given up by his neighbours, who, in three or four days after, has been working in the stone quarry; and several persons are still alive, in very good health at this day, and likely to see some carried to their graves, who had long ago pronounced their doom.'[1]

A considerable number of the writers exhibit a surprisingly modern attitude to hygienic practices. The Banff account, for example, quotes from a printed address written by a former incumbent, Rev Mr Skene, on the care of patients with fevers: 'Among other advice, Mr Skene recommends great attention to cleanliness, washing the chamber of the sick person with soap and water, and, upon recovery of the patient, that his apartment should be white-washed with lime, laid on hot and the windows open every day.'[2] Had this advice been followed more widely, the history of the periodic ravages of such scourges as smallpox and typhoid might have been very different. The account for Cross, Burness and North Ronaldsay, Orkney, makes the same point: 'Fevers sometimes prevail; and when they seize one person in a house, they often affect a whole family. Relapses are frequent, as they are not at pains to wash the bedclothes when they have recovered.'[3] Given the kind of houses the people lived in, and the frequent lack of adequate water supplies, this seems not altogether surprising.

The oft-quoted minister of Clunie, Perthshire, who wrote an outstanding ac-count, adds a note on the generally prevalent fevers: 'When a fever comes here, it generally attacks numbers. This is owing in a great measure to the temerity of those who, from friendly intentions, visit the patient; but who, without observing proper caution, rush upon his breath, imbibe the contagion, and communicate it from house to house, and from village to village. This conduct is to be ascribed partly to ignorance and partly to religious prejudice, both of which are happily giving place to more sensible and enlightened views of things.'[4]

While most of the fevers mentioned are given a name, there are a few enigmatic references about which readers are left to form their own conclusions. The account for Banff, for instance, notes that 'an infectious fever prevailed here, with unusual violence, about the year 1782. Unwholesome food, particularly an immoderate use of potatoes (that year of a bad kind) were among the secondary causes to which this fever was ascribed.'[5] Again in 1782, a mysterious fever visited the parish of Lochlee, Angus: 'In May 1792, after an exceeding cold and wet spring, the wind blowing generally from the northeast, a fever made its appearance in the parish, which, in the space of six weeks, cut off 35 persons. It was attended with symptoms, similar to what accompanies an inflammation of the pleura. The persons affected had their spittle mixed with blood, within a few hours after the fever seized them; they felt a pain at or below their left pap; and died upon the 5th or 6th day.'[6]

A strange fever is reported, too, in the Lochcarron, Wester Ross, account: 'In 1791, there was a remarkable herring-fishing in this loch. During low water, the children of Kirktown went often to the strand, and carried lapfulls of herring with them. The people fed entirely on fish. They were visited by a fever. Their blood was vitiated. When they were let blood in the fever, it had the appearance, when it congealed, of the blood of a boiled pudding, or of an ugly type of jelly. Their breath smelled strong of fish. In proportion as they fed, soberly or voraciously, on the herring, the fever was more or less severe. Such as lived mostly on fish and other strong food, suffered dreadful agony. The poor people, that mostly lived upon water-gruel, suffered very little.'[7]

'No disease has of late years raged here with greater mortality,' declares the Deer, Aberdeenshire, account, 'than the putrid sore throat. It chiefly attacked children, sometimes cutting off 2, 3, and 4 of a family.'[8] This note, presumably referring to diphtheria, is one of several in these accounts, reminiscent of a huge number of poignant references to smallpox, which also quite commonly decimated entire families. (Smallpox is dealt with separately under the heading 'Inoculation', *see* Health.)

Another scourge was tuberculosis, or consumption. The minister of Deer, Aberdeenshire, hoped fervently for the cure, for which Scotland would unfortunately have to wait another 150 years. 'It appears at once striking and melancholy,' he writes, 'that almost one fifth of us are carried off, generally in the prime of life, by consumption. How desirable, a remedy for so fatal a disorder!'[9]

'The rheumatism and sundry fevers' is the reply given by many to Sir John's question on prevailing maladies. Given the climate, and the kind of housing described by a great many contributors, neither is exactly surprising. The account for the remote West Highland parish of Glenshiel offers its own explanation: 'The diseases most prevalent among the inhabitants of this place are rheumatisms, sciaticas and ruptures. They are daily exposed to damps and rains, which are believed to be the cause of the two former; the latter is attributed to the heavy weights which the men are in use of raising to their breasts when they back-load their horses; for, owing to the roughness of the country, and there being no roads, no waggon or cart can be used for any distance.'[10]

The Kirknewton, Lothians, account runs in similar vein: 'The diseases chiefly prevalent are the rheumatism and fevers, occasioned by the poorer people living in cold, damp houses, and resting after labour in wet clothes. When these fevers once begin, they often spread far and wide, as the people, from mistaken notions of sympathy and charity, crowd the house, and even the bedroom of the sick, which is kept close as often as possible.'[11]

For all of the above ills, the Eccles, Borders, account offers a simple panacea – flannel. 'Among the causes which have contributed to lessen the influence of the diseases peculiar to this climate, the incumbent's personal knowledge of its happy effects will not allow him to omit – *the wearing of flannel next to the skin*. Rheumatism proceeds evidently from the perspiration being obstructed on the surface of the body; and nothing but flannel will preserve this discharge uniform and equable, in a climate which is subjected to fogs, and to the vapours which arise from water stagnating on the surface of the ground. Could people be prevailed on universally to adopt this practice, it would do more to alleviate, if not extirpate, nervous diseases than the united powers of the entire *materia medica*.'[12]

A considerable number of accounts – especially in Perthshire – comment on the fact that ague, formerly very common, had disappeared, apparently due to improved drainage. The account for Abernyte, for example, reads: 'Agues, which some years ago appeared in great numbers, both in high and low grounds, have now entirely vanished. This has been attributed to the draining of wet lands, and more nourishing diet of the people. I have been assured, that 30 years ago, if a farmer in the spring wanted four of his cottagers for any piece of work, he generally ordered six, knowing the probability that some of them, before the work could be finished, would be rendered unfit for labour by an attack of the ague.'[13]

It is clearly of considerable nutritional interest to scan the pages of the SA for references to what we now know as deficiency diseases. Of rickets – only too well known in Scotland for centuries, and described medically in the seventeenth century – there is only one mention. This is in the statistical table of diseases for Kilconquhar, Fife, which states: 'rickets . . . uncommon'.[14] This is probably because, the Industrial Revolution being still in its infancy, the vast majority lived in rural or semi-rural conditions, not only enjoying exposure to sunlight but eating a diet which included, at least in times of relative plenty, dairy foods, eggs, oily fish and possibly liver.

The dread disease scurvy, on the other hand, is described in several accounts, sometimes in lurid detail. The Blackford, Perthshire, account, for example, asserts: 'The scurvy is the most predominant disease; and is attended with violent symptoms, such as aching pains in the joints and limbs, and hard livid swellings; in some cases tumours are formed, which suppurate and degenerate into scrophulous runnings; in some instances it affects the judgement, and makes the unhappy sufferers put an end to their own existence.'[15]

The principal interest lies perhaps in trying to ascertain whether the writers of the accounts actually connected the occurrence of scurvy with low intakes of vegetables (fruit, apart from wild berries, being practically unknown in most areas). Some clearly do recognise the connection, some possibly suspect it, and some seem to have no notion of it.

In 1747 a famous controlled experiment had been carried out by a Scots naval surgeon, James Lind. Taking 'twelve patients in the scurvy' on board the *Salisbury*, he proceeded to treat the six pairs with one or other of the popular remedies of the day (elixir vitriol, cider, sea-water, vinegar), while one fortunate pair received two oranges and one lemon each day. By the end of one week, the last-named were fit for duty.

In view of this resounding testimonial to the effectiveness of citrus fruits in the treatment of scurvy, the intriguing question is: to what extent had this percolated through to the doctors around Scotland, or to the ministers? It took, after all, until 1804 – half a century after James Lind published his *Treatise of the Scurvy* – for the Royal Navy to supply its sailors with lime juice as a preventative.

Of a very large number of references to the disease, only a few examples have been selected here, to demonstrate obvious awareness, partial knowledge or total ignorance of the connection between scurvy and a lack of fresh vegetables/fruit. First, the account for Carsefairn, Borders: 'Scurvies are little known, though most of the inhabitants live all the year round on salted provisions, which they use in great abundance. The pernicious consequences of this mode of living are obviated by the plentiful use of potatoes and other vegetables.'[16]

The writer of the account for Orphir, Orkney, cites several factors he believes to be protective: 'The ague is not known here, and scorbutic complaints seldom occur, owing, perhaps, to the abundance of fuel, to the frequent use of vegetables, and of malt liquor; and, above all, to the salubrious sea-breezes which cool the air in summer, and counteract the frosts in winter.'[17]

'Of all the diseases that prevail in this country, the scurvy is the most epidemical, and may justly be called the bane and scourge of human nature,' declares the account for Forbes and Kearn, Aberdeenshire. 'This distemper may primarily be contracted from various causes; idle indolent habits, unwholesome food, impure air, the want of attention to cleanliness, a sedentary life, &c., may occasion it. Sedentary employments are evidently nourishers of this, as well as of all other putrid disorders.'[18] There follows a depressing list of symptoms.

Oatmeal is blamed – and vegetables not even mentioned – in the account from Arngask, Perthshire: 'The scurvy is a common disorder, which originates, as is supposed, from the frequent use of oatmeal.'[19] Interestingly, another Perthshire report, for the parish of Dron, is by no means alone in ascribing anti-scorbutic properties to a mineral well: 'Scorbutic habits are not uncommon, being everywhere, in a less or greater degree, to be met with. But nature has provided a remedy for this disorder in the mineral waters of Pitkeathly in this neighbourhood, which have proved very effectual in some of the worst and most inveterate appearances of this malady.'[20] Despite one's natural tendencies to scepticism, it is difficult to remain unimpressed in the face of the detailed account of 'an Englishman, who had been dismissed from Carlisle Infirmary as incurable.' Suffering from florid scurvy, he came to take the waters in Kirkconnel: 'To say nothing of other effects of the scorbutic habit he laboured under,' asserts the acccount, 'he was quite emaciated, bowed down, feeble and dispirited. But after the regular use of the water, he gradually recruited, till in about 8 weeks he became quite well, and went away stout, and lively, and joyous, because of his unexpected and remarkable recovery.'[21]

Yet another curious note comes across in some of the accounts under the heading of the 'louping ague' – for example, from Craig, Angus: 'A singular kind of dis-temper, called the *louping ague*, has sometimes made its appearance in this parish. The patients, when seized, have all the appearance of madness; their bodies are variously distorted; they run, when they find an opportunity, with amazing swiftness, and over dangerous passes; and, when confined to the house, they jump and climb in an astounding manner, till their strength be exhausted. Cold bathing is found to be the most effective remedy.'[22]

Strangely, the phenomenon seems to be confined to Angus reports. The bizarre syndrome is described thus in the Lethnot account: 'There is a distemper, called by the country people the *leaping ague*, and by physicians, *St Vitus Dance*, which has prevailed for upwards of 60 years in these parishes, and some of the neighbouring ones. The patient first complains of a pain in the head, and in the lower part of the back; to this succeed convulsive fits, or fits of dancing, leaping or running at certain periods. This disease appears to be hereditary in some families.'[23] And also from Tannadice, Angus: 'Twenty or thirty years ago, what is commonly called the *louping ague* greatly prevailed. This disease, in its symptoms, has a considerable resemblance to *St Vitus Dance*. Those affected by it, when in a paroxysm, often leap or spring in a very surprising manner, whence the disease has derived its vulgar name. They frequently leap from the floor to what, in cottages, are called the *baulks*, or those beams by which the rafters are joined together. Sometimes they spring from one to another with the agility of a cat, or whirl round one of them with a motion resembling the fly of a jack. At other times they run, with astonishing velocity, to some particular place out of doors, which they have fixed on in their minds before, and perhaps mentioned to those in company with them, and then drop down quite exhausted.'[24]

Equally bizarre, and appearing perhaps to have something of the same hysterical origin, is the 'condition' described in the Delting, Shetland, account: 'Convulsive fits, of a very extraordinary kind, seem peculiar to this country. The patient is first seized with something like fainting, and immediately after, utters wild cries and shrieks, the sound of which, at whatever distance, immediately puts all who are subject to the disorder in the same situation. It most commonly attacks them when the church is crowded; and often interrupts the service in this, and many other churches in the country. On a sacramental occasion, 50 or 60 are sometimes carried out of the church, and laid in the churchyard, where they struggle and roar with all their strength for five or ten minutes; and then rise up without recollecting a single circumstance that had happened to them, or being in the least hurt or fatigued with the violent exertions they had made during the fit.' And an interesting addendum: 'One observation occurs on this disorder, that during the late scarce years it was very uncommon; and during the last two years of plenty it has appeared more frequently.'[25]

In a neighbouring parish, however, the beadle – clearly an early student of psychology – seems to have found the answer to the same problem, for the account from Northmaven declares that 'convulsions were once very common in this parish, especially during the time of divine service; but are now quite extinct. The cure is attributed to a rough fellow of a kirk-officer, who tossed a woman in that state, with whom he was often plagued, into a ditch full of water.

She was never known to have it afterward, and others dreaded the like treatment.'[26]

Scrofula (scrophula) or the King's Evil – so called because it was believed that a king's touch could cure it – features in several accounts; for example in that for Dundee which runs: 'The most frequent endemial diseases are consumption and the scrophula, by which last, perhaps, the former are principally produced. The scrophula seems chiefly to affect the families of linen-weavers, who sometimes feed poorly, and whose manufacture is carried on in damp and low floors.'[27] And in the account for Elgyn (Elgin): 'The diseases most prevalent, in this town and parish, are fluxes, consumptions, and the King's Evil . . . The progress of the scrophula is alarming, by intermarriage, and the imperfect cure of the lues, with a low diet.'[28] Interestingly, the writer of the account for Canoby (Canonbie), Dumfriesshire, also clearly believes intermarriage to be a perpetuating factor. That there is also a stigma attached to this disease is implicit in his account: 'I am sorry that a regard to truth obliges me to mention another disease, namely scrofula. Whether this direful malady be indigenous, or was at first introduced by inter-marriages, is not for the writer to determine. But it falls under his observation, that numbers in this place are more or less infected with it. And as it is an established fact, that it may be propagated through a series of generations, much caution ought to be used in forming matrimonial connexions, as the only effectual way of preventing the entail of this malignant disorder upon posterity, thus lightening so far the load of human woe.'[29]

Certain other diseases are mentioned less frequently – perhaps in only a single account – but often as the principal ailment suffered in that parish. In Northmaven, Shetland, for example, the account states that 'there is a species of leprosy that has been more prevalent than at present, and of which we have had several miserable instances in this parish; it seldom affects any but the lower class of people. Its symptoms approach nearer to those of elephantiasis, than any other description. It is supposed to proceed from low living, unwholesome or ill-prepared food, and living nastily.'[30]

In Dron, Perthshire, it is worms, an infestation which seems to cause serious effects: 'Another very fatal disease among children, and very prevailing, is that of worms; which cuts off many, debilitates the constitution of more, and is frequently attended with very violent and shocking symptoms.'31 (There is though, perhaps fortunately, no description of these.)

In Kilmallie, near Fort William, it is the dropsy, ascribed to the 'poorer sort of people's feeding so much upon potatoes.' This account also mentions the fact that the itch, formerly a common scourge in the parish, is rarely met with nowadays, because of cleaner ways of living. The writer then goes on to add: 'But this distemper is not peculiar to a Highlander – nor to a Scotchman. It is a *plant* which grows in countries south of the Tweed, else there would be no word to express it in the English tongue; and it is well known to have been one of the plagues incident to the Egyptians.'[32] In Cairny, Aberdeenshire, the account states that the manufacture of linen has introduced 'a certain cleanliness' which has all but banished the itch.[33]

Tetanus is the disease mentioned in the account for Killbrandon and Killchattan, Argyll. Described as 'very fatal to infants, generally attacking before the 8th day after birth . . . It is a fact, that one third at least, of all the children, particularly among the quarriers, die within the time specified. It is supposed that this loss is owing to ignorant midwives. And it must be confessed, that this complaint seldom appears where a bred midwife attends.'[34] One cannot help wondering whether the same unhygienic methods of smearing the umbilical cord prevailed here as on St Kilda, where tetanus continued to account for large numbers of infant deaths until well into the nineteenth century.

In Weem, Perthshire, the disorder singled out for special mention is jaundice: 'The jaundice, before the year 1789, was a very uncommon disorder in this country; but since that period, hundreds have been seized with it of all ages and sexes . . . no change in the way of living can account for this disorder being so frequent.'[35]

Outside of the main towns, hospitals are seldom mentioned in the accounts. A notable exception is that for Montrose, which is of particular interest since this establishment included a 'lunatic asylum' and a department of occupational therapy, which must surely have been unique for the times. 'Several pieces of coarse sheeting have been made, from the yarn spun by the lunatics in their lucid intervals. At such times, they are also occasionally employed in painting, reading, gardening, knitting stockings, spinning, and working with the needle. A piece of painting, in the mistress' room, done by one of the lunatics is, as such, a considerable curiosity. The humanity and frugality of the master and mistress, and the order and cleanliness of the house, merit the highest commendation.'[36]

Unfortunately it need scarcely be added that hospital treatment, or any medical treatment at all, was quite beyond the reach of the vast majority of Scotland's population in that era. The many human tragedies which, at least in the more remote areas, must have been the norm are highlighted in this poignant note from the Isle of Tiry (Tiree): 'The situation of the parish is dismal without a surgeon residing in it. Poor people cannot afford sending occasionally for a surgeon, to a distant country; the raging elements forbid it; or perhaps before the relief arrives, the hope of the family is no more. Too often has the present incumbent seen child-bed women, in particular, fall sad sacrifices without relief.'[37]

To round off this brief review of Scotland's league table of diseases in the late eighteenth century, a few of the morbidity statistics – which some of the reviewers clearly took considerable trouble to provide – are now included. Perhaps the most interesting feature is their total divergence from today's tables with their overwhelming preponderance of 'diseases of affluence'. A representative selection covering the different areas has been chosen.

Highland Area: Alvie, Invernessshire [38]

'Died between 1 February 1792 and 1 February 1793'

fevers	6	inward inflammation	1
consumption	3	old age	1
sudden death	2	hives	1
chincough	1	scurvy	1

'Diseases are stated as the family represent, as a surgeon is not always called upon.'

Central Area: Campsie, Stirlingshire [39]

'Of the last three years of burials, the diseases stand thus:'

fevers	8	bowel-hive	1
small-pox	15	measles	6
consumptions	26	child-bed	1
palsy	2	stillborn	1
asthma	1	mortification	1
chincough	6	old age	26

North-East: Benholme, Kincardineshire [40]

fevers	60	small-pox	43
rush fevers	5	chincough	8
consumption	21	child-bed	7
decay	77	casualties ★	24
dropsy	29	asthma	8
palsy	11	old age	36

★ Casualties:		
	drowned	6
	suffocated	2
	killed in battle	1
	fell from horse	1
	mad dog's bite	1
	fell into fire	1

Fife: Kilconquhar [41]

1. FEBRILE DISEASES

Inflammation of the throat and breast, rheumatism, croup, erysipelas, spitting of blood; consumption of the lungs, catarrh – very common and frequent. Inflammation of the bowels, brain, liver and kidneys – not very frequent. Gout and dysentery – very uncommon. Intermittent fever – very frequent formerly in the village. Continued fever – frequently endemic. Natural small-pox and measles – epidemic from time to time. Inoculated small-pox – very few instances.

2. NERVOUS DISEASES

Apoplexy, epilepsy, cholera morbus – not frequent. Palsy, fainting – not infrequent. Locked jaw, diabetes, canine madness – no instance for 20 years past. Hooping cough – epidemic from time to time. Diarrhoea – very frequent. Insanity – one instance at present.

3. CACHECTICAL DISEASES

General dropsy, dropsy of the belly, scrofula – very frequent. Tympany, jaundice – not infrequent. Dropsy of the brain and breast, rickets – uncommon. Atrophy, lues venerea, scurvy – no instances.

4. LOCAL DISEASES

Iliac passion, suppression of urine – not frequent. Hernia, abortion – not uncommon. Flooding – frequent. Gangrene – rare. Cancer – very rare. Aneurism – no instance.

5. ANOMALOUS DISEASES

Casualties, drunkenness – few instances. Dentition – frequent. Gravel and stone – pretty frequent. Worms – very common.

Health

A great many of the references to health seem to focus upon instances of outstanding vigour or, especially, longevity. Indeed it often looks as though ministers of neighbouring parishes are trying to score points off each other. Although these stories have perhaps to be taken with a pinch of salt – records at the time were by no means always to be trusted – they are nothing if not entertaining.

The first comes from the island of Tiry (Tiree): 'A Tiry man was allowed to be 106, at his death, in spring last. Except for the last seven years, he supported himself and his wife by herding. His liveliness appeared to the last, not only by walking but by dancing.'[42] Another note follows: 'A country man, who died last year about 5ft 10ins high, was employed by the Laird of Coll as post to Glasgow or Edinburgh. His ordinary burden thence to Coll was 16 stone. Being once stopt at a toll near Dumbarton, he humorously asked whether he should pay for the burden, and upon being answered in the negative, carried his horse in his arms past the toll.'[43] (In all fairness, it should be added that the horses of the time were not comparable in size to today's!) Finally, from Tiree: 'The people are very chearful and humorous, and there are not above two or three of either sex corpulent in either isle.'

The stories of two celebrated brothers are related in the accounts for two Border parishes. That for Crossmichael records that 'within these 20 years, at least 12 persons have died in the lower parts of Galloway, of 100 to 115 years old. William Marshall, a tinker in this place, is now 118. He might pass for a man of 60. His faculties are unimpaired, and he walks through the country with ease.'[44] From the neighbouring parish of Borgue, his brother is described thus: 'One person of 89, a tinker by trade, bids fair for rivalling his brother Marshall, celebrated in the annals of Crossmichael. He can drink a glass from the sole of his foot; and in feats of strength and agility, would surpass most men of 60. His teeth were all double and most of them yet remain fast in their sockets.'[45]

Another intriguing note occurs in the account for Inveraray: 'As an instance of longevity in this parish, it may be mentioned, that Provost Brown, late of

Inveraray, when 100 years old, headed one of the contending parties at a shinty match (a game peculiar to North Britain, something like the golf), and carried the town's colours in procession among the victors. He died in the 116th year of his age.'[46]

Unusual longevity is the subject of another account, this time from Kirkpatrick-Fleming, Dumfriesshire: 'The most extraordinary instance of longevity that this parish can boast of was a Thomas Wishart; he was born upon the 26th of September 1635, and died upon the 19th of December 1759, and consequently lived something more than 124 years; he retained the use of his faculties to the last; had lost none of his teeth; and had the use of his sight to such perfection, that he could thread a needle with ease. Not two days before his death, he travelled six miles upon very uneven ground; none ever heard him complain of infirmity, but he frequently expressed much regret at funerals; envying the deceased, he was wont to say: "everybody can die except me".'[47]

A brief note from the Air (Ayr) account runs: 'Many of the inhabitants are between 70 and 100 years of age. One walked to London after his 100th year.'[48] This apparent ability to walk phenomenal distances in old age is a recurrent theme in the parish accounts. So is the ability to carry out manual labour; as in the account for New Kilpatrick: 'There is now living a man near 93, who reaps and threshes his own corn, thatches his own house, and walks to Glasgow, 5½ miles distant, and returns the same day.'[49]

Inevitably the question comes to mind: were they really that vigorous? Even more, were they really that old? A few reports, perhaps anticipating readers' doubts, back up their claims with some kind of documentation, for example in the Buchanan account: 'There is one man living at present who is going on 99; he is remarkably healthy, rises every day by seven or eight in the morning, and if it is a good day, takes a short walk before breakfast; he has no complaint of his sight, hearing or memory; and his hand is as steady as when he was a young man; he was in arms in the year 1715 with his countrymen the Highlanders, and is the only man alive in this part of the country who was out at that time.'[50] Similarly, in the account for Barr, Ayrshire, the 1715 Rising is used as a point of reference: 'There is a poor old woman in the village who must, from her own account, be above 90; she remembers well the young men in this place learning the use of arms in the year 1715, and was reaping a corn ridge, a lass about 18 years of age, when the above men passed by to join the loyalists; she is very healthy, and able to walk about with her staff.'[51]

A different way of reckoning appears in the account for Northmaven, Shetland: 'Most of the old people in this parish, date their age from such a year before or after the mortal pox, which was in 1700 . . . There are at present living, three persons above 90 years old. The kirk-officer, who died in 1791, was aged 95. He calculated, as was usual with old people, from the time of the mortal pox, viz. 1700, and asserted that he was able to run a short errand of a mile or two.'[52]

These anecdotes, while colourful, confine themselves to the extraordinary. Scottish parish accounts today could probably furnish similar stories of certain outstandingly healthy and long-lived persons. It seems altogether more significant to note what minister after minister asserts with confidence about the entire population of his parish: 'They are in general remarkably healthy', or 'of a remarkably sound constitution'. It is hard to imagine this kind of statement being paralleled 200 years later! It does indeed appear that those Scots at the end of the eighteenth century who had survived the perils of an altogether hostile environment were, on the whole, quite remarkably fit and healthy, apart from the prevailing maladies, almost invariably cited as 'the rheumatism and sundry fevers'. The other diseases have already been noted.

It is of interest to look briefly at the various factors to which the writers of the accounts ascribe the health of their parishioners. Some believe it to be due to the quality of the air; for instance the writer of the account for Ardchattan and Muchairn, Argyll: 'The air is salubrious; the people in general remarkably healthy, and strangers to the diseases which spring from idleness and luxury. The different periods of longevity to which many have attained, is a strong presumption in favour of the climate.'[53] The Machlin (Mauchline), Ayrshire, account opts for two other factors to account for the local vigour: 'The inhabitants of this parish, are in general addicted to exercise and temperance, two great sources of long life and good health.'[54] Frugality is the secret, according to the account from Craignish, Argyll: 'The people enjoy good health . . . some of them who are verging towards 80, possess an uncommon degree of bodily strength and mental vigour. Far removed from that intercourse which, while it polishes the manners, corrupts the heart, and undermines the constitution of man, it was their happiness to have led a simple frugal life; and as they were strangers to those excesses to which luxury leads, they are now unacquainted with those distempers which it generates.'[55]

A new element is introduced, among others, in the Shapinsay, Orkney, account as a reason for the local longevity: 'As there is plenty of excellent peat in the parish, and as the air is wholesome, and food in tolerable abundance, the people live long.'[56] Whereas in Birsay and Harray, Orkney, a different set of circumstances is cited: 'In general, our people arrive to a good old age; owing, I suppose, to temperance, drinking beer, and eating some animal food; working hard, and sleeping cheerfully, and following their employments with alacrity.'[57] While beer may be regarded as healthy, tea most certainly is not. It is surprising to see how many accounts are inclined to express anger over the introduction of this beverage; for example, from the parish of Aithsting and Sansting, Shetland: 'The people are not so healthy as formerly, owing to the great alteration in the mode of living. The general use of tea, but lately introduced, has made a very rapid progress. The poorest family in the parish will not now dispense with it, and will sell their clothes, yea their meal, to purchase it. They use a very coarse kind of black tea, and drink it very strong, often without milk and sugar.'[58]

When one looks carefully at the actual statistical tables which some of the writers include for their parishes, it is clear that in general, longevity does not in fact compare with today's figures. What is noteworthy, however, is the way in which those who did live long seem to have retained their faculties so as to be able to live a completely 'normal' life to a remarkably late stage – in many cases, right up to their death. There are indeed so many instances of this phenomenon that it is hard to make the best selection.

The account for Canisbay, Caithness, asserts: 'There are few districts where more good health is enjoyed than in Canisbay. The inhabitants in general live to a good old age. There are several at present in the parish betwixt 90 and 100. Many die at an advanced age, without the recollection of a day's illness in the course of their lives.'[59]

An intriguing note comes from Gamrie, Banffshire: 'Mr Wilson is in his 97th year; and last autumn, at the conclusion of the harvest, the age of him and the two servants that assisted in taking in his crop, amounted in all to 257 years.'[60]

The ability to father children at an advanced age is cited as a characteristic of outstanding vigour; and of this there are several examples. From Halkirk, Caithness: 'The natives are in general very healthy, vigorous, firm, agile, well proportioned, excellently calculated to undergo fatigue and hardships . . . There are besides instances of longevity not a few. In the course of my incumbency, there have been several men and women who survived 100 years and upwards . . . Here I should not omit observing, that there is a man in my near neighbourhood, on the borders of 80 years, who can number upwards of 120 persons of his own progeny, besides those who died. The number is still increasing by his children, grandchildren, great grandchildren etc., and what is of particular remark, he is still healthy and vigorous, and is as able to add to the number by his own personal exertions, as he was several years ago; so that if he is spared but a few years, I have no doubt but he may see the number doubled.'[61] Another amusing anecdote along the same lines comes from Parton, Galloway: 'A few years ago, a man died above 90, who, about eight months before his death, got a complete set of new teeth, which he employed till near his last breath to excellent purpose. He was four times married, had children by all his wives, and at the baptism of his last child, which happened not a year before his death, with an air of complacency expressed his thankfulness to his Maker for having "at last sent him the *cled score*" [the twenty-first].'[62]

Again from Galloway (Kirkpatrick-Durham), comes this account: 'The inhabitants, who are naturally of a sound constitution, and who meet with no remarkable occurrences to waste their strength, generally enjoy the blessings of life to a remote old age. There died lately in the parish, a woman aged 108 years, whose faculties were fresh, and almost unimpaired to the last; and there are living in it, just now, a number of persons on the borders of 90, who support the fatigues of their respective employments, with an astonishing degree of strength and agility, and who tell the tales of former years, with a vivacity and cheerfulness, almost approaching to the gaiety of youth.'[63]

The account for Orwel, Kinross-shire, makes the bold claim that 'the inhabitants of this parish are not only entirely free of all disease, but are strong, robust, and of a healthy constitution. Many of them live to a great age. One woman in particular may be mentioned, who, though upwards of 94 years, is in good health, and supports herself by spinning.'[64] And from Sorn, Ayrshire, comes this account: 'Within a very small distance of the church, there are just now living a shoemaker in the 90th year of his age, and who still occupies the house in which he was born; the church-officer, who is in his 85th year; a gardener in his 95th, and his wife, nearly of the same age; also the possessor of a small farm, who is now in his 97th year. The last of these is the most vigorous of them all, and walks two or three miles every day.'[65]

Finally, a note which seems to encapsulate much of what has come through in many accounts, from Colmonell, Ayrshire: 'The inhabitants, in general, are not only long-lived, but healthy in their old age.'[66] This would certainly seem to have been true of the subject of the following account from Lyne and Meggett, Borders: 'The only remarkable instance of longevity that can be remembered, is that of the late minister, the Rev Mr Johnston. Though his age cannot be fully authenticated, as the register of the parish where he was born is lost, yet there is good reason to believe, that he died at the advanced age of about 102. In his diet and dress he was very homely and simple. He had a strong antipathy to medicine of every kind, and it is doubtful if he ever made use of any in his life, except once. He enjoyed a good state of health almost uninterrupted, officiated in public the Sabbath before his death, and was getting out of bed, in order to prepare for the duties of the next Sabbath, when he expired suddenly, in a fainting fit, without a groan.'[67]

Why was it, though, that those who had survived the undoubted hazards of life in the late eighteenth century were still pursuing their normal occupations some 20 or 30 years after today's accepted retirement age? Was it simply because nobody had told them it was time to stop and take things easy? From all over Scotland – from Shetland to the Borders, from Aberdeenshire to Tiree – we have reports not simply about old *people*, but about old shoemakers, shepherds, spinners, blacksmiths, farmers, still supporting themselves by the trades they had pursued all their lives. Nor was this phenomenon confined to manual workers; mention is also made of schoolmasters, ministers and doctors still active in their late years. And in the accounts for the Western Isles in particular, whether one is reading of the hard labour of potato planting or peat cutting, or of the dauntingly laborious task of dragging vast quantities of seaweed on to the barren land as fertiliser, it often becomes clear that the old in the community played a very active part.

This picture of a hardy people covers much more than the older age-groups; it is also reinforced in the writings of various early 'tourists' of the time. These frequently profess themselves 'astonished' by the feats of endurance of which the Scots folk were capable, usually in relation to the extremely frugal diet on which they lived. It seems that this last may well hold the key. Although food – comprising mainly dairy products, cereals and potatoes, with a few vegetables, pulses and eggs, a variable amount of fish but for most, hardly any meat – was not only frugal but decidedly monotonous, its high nutritional rating is quite clear.

When, in contrast, one looks at Scotland's deplorable health record today, with the depressing list of 'diseases of affluence', and reflects at the same time that these ancestors of ours lacked not only our medical service but also even the benefits of dry, warm housing, the health decline which has taken place over the intervening 200 years must surely give serious food for thought.

Inoculation

Surely no subject, with the possible exception of the agricultural improvements, could present a more intriguing picture of the seemingly haphazard spread of new and challenging techniques in eighteenth-century Scotland than inoculation. In reading through the parish accounts – of districts north and south, accessible and remote, urban and rural – one looks for some kind of tidy overall pattern. It would seem reasonable to expect, for example, that the knowledge and acceptance of the benefits of inoculation might have spread first within the larger centres of population, then to the areas around, generally perhaps from south to north, and eventually to the most remote townships of the Highlands, and the Western and Northern Isles. It requires no more than a few accounts to make it abundantly clear that this was not the case.

What was it then which dictated wide acceptance of inoculation in the Shetland Isles while parts of urban Lanarkshire rejected it? Why should relatively accessible Easter Ross generally oppose it, while remote districts like Applecross and Glenshiel in the west were practising it with enthusiasm? For that matter, how is it possible that even adjacent parishes could at times display completely opposing attitudes? Could it have been some keen medical man who introduced the life-saving technique, or perhaps a crusading laird, or a new minister who had seen its benefits elsewhere? Or did the acceptance come through sheer desperation, in that an earlier smallpox outbreak had been so devastating?

Answers to these tantalising questions do come through in a few of the reports; often, though, one is left wondering. No explanation is offered, for example, in the account for Kilfinichen and Kilviceuen, Mull: 'The inhabitants of I[ona], Ross, and Brolas [Mull], inoculate their children; but the people of Airdmeanach have not yet got over their prejudices, which occasion the loss not only of many young children, but sometimes of grown persons.'[68] Death rates from smallpox were certainly appalling, in some cases involving the loss of entire families of children, as the Lochalsh account notes: 'About 40 years ago, when inoculation was not practised here, this virulent distemper, visiting them in the natural way, gave cause to many unhappy parents, to bewail the loss of a whole family of children.'[69] The Lochalsh people had, by the time of the compilation of the SA, accepted inoculation; not so the equally hard-hit parishioners of Tarbat, Easter Ross: 'The small-pox is the disease which has proved most fatal to the rising generation. Its effects were particularly calamitous in 1756, when it carried off 75 children. In 1768 it cut off 46, and 38 since in the month of October last [1791]. Some families at those different times lost their whole children. Inoculation when tried failed in only one instance, and there are families in the place, in which there was not an instance of recovery until this method was taken; notwithstanding which, the people still retain a strong prejudice against it, and seem deaf to all arguments used to shew its lawfulness and expediency, as a mean which Providence has blessed for saving thousands of lives.'[70]

But this last was precisely what many people could not or would not accept. Strongly prejudiced against anything which appeared to them to usurp the prerogative of God, they were prepared to oppose inoculation even if it did indeed mean losing their entire families. That the ministers themselves, with very few exceptions, had been well and truly won over to inoculation comes across very clearly. The laconic statement offered without comment in the Golspie account is unusual: 'Number of burials, 49. But, it is to be observed, that this exceeds considerably the average number of deaths in the year. Children who died of the small-pox make a great part of the number.'[71]

In contrast, most of the ministers express keen interest, detailed knowledge, compassion and conviction on the subject. Some write passionately, raging at the tragic waste of young lives through blind prejudice, clearly frustrated at their own inability to prevent it (something which is surprising in view of the very considerable influence which they exerted over their congregations at the time). One such is the minister for Kirkmabreck, Galloway: 'General as the practice of inoculation is become, yet, still there are many of these little innocents, that fall victim to the inattention, stupidity, and superstition of their parents, who are so wedded to the ancient prejudices, that rather than part with them, they will consign over half a dozen fine children to the ravages of this terrible disorder, or, perhaps, to the gloomy mansions of the tomb.'[72]

The East Kilbride minister sounds equally angry and frustrated: 'The small-pox sometimes rages here with great fury. Inoculation, the best remedy for that mortal contagion, meets here with a bad reception. Rooted prejudices, founded upon arguments, some of which are trifling, and others absurd, influence the minds of the people so much against it, that they sit still, in sullen contentment, and see their children cut off in multitudes.'[73] The Chirnside, Borders, account unhesitatingly blames the women: 'Fatal here was the visitation of the small-pox at the end of the year 1791, when, by a contagion in the natural way, between 30 and 40 children [out of a total population of only 690] were carried off. The preservative means of inoculation might have been, at no expense, obtained; but from the prejudices of a superstitious kind still remaining with some female parents, there was no application made for the remedy, until it could not be safely used.'[74]

Interestingly, though, in other parts of the Borders, such as Dumfries, there was a long-standing record in the use of the technique: 'The practice of inoculation for the small-pox became frequent here as soon, or sooner than in many other parts of Scotland. It began as early as 1733, about seven years after its introduction into Britain.'[75]

Not all of the parish ministers were unsuccessful, however, in their efforts to eliminate prejudice. Thus the Melrose minister: 'The writer of this account, as well as his predecessors, has, in his intercourse with his parishioners, laboured to obviate their scruples, and recommended the practice. Through such persuasion, several children have been inoculated, whose parents have afterwards expressed their gratitude. It is hoped, that in a short time, a practice will become universal, which has already begun, and through the blessing of God, will continue to be a mean of saving many infants from an early grave.'[76]

But some went further. Not content with exhortation, they decided to become inoculators themselves. More than one strong-minded clergyman was bold enough to begin with his own family. 'Inoculation has taken place in part here,' declares the Kirkpatrick-Irongray account. 'The minister while in another charge, inoculated five children of his own, at two different times, with his own hand. Upon inoculating three at first, the people seemed to be shocked and offended; but when he came to have two other fit subjects, he warned his neighbours of his intention to inoculate these also. The example was followed immediately then, by the inoculation of 30 children in the parish, by the hands of a common blood-letter from another parish, who had performed at home.

They all did well.'[77] And in the account for Kirkgunzeon, Galloway: 'Besides those that were inoculated in this parish by medical gentlemen in the year 1788, the minister inoculated about 50 of the children of his parishioners, all of whom did well and recovered, without ever having the least appearance of danger; besides 40 more last winter, with equal success.'[78]

In Shetland – where inoculation was very widely accepted – there was even a suggestion that ministers should be taught in their divinity course how to carry out inoculations. The account for Tingwall runs: 'The late incumbent, Mr Wm. Mitchell, finding that the common people declined to inoculate their children, in consequence of the expense attending it when a regular surgeon was employed, resolved to undertake it himself, without charging them anything; and carried it on with great success, having inoculated no less a number than 950, between the years 1774 and 1793. As it requires no great skill and dexterity, it is extremely desirable that his brethren, in other remote parts of the country, would imitate so laudable an example. Young students of divinity might easily acquire this branch of the medical art, when attending the various universities.'[79] The New-Abbey account takes this idea further: 'It is to be believed, that a plan is now in agitation, for instructing the students in the art of inoculation, which the physicians of that city [Edinburgh] generously and humanely propose to do without putting them to any expense.'[80]

In a number of accounts, it appears that parents took matters into their own hands, for example in Blackford, Perthshire: 'Formerly the small-pox never appeared in the parish without proving fatal to one out of every three whom they seized. But the country people have been taught to change their way of managing children in that disease; and some are so hardy as to inoculate their children with their own hand, so that very few die of that distemper.'[81] Similarly in Peebles: 'Above a thousand have been inoculated, without one dying. Nay, some parents have even inoculated their children themselves, and have perfectly succeeded.'[82]

In some districts it was the gentry who tried to set an example. In Urray, Easter Ross, however, there was generally great resistance: 'The gentry inoculate their children for the small-pox with success. But the great body of the people have not surmounted their religious prejudices against that innovation.'[83] A few offered more than mere example. It is clear from many accounts that for the poorer folk expense was a potent deterrent; however in Jedburgh some of the local heritors paid for the children of the poor to be inoculated – the writer of the account adding that 'this generous design was attended with the happiest success.'[84] In several accounts, ministers urged that financial help be given to the poor. In Kirkwall and St Ola, Orkney, 'the kirk session, on a motion made, agreed to bear the expense of inoculating the children of such parents as could not afford to pay for that salutary operation.'[85] And from Tongue, Sutherland: 'The small-pox used to make terrible havock, till, about five years ago, a gentlewoman, by introducing inoculation, was the means of preserving many lives. She inoculated 99 with her own hand, and paid them such attention during the progress for the malady, that, except one, they all recovered.'[86]

Enthusiasts are seen to come, however, from all classes and backgrounds. One of the most fascinating aspects of this whole subject is, in fact, the emergence of ordinary folk who had obviously acquired great skill as inoculators. Perhaps the most colourful is a man from Mid and South Yell, Shetland: 'Inoculation is successfully practised, even by the common people, but in particular by a person whose name is John Williamson, who, from his various attainments, and superior talents, is called *Johnny Notions*, among his neighbours. Unassisted by education, and unfettered by the rules of art, he stands unrivalled in his business. Several thousands have been inoculated by him, and he has not lost a single patient.' There then follows a lengthy account of Johnny's technique, which certainly bears all the marks of the true specialist. It states that he 'uses only the best matter, and keeps it a long time before he puts it to use – sometimes seven or eight years. And, in order to lessen its virulence, he first dries it in peat smoak, and then puts it under ground covered with camphor . . . The only plaister he ever uses, for healing the wound, is a bit of cabbage leaf.' It is not clear whether he was actually paid for his services. Probably not, since he had a variety of other occupations from which to earn his living, being 'a tailor, a joiner, a clock and watch mender, a blacksmith, and a physician.'[87]

In other places local inoculators are mentioned casually in passing, for example in Applecross: 'A man in no respect noted for acquired knowledge, inoculated about 700 persons, of which number only eight died.'[88] Inverness could boast of another remarkable inoculator – not least remarkable in that he charged nothing for his services: 'A square wright, who resides at the distance of two miles from the town, and who suffered in his family by the natural small-pox, is now become, with the lower class of people, an inoculator. The first he inoculated was a child of his own, and an only child. He forcibly inculcates a sedulous attention to light bedclothes, fresh air, cleanliness, and simple diet.'[89] Clearly an exceptional character, who in some ways may well have been ahead of many of the physicians of his time!

Somewhat in line with this is an interesting account of an alternative type of treatment, from the account for Birsay and Harray, Orkney: 'The small-pox generally visits us once in four or five years; when I and my good neighbours generally visit the children and we apply plain washing and lukewarm water, which I never saw fail, especially when accompanied with clean linen. I have seen hundreds treated in this manner, none of which failed.' The contrast with the normal treatment, in which the unfortunate patients sweated in stifling rooms under suffocating mounds of blankets, could scarcely be greater; the account continues: 'The children slept well, wakened refreshed, and soon got through the fever without any danger.'[90]

But what of the medical profession's own role in this massive public health exercise? Did they not object to this invasion of their precinct by wrights and blacksmiths, or indeed ministers and gentry turned inoculators? No hint of an answer is to be found in the accounts. It would be wrong, all the same, to suppose that their own involvement was minimal – although, predictably, the overall picture is far from clear-cut. In many accounts no mention of doctors is made at all; in others it is clear that they are the prime movers. One example is from Greenlaw, Borders: 'The people, in general, are become reconciled to this practice, by seeing the remarkable success with which it is attended. Mr Alexander, surgeon in this place, has, in the course of the last 10 years, inoculated upwards of 500, of which number only one died.'[91] Similarly there is mention of 327 being inoculated by a physician in Aithsting and Sansting, Shetland;[92] and large numbers by 'many eminent gentlemen of the faculty'[93] in Doune.

Some interesting observations on a prevailing outbreak are included in the account from Sir John Sinclair's own parish of Thurso, written by another John Williamson, the surgeon to the Second Battalion of the Rothesay and Caithness Fencibles: 'After much difficulty, when with the assistance of the clergy, I had overcome any unfortunate religious prejudice, I recommended their collecting the inhabitants of a district to one place, and thus in one day, seldom less than 20 were inoculated. Indeed, when not prevented by particular business, I have arrived at the number of 120 in a single day.' He ends his brief treatise on a complimentary note: 'I have thus far continued to give my opinion, collected from practice, with the sole view of introducing the most favourable method of inoculation, and to preserve, from so fatal a disease, many of a valuable race, the Highlanders of Scotland.'[94]

One question remains: to what extent, if at all, could the advent of inoculation be considered a factor in the population increase of the latter half of the eighteenth century? That some writers believed it to be so comes across in several accounts – for example in the Snizort, Isle of Skye, account, this assertion is made: 'The population seems rather on the increase. This, I think, must be attributed chiefly to the introduction of inoculation, which of late years, is practised with great success.' Nevertheless, the generally late dates of adoption of the technique would seem to indicate that the 1790s should still be regarded as a period of transition. Examination of some of the death rates quoted for smallpox epidemics does appear, however, to reveal in some places a decline in the virulence of the outbreaks.

Repeatedly in the accounts, deep gratitude for the benefits of inoculation is expressed. The account for Clunie, Perthshire, states: 'The prejudices against it are every day giving way, and the more rational part of the people begin to feel a becoming gratitude to Heaven for having been pleased to communicate to man such an important discovery.'[95] In none is more fulsome praise given than in the account from North Yell and Fetlar, Shetland: 'Traffick produces riches, and riches luxury, and luxury diseases; and maladies of every kind prevail here perhaps with more violence than anywhere on the Continent. But within these 22 years by-past, the great Giver of every good and perfect gift to mankind, has been pleased to vouchsafe this poor land one of the most merciful discoveries ever bestowed upon sinful mortals (the sending of a Saviour excepted); I mean inoculation, which is here practised with very great success.'[96]

At first sight one might perhaps be tempted to write this off as a somewhat unbalanced outburst – until one considers that this writer had doubtless watched many of the children in his parish, quite possibly including his own, die from the disease. It can take an effort of imagination to bring statistics to life, but if one considers, for example, the plight of the small community of Tarbat, Easter Ross, which lost no fewer than 75 children in a single smallpox outbreak in the year of 1756, it becomes a sobering exercise to imagine the total sum of human misery caused by this disease alone. Small wonder then that this minister is by no means alone in hailing inoculation as an altogether miraculous gift to mankind.

1. X, 759
2. XVI, 43
3. XIX, 27
4. XII, 220
5. XVI, 43
6. XIII, 428
7. XVII, 571
8. XV, 100
9. XV, 106
10. XVII, 406
11. II, 334
12. III, 154
13. XI, 17
14. X, 459
15. XII, 87
16. V, 73
17. XIX, 156
18. XV, 139
19. XI, 33
20. XI, 125
21. IV, 277
22. XIII, 127
23. XIII, 373
24. XIII, 650
25. XIX, 403
26. XIX, 469
27. XIII, 148
28. XVI, 604
29. IV, 31
30. XIX, 469
31. XI, 125
32. XVII, 117
33. XV, 52
34. VIII, 172
35. XII, 804
36. XIII, 542
37. XX, 266
38. XVII, 6
39. IX, 250
40. XIV, 40
41. X, 459
42. XX, 266
43. XX, 266
44. V, 97
45. V, 39
46. VIII, 155
47. IV, 323
48. VI, 22
49. IX, 55
50. IX, 186
51. VI, 59
52. XIX, 469
53. VIII, 1
54. VI, 450
55. VIII, 73
56. XIX, 293
57. XIX, 9
58. XIX, 375
59. XVIII, 11
60. XVI, 187
61. XVIII, 64
62. V, 298
63. V, 241
64. XI, 665
65. VI, 530
66. VI, 83
67. III, 816
68. XX, 284
69. XVII, 645
70. XVII, 645
71. XVIII, 437
72. V, 229
73. VII, 414
74. III, 75
75. IV, 134
76. III, 568
77. V, 252
78. V, 221
79. XIX, 480
80. V, 280
81. XII, 87
82. III, 873
83. XVII, 678
84. III, 486
85. XIX, 143
86. XVIII, 480
87. XIX, 542
88. XVII, 29
89. XVII, 83
90. XIX, 3
91. III, 196
92. XIX, 389
93. XII, 499
94. XVIII, 169
95. XII, 220
96. XIX, 552

Fishermen and their Wives
E. Burt, *Letters from a Gentleman in the North of Scotland*, London, 1754
(The Trustees of the National Library of Scotland)

12   FISHING

It would be difficult to read the SA without becoming aware of the vital importance of fishing to the ordinary folk of Scotland during the late eighteenth century. In times of real scarcity, indeed, even the shellfish gathered on the shore could have meant the difference between life and death.

In some of the accounts, the fishing industry is quite clearly the most important aspect of local life; while the extent of the fisheries, the size of the catches, and the sheer courage of the men who covered vast distances in their frail craft, are all quite surprising. Surely, though, hyperbole must have crept into the account from Edderachylis, North-West Highlands: 'There has not only been a greater quantity of fish killed on the coast of this parish, for some years past, than on the coast of any other place in the Highlands, but more herrings than what have been killed on all the coasts of all the Highlands put together.'[1]

Feats of seamanship abound, in these humble parish accounts. The account from Avoch, Black Isle, for example, states: 'In addition to the active enterprising spirit of these honest men, we may add, that three of the seatown crews having engaged in spring 1791, to fish for several months on the coast of Northumberland, coasted it in their little open boats the whole way from Avoch to Beaduel, without either chart or compass, and returned home in like manner, with no other accident, except splitting one of their sails.'[2]

But what, one wonders, did the Northumbrian fishermen think of this? In these most human of documents, it seems that there is nothing new under the sun. Consider, for example, this entry in the account for the fishing town of Fraserburgh: 'The Dutch are in the practice of fishing in summer on this coast; and in 1786, came so near as to preclude the inhabitants from their usual stations. This practice has long been followed by them.'[3]

The distinctiveness of the fisherfolk in the numerous fishing villages, especially those of the east coast, is the subject of many comments in the accounts – something which is highlighted by the minister of St Vigeans, Angus: 'In Auchmithy, as perhaps in most fishing villages, the accent of the inhabitants differs remarkably from that of their neighbours, even to such an extent, that the writer of this can easily distinguish the voice of any person belonging to that village, though speaking in a different room.'[4] As to their character, it is of the women that most of the ministers write. The account from Rathven, for example (taking in four fishing towns – Buckie, Port-easy, Findochtie, Port-nockie), states: 'The fisher-wives lead a most laborious life. They assist in dragging the boats on to the beach, and in launching them. They sometimes, in frosty weather, and at unseasonable hours, carry their husbands on board, and ashore again, to keep them dry. They receive the fish from the boats, carry them fresh, or after salting, to their customers, and to market, at the distance, sometimes, of many miles, through bad roads, and in a stormy season . . . The men and women are in general remarkably stout and well-shaped. Many of the former are above the common stature; and of the latter, many are pretty, and dress to advantage on holidays.'[5] Holidays must surely have been rare events for those involved in fishing, such as the women of Nigg, Kincardineshire: 'The woman, who has been from three or four o'clock carrying home fuel, or engaged at the rocks, bears the fish to market, five miles distant to some, and comes back to household affairs . . . During some later months of winter, the subsistence of the family has depended much on the work of the females . . . The whole female part of the parish, when not occupied by these engagements, or harvest, the moss [peats] and domestic affairs, work at knitting woollen stockings, the materials of which they generally receive from manufacturers in Aberdeen.'[6]

Most remarkable of all, it would seem, were the fisherwomen of Inveresk near Edinburgh. They were remarkable not least in attaining a state of independence which could confidently be called unique for the times: 'The fish-wives are particularly distinguished by the laborious lives they lead. They are the wives and daughters of fishermen, who generally marry in their own cast, or tribe, as a great part of the business to which they have been bred, is to gather bait for their husbands, or bait their lines. Four days in the week, however, they carry fish in creels to Edinburgh; and when the boats come in late to the harbour in the forenoon, so as to leave them no more than time to reach Edinburgh before dinner, it is not unusual for them to perform that journey of five miles, by relays, three of them being employed in carrying one basket, and shifting it from one to another every 100 yards, by which means they have been known to arrive at the Fishmarket in less than 3/4 of an hour . . . The fish-wives who carry to Edinburgh, gain at least 1s. a day, and frequently double and triple that sum.

'From the kind of life these women lead, it may naturally be concluded, that their manners are peculiar, as they certainly are. Having so great a share in the maintenance of the family, they have no small sway in it, as may be inferred from a saying not unusual among them. When speaking of a young woman, reported to be on the point of marriage, "Hout!" they say, "how can she keep a man, who can scarce maintain hersel?" As they do the work of men, their manners are masculine, and their strength and activity equal to their work. Their amusements are of the masculine kind . . . It is remarkable, that though a considerable degree of licentiousness appears in their freedom of speech, it does not seem to have tainted their morals, there being no class of women, it is believed, who offend less against the seventh commandment.'[7]

Repeatedly the accounts emphasise the hardness of the lives of the fishermen and women, and the risks they faced daily. Some, however, tell of a more sinister peril which led to untold misery for these people, for example, in the account from Nigg, Kincardineshire: 'After the necessary expenses of bait and lines, a man in this hazardous manner of life, with his wife and child, has gained in these seven past unfavourable years, scarce £10 annually. Since the commencement of the American and French wars in 1778, 24 men have been impressed or entered to serve their country in the fleet from the fisher families. In these late armaments, their fishing has been interrupted from fear of young men being seized; and to procure ten men, instead of one from each boat, who have been demanded from them, the crews have been forced to pay £106.14s., which exhausted the substance of some families, and hung long debt on others.'[8]

The same story of the oppression by the press gangs, and the 'racketeering' by which many fishermen were brought to penury, is reported in the Benholme, Kincardineshire account: 'As the boats were returning from sea in 1756, a tender intercepted three of them, and impressed the stoutest of their men. A demand from government of every fifth man to serve on board the fleet soon followed. The fishers were obliged to comply with the necessity of the times, by either going themselves, or bribing others in their stead; and thus purchased protections for those who remained, at a great expense. Reduced in men and money, they were unable, by the end of the war in 1763, to fit out more than eight large boats, and as many small. In 1768, they were harassed by Press-gangs, and forced to raise a new levy, at the rate of £10 or £12 a man. Distressed with so many demands, and deprived of the means of supplying them, many stout young men abandoned the fishing, and bound themselves apprentices to colliers, in order to avoid serving in the navy . . . The exactions made on the fishers, during the last war, gave a decisive blow to the fishery at Johnshaven, and deprived the nation of a valuable nursery for hardy seamen.'[9]

No wonder the writer of this account gives prominence to a dissertation on the reasons for the decline of the fishing industry, which included the port of Johnshaven in his parish. The loss of three boats at sea, the activities of the press gangs, and the unsafe state of the harbour at Johnshaven in winter are the three main reasons he cites for this decline. In this case, the vessel owners have transferred to Montrose; in other areas too, the lack of safe harbours is seen as being a prime disadvantage to the industry.

Another important disadvantage was the lack of salt. Deep resentment was caused, particularly in the Western Isles, by the scarcity of this vital commodity, for example in Portree: 'It would insure to the inhabitants a certain provision to their families for the year, and prevent a vast consumption of meal imported into the country, if a report was annually given in of the number of the small class of tenants, to whom a barrel of salt might be distributed upon oath, for the purpose of curing the relative quantity of herrings to eat with their potatoes; even one barrel would totally change the face of affairs, where subsistence is so scanty, and population so overbearing. This trifling indulgence would contribute to the necessities of many thousands.'[10] And from South Uist: 'The herring-fishing is the great object in the fishing trade, to the inhabitants of this parish. Notwithstanding, this branch of the fisheries cannot be carried on to any great degree, while the salt laws continue in their present form. The severe laws, with respect to the importation of salt to these remote parts, is the greatest shackle that the invention of man could find out, to put a stop to the industry of the poor inhabitants of the earth.'[11]

It is not surprising, therefore, that the writers constantly use the word 'iniquitous' when describing the salt laws. Like the ill-judged coal tax, which precluded many poor people from importing enough fuel to see them through the winter – and even, for some, meant having to burn their own furniture – this is an example of poor legislation which blighted the lives of large numbers of people. To be unable to preserve a bumper catch of herring, in remote areas where the ordinary folk always lived on the edge of starvation, must have been hard indeed. (Some of the later reports, however, record their gratitude that the hated tax had at last been repealed.)

To illustrate something of both the extent and the diversity of fishing catches, it seemed best to quote directly from the various accounts, chosen at random from around the country:

1. Fife; Kilrenny

The incumbent was born, and has spent the greatest part of his life, in this parish; and, within his remembrance, vast quantities of large cod, ling, haddocks, herrings, halibut, turbot and mackerel, have been caught here; but the fisheries are now miserably decayed. He can remember, when he was a young man, that he numbered no less than 50 large fishing boats . . . he can recollect that he saw such a number of boats throwing their nets at one time as he could not number, but heard that the Collector of the Customs of Anstruther at that time, said they amounted to 500 . . . So strong is the contrast between that time and this, that not only few or no fish are caught, but the haddocks seem to have deserted this coast.[12]

2. Aberdeenshire; Fraserburgh

Cod, ling, skate, turbot, whitings, haddocks, mackerel, lobsters, and many other kinds of fish, all of the best quality, and often in great quantities, are caught here in their seasons.[13]

3. Angus; Craig

(Two fishing villages: Ferryden, with six boats; Usan, with three boats.)

Cod, ling, haddocks, skate, flounders, turbot; also mussels, lobsters, crabs. Salmon fishing on the Southesk.[14]

4. Angus; Dundee

Sea coast: haddocks, whitings, cod, ling, plaice, dabs, flounders, soles, turbot, halibut, skate, mackerel, herrings.
Channel: smelts.
Fresh water streams: trout, pike.
Banks: shrimps, periwinkles.
Tay: salmon.
Sands of river: crabs.[15]

5. Argyll; Inveraray

In some years, when herrings came in a considerable body, there have been at least 500 boats employed in catching them, each boat having four men at an average. From the best information, it is believed, there have been caught and cured in some seasons 20,000 barrels, valued then at 15s. per barrel.[16]

6. Borders; Kirkcudbright

Besides salmon, sea-trouts and hirlies, the following sea fish are to be found in the harbour: cod, scad (called here lyth or lyd), blochan, mackerels, whiting, flounders, soles, skate, eels, sand-eels, clubbocks or codlocks, shrimps, lesser spotted sharks, called here dog-fish, angel sharks, bull's heads or miller's thumbs, porpoises, and herrings. The shell-fish are, rock oysters, lobsters, cockles, mussels, wilks, buckies, limpets, and crabs.[17]

7. Easter Ross; Avoch, Black Isle

Herring, whiting, flounders, sprats, oysters, crabs, and abundance of other shellfish; a considerable amount of cured herring exported. It is not unusual for each boat to bring in 18-25 barrels in one night.[18]

8. Wester Ross; Gairloch

Gairloch has been for many ages famous for the cod-fishing. Sir Hector McKenzie of Gairloch, the present proprietor, sends to market annually upon an average, between 30,000 and 40,000 cod, exclusive of the number with which the country people serve themselves. Gairloch hath also from time immemorial been remarkable for the herring fishing.[19]

9. Wester Ross; Glenshiel

Huge shoals of herring . . . also haddock, skate, cuddies, flounders; and many shell-fish.[20]

10. South-West; Ayr

Formerly there were great herring fishings at this place, much to its emolument; but nothing of that kind has appeared for these 28 years last past.

Mentioned: cod, ling, haddocks, whitings, skates, flounders. Also seven cobles, four men to a boat, on the rivers Ayr and Doon.[21]

The history of herring fishing in Scotland is a long one. The Greenock account states that in the reign of Charles II a piece of ground, known as 'The Royal Close' was enclosed for the curing of herrings. The 'Society of Herring Fishers' set up there was later dissolved, and at the time of the accounts being compiled, the buildings were being used as storehouses for tobacco. The herring fishing was, however, continued by individuals 'but without success.' In 1750, the Free British Fishery granted a bounty to herring fishers of 30s. the ton; in the year 1791-92, 53,488 barrels were recorded at Greenock.

Generally speaking, herrings were the mainstay of the west coast. The Stornoway account underlines their importance: 'The attention and industry of the principal inhabitants are chiefly directed to fishing of herrings, of which, in successful years, they take some thousand barrels, and have about 35 vessels from 20 to 80 tons burden, annually fitted for the bounty at a great expense; and by the profits arising from them they are chiefly supported.'[22]

One has only to read some of the Highland reports to glimpse something of the significance of this fish – providing, along with the potato, a truly nourishing diet – to a largely poverty-stricken people; from Urray, Easter Ross: 'The body of the people are indebted for their support, to the shoals of herrings which, for the most part, appear annually in the Firth of Beauly, at the ferry of Kessock. They visit us at the beginning of harvest, and sometimes continue till February . . . They serve the adjacent parts of the counties of Ross, Inverness, Nairn, and Moray. People from the braes of Banff, Aberdeen, and Perth shires, come to purchase them.'[23] An immense boon – if only they could have been depended upon to appear without fail! But sadly they were always known to be capricious in their visitations. The Wick account mentions simply that 'the success of the herring has been various.'[24]

The same complaint is sometimes made about the cod – for example in the account for Walls and Flota, Orkney: 'The cod fishing here is extremely precarious, the fish being in some seasons remarkably plenty, and at others equally scarce. At some periods, for months together, there will be so many fish caught in a boat as, on a division, to be a fish for each man. At other periods, on the same ground, and in the same space of time, the boats will be loaded as deep as they can swim. From 50,000 to 70,000 cod have often been cured here in one season.'[25]

A surprisingly modern note is struck when the Kinfauns, Perthshire, account reports that salmon is actually sent to London packed in ice: 'The salmon are carried to market fresh, pickled, and salted. Very few, of late years, have been salted; a good many are kitted or pickled; but by far the greatest quantity is run up fresh, in ice, to London, where they are now often eaten almost as fresh as on the banks of the Tay.'[26] And in Perth, where the salmon fishing is a huge enterprise, worth £7,000 per annum, the account declares that 'in the spring and part of the summer fish go fresh, packed in ice, to the London market; and when plentiful in warm weather, they are pickled for the same market. No town in Scotland is better appointed for intercourse with London than Perth, as every four days, at least during the fishing season, one smack sails, and in general, makes the passage up within the week, if the weather be any way favourable; and the passage to London has often been performed within 60 hours; the vessels return with porter, cheese, groceries, and other goods, for the consumpt of the town.'[27]

A diverting aspect of these accounts is the ingenious methods of catching salmon. In Lairg, Sutherland: 'The old method of killing the salmon of the Shin, was by thrusting a long creel or basket in behind the cascade, at the foot of the rock, and every fish that jumped to get up, was sure to fall into the basket, and kill itself by the fall.'[28] A similar device was used further south, in Glenorchay (Glenorchy) and Inishail, Argyll: 'Four miles beyond the church, at a place called

Catuish, shoals of salmon are taken in Urchay, by a simple but fatal device. A bold projecting rock crosses the bed of the river, nearly from side to side. Its height is such, that few fish can overleap the torrent, which, after rains, rushes forcibly into the pool below. Many salmon, in attempting to leap, fall into the creel, or basket, fixed transversely with the stream.'[29]

An anecdote concerning Lord Lovat provides a bizarre variation on this theme: 'This river, from the Firth to Beaufort Castle, abounds in salmon . . . A little below the Falls of Kilmorack is a stream reckoned among the best in Scotland for angling salmon; from 20 to 30 have often been taken by one person in the course of a day. The late Lord Lovat, who, with pleasure, often visited these Falls, once made a very uncommon and surprising experiment. Alongside one of them he ordered a kettle full of water to be placed over a fire, and a few minutes later, a large salmon leaped into it. Fabulous and incredible as this may seem to those who never were at Kilmorack, it is what would undoubtedly happen a hundred times any season, were the experiment tried.'[30] On the River Beauly, 'cruives' were employed to trap the fish, as the Kiltarlity account illustrates: 'The salmon are kept from getting up this length by the cruives on the Beauly, till end of August, when the fishing stops, and the cruives are opened. Then thousands of them get up to these rivers to spawn and not a few of them are at that time killed by the Strath-glass people by fishing on the said rivers with spears and torches in the night time.'[31] While in the south, in Tongland, Galloway, the salmon were caught thus in the River Dee: 'They take the salmon by a boat with drag-nets; but, in general, by far the greatest number of salmon, grilse, and sea trouts, are caught in the night time, by what they term fishing with the shoulder-nets . . . In certain places of the river, great numbers of fish are taken by this mode of fishing. For this purpose there are two shoulder-net men, and one man to kill, generally employed through the fishing season.'[32] As a final example, in Balmerino, Fife: 'There are eight salmon-fishings in the parish upon the banks of the Tay. These fishings are carried on by means of yairs or scaffolds with poke-nets and in summer with sweep and toot nets. The first are hauled when the fish strike the nets in their way up with the flowing tide. The second are payed off and drawn in at a certain time of the tide, without knowing whether there are salmon or not; and the last are set in the water, and never drawn till the watchman, or *tootsman*, as he is called here, observes the fish to have got within the net.'[33]

Flounders are the fish most frequently mentioned in the account for Ruthwell, Dumfriesshire: 'The flounders are caught in what is called a *pock-net*, and sometimes the people grope for them with their feet in the sand, and kill them with a spear; they frequently weigh from three to seven pounds, and are remarkably delicate.'[34] In a few accounts, eels receive mention. The account from Peterculter, Aberdeenshire, has a great deal to say about them (although in many parts of Scotland they were abhorred because of their similarity to snakes): 'Tenants who live on the banks of a burn sometimes build a fish-garth, or dam, with an opening to receive a kind of osier basket, or what they call an hose-net for catching fish. They catch some trout and some pike, but eels in great abundance, and sometimes cure them in large earthen jars, or in small casks for winter provision.' This account then proceeded to attempt to calculate the probable number of these creatures passing through at a given time: 'Some assert that two eels, at least, pass in one second; say three in two seconds, or 90 in a minute; or 37,800 in an hour; which, being doubled for both sides of the river, makes 75,600 in an hour, or 1,814,400 in a natural day.'[35]

Lobster fishing is clearly important also, particularly on the east coast. The account for Rathven, Banffshire, mentions a 'large lobster fishery.'[36] All the same, as in other aspects of the industry, there does appear more than a hint of decline – for example in the Peterhead account: 'The lobsters formerly were more frequent, and purchased in great quantities for the London market; there are at present no more than 4,000 annually sent from this parish.'[37]

Oysters are given prominence in the more sophisticated areas round Edinburgh, where they were in popular demand in the taverns and coffee-houses. In the North Leith account 'there are abundance of lobsters, oysters and mussels in the neighbourhood;'[38] although in Cramond 'the oyster fishery is much degenerated from what it was about 50 years ago.'[39] It still thrived, however, in Prestonpans, where there were 10 oyster boats, regularly bringing 400-500, the going price being 15d. per 100.

On the east coast, a thriving industry of drying and curing had arisen at an earlier time; in Peterhead 'great quantities of large cod and ling are catched in the spring on Rattrayhead, and on a bank which lies from 30 to 40 miles east of this town. They are dried on the rocks, and after supplying the demand in this part of the country, are sent to the south country, where they find a ready market.'[40] A description of the process used for curing fish is offered in the Northmaven, Shetland, account: 'Old men and boys are employed at the fishing station for curing the fish. The old men cut out the back bone, after which the boys wash the fish in the sea, bring them again to the old men, who salt them in tubs or vats for the purpose, where they lie a competent time soaking in brine. When taken out of these vats, they must be carefully washed with a broom in salt water. They are then laid in heaps for a day or two, and then, at proper intervals, exposed to the sun, till perfectly dried, taking care gradually to increase the piles or stiples into which they are built as they harden. In this way, they are kept on the beach for six, eight, or ten weeks until cellared or shipped.'[41] And in Unst, Shetland: 'By the sale of the ling, cod, and tusk which they take, the tenants obtain money to pay their rents. About 80 tons of these fish have, upon an average, been annually taken, for these last seven years. These are salted and dried, and in this state exported to Barcelona, Ancona, Lisbon, Leith, and Hamburgh.'[42]

To anyone with an interest in the history of nutrition, reference to the extraction of oil from the livers of sharks (also known as sail-fish) is notable, these being of course extremely rich in the anti-rachitic vitamin D – not that rickets received much mention in the accounts, possibly because the population was still predominantly rural at the time. The account from South Uist states: 'The sail fish, or basking shark, appears on the coasts of the parish early in the month of May . . . The inhabitants to the east side of the island (such as are able to fit out boats, lines, and harpoons) have been for some years very successful during the summer months, in this branch of business, owing entirely to the laudable exertions of the trustees for managing the fisheries in Scotland, in granting premiums to the owners of boats, that extract the greatest quantity of oil from the liver of the basking shark. The lucky adventurer in this fishing, should he chance to harpoon a large one, may have nine or ten barrels of liver, from which the return in clear oil is about eight barrels.'[43] A similar note comes from the account for Delting, Shetland: 'The voes, by which the parish is intersected, furnish, in most years, plenty of sail fish, from the livers of which a considerable quantity of oil is made. This fishing is the most beneficial to the poor tenants, and brings not only wholesome food to their families, but oil, which generally sells at 30s. or 35s. and sometimes at 50s. a barrel.'[44]

It is intriguing to come across the roots of today's issues in these accounts. The writer of the Hutton and Corrie, Dumfriesshire, account, for example, may be seen as an early conservationist: 'Grilses and salmon come far up in the spawning time. They do not meet with the same protection they do in most other waters in Scotland at that season. It is little wonder they should not, in the small waters of this parish, where the people are not benefited by them when the fish is of more value. But it is surprising, that even proprietors of fishings upon Annan kill salmon down to November, and see them destroyed under their eye with the leister or spear, upon the spawn bed. The destruction of the ewe in lamb, or the hen upon eggs in March, would not more demonstrate the impolicy and depravity of man.'[45]

Similarly there is condemnation of unacceptable practices in the account from Channelkirk, Borders: 'The streamlets which fall from our mountains, indeed, abound with very fine trout; but the infamous practices of taking them with nets, and destroying them with lime, which have for some years past been very prevalent, have greatly diminished the different species of this excellent fish.'[46]

From Kintail, West Highlands, however, comes a more sinister note, typical of the kind of oppression of the poor people which was too common a feature of Highland life. As is well known – and many amusing tales about it were told by the early 'tourists' – salmon, because it was so plentiful, was not greatly appreciated in those times. In employment agreements, stipulation was often made that it should not appear more than two or three times a week on the menu. But the situation changed: 'Both the rivers were once famous for salmon; and the fishings were common to the inhabitants, till they were laid under strict prohibition, soon after 1745 . . . a novelty which the people did not relish. They acted under the idea, that hunting and fishing were privileges handed down to them by their ancestors; and that these immunities ought never to be monopolised nor wrested from mankind.'[47]

Finally, of an altogether more exotic kind of fishing, the Kells, Galloway, account states: 'There is another fishing in this parish, claimed as no man's property, that cannot be easily estimated. I mean a pearl fishery. In dry summers, great numbers of pearls are fished here, some of great size.'[48] Some of the Perthshire accounts also refer to pearl fishing – the Callander one, for example, offers a description of the method in use: 'They are fished with a kind of spear, consisting of a long shaft, and shod at the point with two iron spoons, having their mouths inverted; their handles are long and elastic, and joined at the extremity, which is formed into a socket, to receive the shaft. With this machine in his hand, by way of staff, the fisher, being often up to the chin in water, gropes with his feet for the mussels, which are fixed in the mud and sand by one end, presses down the iron spoons upon their point; so that by the spring in the handles, they open to receive the mussel, hold it fast, and pull it up to the surface of the water.'[49]

The Cargill, Perthshire, account adds an interesting snippet about the 'catches' in that area: 'Besides salmon, the rivers in this parish produce also a number of horse or pearl mussels. About 20 years ago, there was a great demand for pearls; many people were occupied in fishing for them; considerable numbers were caught, for which there was a ready market, and good price. The demand however ceasing, this species of fishing has been dropped for some time. There is now in the custody of the Hon. Mrs Drummond of Perth, a pearl necklace, which has been in the possession of the ladies of that noble family for several generations, the pearls of which were found here.'[50]

1. XVIII, 394	14. XIII, 128	27. XI, 497	40. XV, 374
2. XVII, 316	15. XIII, 152	28. XVIII, 453	41. XIX, 467
3. XV, 169	16. VIII, 142	29. VIII, 118	42. XIX, 504
4. XIII, 620	17. V, 199	30. XVII, 167	43. XX, 120
5. XVI, 393	18. XVII, 302	31. XVII, 180	44. XIX, 405
6. XIV, 224	19. XVII, 400	32. V, 329	45. IV, 244
7. II, 295	20. XVII, 407	33. X, 83	46. III, 29
8. XIV, 224	21. VI, 34	34. IV, 453	47. XVII, 520
9. XIV, 41	22. XX, 19	35. XIV, 668	48. V, 145
10. XX, 205	23. XVII, 673	36. XVI, 369	49. XII, 162
11. XX, 130	24. XVIII, 245	37. XV, 373	50. XI, 54
12. X, 476	25. XIX, 350	38. II, 15	
13. XV, 169	26. XI, 267	39. II, 170	

13   INDUSTRY AND OCCUPATIONS

The period covered by the SA is an extremely significant one, representing as it does a time of unprecedented expansion in both heavy industry and, especially, the textile trade. Although the latter, by far the most important industry in Scotland during the eighteenth century, was largely carried out by people working in their own homes, mechanisation was proceeding apace. The huge cotton mill at New Lanark had, for instance, been set up a few years earlier, in 1786. Heavy industry was also growing; a great expansion in iron working had led to the establishment of the Carron Iron Works in Falkirk in 1759; smaller furnaces were in use in other places, such as Bonawe in Argyll.

One of the first points of interest, therefore, in investigating the accounts, is to attempt to gauge the attitudes of the writers to the great changes taking place around them, changes which in some places had already brought into being an industrial society. The Falkirk writer, who includes a detailed, and highly knowledgeable, description of the Carron works, with its blast furnaces, its cast-iron products, its celebrated 'Carronade' cannons, was clearly excited by the advent of this, the first works in the country to use coke to smelt iron. He writes dramatically: 'In the darkness of night, the flashes of light from the iron-works at Carron, appear in awful and sublime majesty.'[1] Reactions, however, were diverse. In the Fintry account the writer took a less than enthusiastic view of industrial expansion in the cotton trade: 'Notwithstanding present opinions, it still remains a doubt, whether this revolution in the state of a country, will in the end prove a national advantage. Whether a pallid and sickly race, brought up in the confined air of cotton mills, with few attachments, and little education, will compensate for the sturdy sons of our hills and mountains, or afford a set of as loyal and virtuous subjects, is a question which we leave posterity to answer.'[2]

Opposing attitudes are also highlighted in accounts from Renfrewshire. The Kilbarchan account enthuses about the new cotton mills: 'The most splendid establishment in the cotton spinning business, perhaps in Britain, is the Linwood Mill . . . the house is six storeys, with garrets.' There follows details of the enlightened way in which the entire operation is conducted; and then: 'If equal attention is paid to the instruction of the children, I should consider a work of this sort as a school, where the children of the poor, otherwise a burden on their parents, may be trained in industry and virtue.'[3] But at nearby Neilston, the view was altogether less rosy: 'It is apprehended that the rapid increase of manufactures is neither friendly to the health nor morals of the people. In cotton mills a multitude of children are employed, before they receive even common education. They there spend, perhaps, a considerable part of their life, without

View of New Lanark cotton mills, early nineteenth century

any other principles in the direction of their conduct, but those which natural conscience dictates. The lower ranks of mankind, however, when collected and confined together, are too apt to corrupt one another.'[4] The Paisley account also deplores the conditions in the mills: 'The numbers that are brought together, the confinement, the breathing of an air loaded with the dust and downy particles of the cotton, and contaminated with the effluvia of rancid oil, arising from the machinery, must prove hurtful, in a high degree, to the delicate lungs of children.'[5]

Some ministers express a similar concern about the possible consequences to both the health and morals of young people working in their own homes. For example, writing of the local weavers in the account for Avendale or Strathaven, the minister affirms his belief that 'they set their boys too early to that business, which stints their growth, and hurts their morals, by rendering them too soon independent of their parents. The same temptation is presented to the girls by the flowering of muslin, which, by confining them too soon to a sedentary life, makes them pale and sickly.'[6]

Cotton

All over Scotland, capitalists were setting up cotton mills. The one which gave rise to the most interesting account, however, is undoubtedly the New Lanark mill, established by David Dale in 1786. This was sold in 1787 to his son-in-law, Robert Owen, a well-known philanthropist who was noted for the interest he took in the welfare of his employees. The Lanark account includes a description of the 1,334 workers, aged from six years, who toiled from six in the morning until seven at night, with an hour and a half off for meals, and then went to school until nine. If this sounds scarcely an enlightened regime, it does at least seem to have been infinitely better than most. Owen took a particular interest in the children's diet, which consisted of generous amounts of milk, cheese, bread, herrings, potatoes, beef, barley broth, and oatmeal – vastly superior to what the rest of the child workers of the day would have had to eat. In addition, the account asserts: 'They sleep well in aired rooms, three in a bed; and proper care is taken to remove those under any disease to separate apartments.'[7]

Another centre of the cotton industry was Balfron, Stirlingshire, where a colony of cotton weavers had had a village built for them, each having a house and garden: 'The village now consists of 105 new houses, in which there are upwards of 430 rooms and fireplaces. The houses in general are substantial. Most of them are covered in slate, and some of them are three stories high.'[8] A printfield and bleachfield were then established on the other side of the river Endrick. Another account which took an optimistic view is the account for Auchtergaven, Perthshire, which includes a report of the celebrated Stanley cotton works: 'Near an hundred families, now reside in the village at Stanley. Above 350 persons are employed about the cotton mill – of this number, 300 are women or children under 16 years of age. The boys and girls, although confined at work in the mill for many hours of the day, and, at times, during the night, are, in general, very healthy.'[9]

Linen

It was, however, the manufacture of linen which, apart from agriculture, had become Scotland's chief industry in the eighteenth century, and it is mentioned in many of the accounts. 'Weaving of linen cloth has become the principal employment,' asserts the account from Liff and Bervie near Dundee, which goes on to give a detailed picture of the small pieces of land feued out to families in the linen trade; of the stream running through, supplying water for boiling and bleaching; and of the 'merchant weavers' who dyed the linen before selling it in Dundee and Perth.[10] Linen manufacture, beginning with the growing of flax plants – requiring a damp, temperate climate – was a complex business. It needed only one of the processes to go wrong for the quality of the product to be affected. Standards therefore had to be carefully maintained. The account for Barrie, Angus, illustrates the strict system of quality control which was in place there: 'Every householder, almost, is a manufacturer of brown linen . . . It will not be denied, that to the cloth made at Barrie, which has long been distinguished for the goodness of its materials, and the superiority of its workmanship, the stamp of Aberbrothock is indebted for part of its fame. By introducing honour as a prompter to excellence, the manufacture of Barrie has reached its present perfection. For more than 40 years, the inspection of the weaving, by the unanimous consent of the manufacturers, has been assigned to an annual officer, who is allowed to choose two assistant counsellors. The officer with his assessors, are eagle-eyed to discover every blemish. A pecuniary fine, or, what is more dreaded, the correction of ridicule, overtakes everyone who is at fault. These circumstances have contributed to fix such habits of attention and accuracy, that instances occur of workmen whose cloth has not been cast at the stamp-office in a period of twenty years.'[11]

The east coast generally, and the county of Angus in particular, was deeply involved in the linen trade. Around Arbroath, the fabric produced was known as 'osnaburgh' after the German town where it originated. In Forfar, the account states that between 400 and 500 looms were working: 'The knowledge of the art is so easily acquired, and the call for hands is so great, that almost every young man here betakes himself to it.' A familiar note is then added, in that the linen trade paid so well that others suffered: 'There has not been above one or two apprentice taylors in Forfar these seven years past.'[12]

Bleaching was an important industry in some parishes, notably in the Vale of Leven – the first area to have a large-scale bleaching operation, which had begun as early as 1728 in Dalquhurn. The Bonhill report states that nearly 100 people, including women and children, were employed there on three printfields.[13] A huge bleachfield near Perth is the subject of the Redgorton account: 'For more than 30 years past, there have been 80 acres and upwards covered with cloth, which has been whitened and dressed either after the Dutch or Irish mode, in so perfect a manner, that as yet is unrivalled in Britain.'[14] No fewer than half a million yards of cloth were bleached annually. In contrast, the industry seems to have played a minimal part in the Highlands. It is, however, mentioned in the Kiltearn account, which states that the Culcairn bleachfield, the only one in the County of Ross, was set up in 1751, and in the year of the account being written, had bleached 2,242 pieces of cloth.[15]

Muslin

In addition to the principal branches of the textile trade, mention is made of other smaller off-shoots which provided employment, mainly for women and girls, and principally in rural areas. 'Tambouring' of muslin, for example (a tambour was a frame on which muslin was stretched for embroidering), is a feature of the account for Kippen, Stirlingshire, among others. The account mentions that between 20 and 30 young girls were employed there, by a Glasgow firm, in tambouring muslins.[16]

Hemp

In Inverness, for example, hemp was imported from the Baltic and products from it were exported. Cromarty was one small town in which hemp-working became an important industry; the account states that there is 'an extensive manufacture of hemp', which was begun in 1773, and employed 200 men, women and children, the fabric being used chiefly for coal-bagging.

Silk; Cotton thread

The Paisley account states that a vast amount of silk gauze, lawn and linen gauze was produced, as well as the more celebrated sewing thread.[17] In all, no fewer than 26,000 persons were engaged in these branches of industry. Dalry, Ayrshire, is another place in which silk weaving is mentioned; 36 women were employed in this way.[18] The account for Erskine, Renfrewshire, includes the extraordinary story of Christian Shaw, the daughter of a local landowner, who at the age of 11 claimed to have been bewitched. As a result of the ensuing trial, a notorious case which was conducted in 1696-7, three men and four women were eventually convicted of witchcraft, and executed in Paisley. Later, however, this young woman was in the news again, this time on the industrial scene. The writer of the account takes up the story: 'Having acquired a remarkable dexterity in spinning fine yarn, she conceived the idea of manufacturing it into thread. Her first attempts in this way were necessarily on a small scale. She executed almost every part of the process with her own hands, and bleached her materials on a large slate placed in one of the windows of the house. She succeeded, however, so well in these essays, as to have sufficient encouragement to go on, and to take the assistance of her younger sister and neighbours. The then Lady Blantyre carried a parcel of her thread to Bath, and disposed of it advantageously to some manufacturers of lace, and this was probably the first thread made in Scotland that had crossed the Tweed.' The story then continues. A friend of the family managed to learn the secret of thread-making in Holland. He returned to her home and – not very creditably, it has to be said – passed on all that he had picked up. Subsequently the young women of the neighbourhood were trained to spin fine yarn, twining mills were erected, and a profitable business, 'Bargarron thread', grew up. The secrets, however, were gradually divulged by assistants and apprentices; finally, a large thread manufacture was set up in Paisley by a Mr Pollock.[19]

Stockings

An intriguing note to be found in some of the Aberdeenshire accounts suggests that the people there managed to survive the disastrous food shortages of 1782-3 through the industry of the women in knitting stockings. (The men, apparently, were not idle either – they built dykes.) This home industry also flourished in the Shetland Isles. The Tingwall account states: 'The women, when not busied about farm work, are employed in knitting coarse stockings. This has of late become an object worthy of their attention. Formerly the stockings of Shetland were sent to Holland and Hamburgh; but the difference of their value since they found their way to other markets, particularly the English, is said to be nearly equal to the land rent of the country; and this difference must be ascribed to the patriotic and benevolent exertions of Sir John Sinclair.'[20]

Iron

In referring to heavy industry, several mentions of iron working, apart from the celebrated Carron Works with which this chapter began, are made. One of the sources, from which the Falkirk company derived its raw materials, was in Dunfermline. The account for that town declared that the local ironstone had been worked, by around 60 miners, since 1771. It is 'of an excellent quality for making cannon, and has been exported to the Carron Company for that purpose.'[21] The account for Cramond, near Edinburgh, also includes a knowledgeable description of the local iron manufacture, which consisted of three forges and two steel furnaces at which were produced boiler plates for fire engines and bolts for ship-building, as well as more mundane items like spades and nails. For these, though, the iron was imported from Sweden and Russia.[22]

Coal

During the earlier part of the eighteenth century, most of the coal was mined in Ayrshire, Fife, Midlothian, and the Glasgow area. The mines, owned by the landowners and generally run by managers, were very primitive; conditions were abysmal for the workers. The coal was cut by hewers, while women bearers took it back from the face. In some cases they carried their heavy loads up staircases to the surface. From 1606, when an act passed by the Scots parliament had decreed the pit workers be bound for life to the mine in which they worked, this state of servitude had continued. By the eighteenth century things were even worse, since it was taken for granted that the children of mining families would follow their fathers into the pits. Working conditions were not improved by the appalling state of the mines; and it seems surprising that none of this is really reflected in the accounts – illustrating, perhaps, the extent to which colliers in their isolated communities were shunned by the rest of the population. Most of the accounts which refer to coal mining content themselves with a description of the actual workings. Something of the nature of the labour involved is conveyed in the Alloa account: 'There are traps, or stairs down to the pits, with a hand rail to assist the women and children, who carry up the coal on their backs. The price given is 4d. per chalder, of 30 cwt . . . A diligent bearer often brings in, from the bottom of the pit, 6 chalders, or 9 tons of coals in the week.'[23] In fact it was estimated that the daily load of some of these women was equal to carrying a hundredweight of coal from sea-level to the top of Ben Lomond. That neither opposition, nor even comment on this exploitation, comes across in the accounts is indeed strange.

Detailed notes on the mechanical aspects of mining, far too long for inclusion, are to be found in the Campsie account. This whole belt, centred on Kirkintilloch, was largely devoted to the industry.[24] The Dunfermline account also offers a lengthy description of the local workings, which employed 180 colliers, 140 bearers, 300 above-ground workers – in all, 400 women and children, and 200 horses. Several Ayrshire accounts also mention it, each pointing out the existence of an export trade to Ireland; for example that of Air (Ayr): 'The most considerable branch of trade is . . . the exportation of coal to Ireland (in 1790, 12,627 tons). This trade is chiefly carried out by vessels belonging to Ireland, which import a considerable quantity of limestone of an excellent quality. The articles chiefly imported from Ireland are grain, linen cloth, and hides.'[25] And finally, the Canoby (Canonbie), Dumfriesshire, account, states that 'the coal here is wrought by a water engine upon a new construction, the invention of Mr Keir of Millholm.'[26]

Ships

At the time, building ships was only one of several industries in Greenock. Those named are: one ropework, three soap and candle works, one saddle and shoe manufacture, and two sugar houses. In addition, though, the account states: 'Since the Americans established their independence, ship-building has gone on briskly in the ports of Clyde . . . the largest merchant vessel ever built in Scotland, was launched in Greenock about a year ago.' In this context too the notes on goods imported and exported at Greenock are of interest; the variety is considerable:

> From the West Indies – rum, sugar, cotton, mahogany;
> From America – rice, naval stores, potash, oil, timber;
> From France, Spain, Portugal – wines and fruit;
> From Greenock – herrings, coals, all kinds of British manufactures.

Finally, the account asserts that 'there are, by the Canal, 44 packets, to Leith, Dundee, London, to all parts of the Northern Highlands and Islands, as far as Orkney; and packets to Liverpool, fine sloops of 80 tons and upwards, well fitted up for the accommodation of passengers.'[27]

The account for Tulliallan has a fairly lengthy entry about ship-building: 'Kincardine is a creek within the precincts of the custom-house of Alloa. For these 40 years past, a considerable number of ships' carpenters have resided here, who built annually several sloops and brigantines. Vessels of 200 and 300 tons have been built here, for the West India trade, and the Greenland fishery. In 1786, there were nine vessels upon the stocks at one time, and the number then belonging to this place was 91, and their tonnage 5,641 . . . The number of sloops and brigantines belonging to Kincardine at present, is 75, and their regular tonnage 4,043 . . . they require about 300 sailors to navigate them. They import a great quantity of wood, iron, flax, and lintseed from the Baltic and Holland, and barley from England and the Carse of Gowrie, etc., and they export coals from Alloa, Clackmannan, and the other collieries on the Frith, to Dundee, Perth, Norway and Sweden.'[28]

'The principal manufacture in this place is ship-building,' declares the North Leith account, 'and a number of fine vessels from 200 to 300 tons have lately been built. There are 5 master-builders, who employ about 152 carpenters, whose wages are about 1s.10d. a day each. There have been two dry docks erected within these 16 years. The great bulk of the inhabitants are carpenters, sailors, and fishermen; there are a few anchor smiths, and weavers.'[29]

On a smaller scale, mention is also made of the ship-building carried on at the mouth of the River Spey, in the account for Speymouth; the yard was at Kingston, the area being famous for its timber trade.[30] To the Abernethy and Kincardine account is appended a list of all the ships built at Speymouth of the timber floated down-river from the Glenmore Forest.[31]

Timber

The descriptions of logging operations in the accounts make intriguing reading. As might be expected, these come chiefly from the valley of the Spey with its extensive woodlands; from the Speymouth account: 'At Garmouth, or at the mouth of Spey, there is a wood trade, the most considerable, it is supposed, of any in Scotland, for home wood. The wood is mostly fir, with some little oak and birch. It comes from the extensive forests in Strathspey and Badenoch, belonging to the Duke of Gordon, Mr McIntosh of McIntosh, and Mr Grant of Rothiemurchus; and is floated down the River Spey in deals, planks, logs and spars . . . The wood is partly sold at Garmouth, to the people of the adjacent country; but the greater part is carried coastwise by shipping . . . The planks, deals and masts are sent down the Spey in rafts, conducted by two men, at the rate of 30s. per raft. The logs and spars are, for the most part, floated down the river loose, to the number of, perhaps, 20,000 pieces at a time, with men going along the side of the river with long poles, to push them on, as they stick on the banks. These men have 1s.2d. per day, besides whisky; and there will sometimes be from 50 to 80 employed at once in the floating.'[32] Higher up the river, too, the timber trade was the predominant one for the area, the sawmills being described in the account for Abernethy and Kincardine.[33]

Clearly, the operation by which logs were floated down the Spey was a huge one; its extent takes one by surprise. Although on a smaller scale, a similar industry had arisen on the estates of Lord Lovat and other landowners around the Beauly area, as stated in the account for Kilmorack: 'Many thousand fir trees are annually cut in Lovat's, the Chisholm's, and Struie's woods. These are sawn into square timber, planks, deals, etc., for the home and English markets.'[34] The logs here, too, were floated down to the (water-driven) saw-mills.

Kelp

To all who are aware of the exploitation associated with the making of kelp, the very word is emotive; for example, many of the landlords actively opposed emigration when the rates paid for the product in this labour-intensive industry were high, but swiftly changed their attitude – indeed, made haste to get rid of as many tenants as possible – when the trade was no longer lucrative. The story is perhaps best illustrated by the accounts for Orkney, where the economy was dominated by the production of kelp. These were still the boom years for the industry; Orkney produced some 2,000-3,000 tons a year. At almost £110 a ton, this represented vast fortunes for the landlords. For the people, it meant back-breaking toil for the merest pittance. An example of the kind of profits accruing to the landlords is given in the Kirkwall and St Ola account: 'In the space of 50 years, the proprietors of these islands have received in addition to their estates the enormous sum of £370,000 sterling.'[35] They would have been billionaires today.

The Kirkwall and St Ola account also relates something of how kelp was made and the uses to which the product was put: 'The kelp which constitutes the chief ingredient in the manufacture of glass, soap, allum, and of some others, is formed of the ashes of the different species of seaweed, burned in a round hole in the earth made for the purpose.'[36] And the account for Cross, Burness and North Ronaldsay asserts: 'It is about 70 years since kelp was first made here. The quantity at first was inconsiderable, and the price low. For 30 years past it has been the staple commodity of these islands, and by the superior skill in making it, the quantity is doubled . . . The value of estates has been so raised by this commodity, that an estate which 70 years ago was not worth £40 sterling a year, is now worth £300 yearly.' This same account explains one of the chief disadvantages of the trade to the common folk: 'No fish of any kind, or oil, are exported to any foreign market; the people being employed in making kelp during the summer season, have not time for fishing. Lobsters are caught, and brought to the London market by smacks; but none of the people of these two islands are engaged in catching them, for the reason already mentioned.'[37]

Some of the other accounts describing kelp-making make it clear also that none of the profits were used for further improvements; instead, the landlords' standard of living rose dramatically. In the Western Isles, where the industry was also prominent, it is the agricultural deterrence for the labour force which is stressed rather than the fishing; as for example in the reports from the Uists. There, the people were busy making kelp from June right through to August, the very time when they desperately needed to be at work on the crops which were to keep them alive. Thus there was a rush to sow their corn in advance of the kelp season; peat-cutting and harvesting had to be done late; nor was there any time left for the fishing which might so greatly have improved their lot.

Altogether the story of the making of kelp is a sad one of wholesale injustice which must have caused widespread misery and deprivation.

Mills

Water power was used all over Scotland to drive mills of every description. Something of the prodigious extent to which these were used may be gleaned, for example, from the account for Mains, Angus: 'Dighty, the only river in the parish, drives more machinery for its size than, perhaps, any water in Britain; every fall upon it turns a mill; so that within this parish, though not above four miles in length, there are no fewer than 33 mills erected for different purposes. There are several corn mills, barley mills, and mills for washing and cleaning yarn . . . There are also upon the water of Dighty, a waulk mill and a snuff mill.'[38]

Distilling and Brewing

In many rural areas distilling had become an important industry employing considerable numbers of men; this was true especially in the North-East. One account which stresses this trade is from Urray, Easter Ross, where the bulk of the barley crop was used for distilling; in this account the beginnings of local co-operatives can be seen: 'The only article in this and the neighbouring parishes that can be called a manufacture is distilling of aquavitae. There are nine licensed stills in the parish, at 30 gallons each . . . From five to ten or twelve tenants join about one of these stills, by which means each has an opportunity for manufacturing his own growth of barley . . . The principal or only profit resulting from the distillery is keeping up the price of grain, and converting it speedily into money.'[39] The last point is important, since virtually the only other source of money was black cattle.

The most interesting story by far to emerge from the accounts under this heading concerns the celebrated Duncan Forbes of Culloden. Following his service to the Crown in the Risings of 1715 and 1745, this gentleman was granted the unusual privilege of immunity from paying excise duty on whisky distilled in Ferintosh, the Black Isle, where he was the landowner – a privilege which he and his successors enjoyed until the year 1786, when the government decided instead to pay an estimated 16 years' total of duty. It was of course the local folk who were adversely affected by this decision, as the Urquhart account explains: 'It was not solely the population of the parish, that was affected by the Government's resuming of the Ferintosh privilege. The people of that district, who constitute the great body of the parish, underwent in general a great deterioration, as to their circumstances and mode of living, from that event, against which few of them comparatively had made any provision . . . But the business of distillation is now resumed.' [1792.] Later, it states: 'There are, however, very few who derive from it any benefit; but the mischief resulting from it is manifest.'[40]

Another area in which distilling played an important part was Campbeltown in the Kintyre peninsula. The account described it picturesquely: 'Next to the fishing of herrings, the business most attended to in Campbelton is the distilling of whisky . . . This business is undoubtedly gainful for a few individuals, but extremely ruinous to the community. It consumes their means, hurts their morals, and destroys both their understandings and their health.' It goes on, however: 'In this place all the same, very few, comparatively speaking, are given to drunkenness, as people are seldom guilty of excess in what is their daily fare. But, abstracting from this consideration, the trade, when carried on to such an extent, is extremely hurtful to the parish in another point of view. To it we owe the want of wheat or flour of our own, which takes yearly out of the place above £2,000, besides the want of a sufficiency of meal to serve the inhabitants, for which we send away about as much more. Both these sums might be saved, if we could be kept from destroying so much of our own and our neighbours' grain. But the project of enormous gain, first tempts the indigent to convert their little crop into a pernicious liquor, and then the law obliges them to drink it themselves, as it cannot be sold where they have equal poverty and equal liberty. Thus, in the trite story, the two publicans, who went alternately to each others' houses, with the same twopence, drank both their cellars dry.'[41]

Distilling receives mention too in other areas. An example is Beith, Ayrshire, where it is listed among the town's productions. Distilleries and breweries are also referred to in several reports. Linlithgow boasted no fewer than four distilleries and three breweries;[42] Crieff had two distilleries and one brewery.

Apart from the main industries outlined above, there is a huge miscellany of other products – some mentioned in several reports, some in only a single one. It has to be said that it is these which, on the whole, provide much of the fascination in the perusal of the accounts.

Pistols

Who would have imagined, for instance, that a colourful addition to the list of industries in a rural parish would be pistol-making? Yet this is what the Perthshire village of Doune had been engaged in many years before the 1790s: 'The only remains of any of the ancient branches of trade is the making of Highland pistols . . . This art was introduced to Doune about the year 1646, by Thomas Caddell. This famous tradesman possessed a most profound genius, and an inquisitive mind; and, although a man of no education, and remote from every mean of instruction in the mechanical arts, his study and persevering exertions brought his work to so high a degree of perfection, that no pistols made in Britain excelled, or perhaps equalled, those of his making, either for sureness, strength, or beauty.'[43]

Girdles

An outstanding example comes from the Culross report. After a long line of accounts of rural parishes, with a predictable list of occupations – of which farming and weaving form the main part – it takes one by surprise suddenly to come across this: 'The following are assigned for the decrease of the town: first, the loss or decay of several branches of manufacture carried on here, particularly girdle-making i.e. iron girdles used for baking over an open fire is now supplanted by the Carron work.' This highlights a problem which must surely have reared its head in hundreds of instances since that time – and does, indeed, in many countries today – in that mass production virtually destroys a cottage industry which may have held sway for centuries. The account continues: 'There was formerly a species of manufacture in some measure peculiar, if not altogether confined, to the place, from 30 to 40 hands being usually engaged in it. This branch was that of the making of girdles, a kitchen utensil well known in Scotland for toasting unleavened bread. By two royal grants, one of James VI and the other Charles II ratified in Parliament in the year 1669, the girdlesmiths of Culross had the sole and exclusive privilege of making girdles, which were invented by them; but, in the year 1727, the Court of Session found that no monopolies of this kind could be granted, in prejudice of any royal borough. The decline of manufacture in Culross, which has now dwindled almost to nothing, is, however, not so much to be ascribed to the loss of the patent, as to the cheaper mode of making girdles by the Carron Company from the power of machinery, the more frequent and general use of ovens, together with the preference now pretty generally given to wheat bread in every part of the country.'[44]

Nails

An unlikely specialisation appears too in the account for Dysart, Fife: '43 smiths make six million nails annually'[45] – these being fashioned from old iron imported from Holland.

Salt

Salt is another product of the enterprising parish of Dysart; salt manufacture was said to date from the fifteenth century. Another Fife town, Inverkeithing, had a larger salt output: 'There are a few salt-pans that make annually 12-15 thousand bushels.' (Also produced here, in a small iron foundry, were 'beautiful iron grates, waggon wheels, and all kinds of cast iron work for machinery and house utensils.')[46] Brora, Sutherland, and Portsoy, Banffshire, were two other small towns producing salt, while the account for Ruthwell, Borders, states that 'the people on the coast employ themselves in making a kind of coarse salt.' The account then offers a detailed description of the long and wearisome process involved, and ends by stating that, despite its having been exempted from duty by a former king of Scotland, 'the tenants on the shore who practise this manufacture are supposed to be no considerable gainers'[47] – a fairly familiar situation. Prestonpans, as its name suggests, was also engaged in this trade. 'When the sea is good, a Scotch gallon of it will yield of salt one pound avoirdupois.'[48]

Shoes

The making of shoes – no fewer than 24,000 pairs annually – kept around 100 persons busy in Linlithgow.[49] A colourful note from Langton, Borders, states that 'three brothers in the village of Gavinton, without any stock to begin with, and without friends, have, by the making of shoes, in less than 20 years, acquired upwards of £800.'[50] No mean sum for those days. But of course every village had its quota of shoemakers; to quote a single example: in the table of occupations given for Errol, Perthshire, the number of these is 21!

Slates

The old slate-making industry of Argyll is mentioned in several accounts. The account for Killbrandon and Killchattan gives some idea of the size of the operation in that district: 'The Easdale slate quarries are well known over the most of Britain. They are within a few hours' sailing to every vessel that passes through the Sound of Mull, round the western coast of Scotland, whether bound for the Baltic, Ireland, Leith, or London . . . The manufacturing of slates at Easdale commenced near a century ago. The quarries are of late increased to about 300 men. From the company's books, it appears that about 5,000,000 of slates are quarried annually.'[51] The Lismore and Appin account states that 'the slate quarry at Bailechelish, at Laroch in Glenco, is the only quarry of this nature in the parish that has turned out to any material advantage. There are 74 families in the quarry, containing 322 souls.'[52] Slate was by this time replacing thatch in the better houses all over Scotland.

Tiles

The making of blue tiles is another small industry mentioned in the account for Old or West Monkland, Lanarkshire: 'Near the bank of the Monkland Canal, was erected in 1785 a large brick and tyle work, where are manufactured blue, pan, and slate tyles, the first of the kind in Scotland. These tyles are preferable to red ones, in point of durableness; and so similar are they, in shape and colour, to slate itself, that it requires a nice eye to discover the difference, when put on the roof.'[53] This would seem to highlight yet another problem in industry – one which indeed has been repeated in many ages and parts of the world; just as the traditional iron girdles of Culross had been threatened by the mass production of the Carron Ironworks, so surely must the old slate industry of Argyll have trembled at the competition from 'slates' made from what might be termed an ersatz product, which closely resembled the real thing. Brick and tile works are referred to also in other accounts, for example those from Alloa[54] and Banff.[55]

Lead

Ancient lead mines feature in the Crawford, Lanarkshire, account. 'Leadhills contain the most famous and ancient lead mines in Scotland. There are nearly 200 men employed by the Scotch Mining Company. These are sub-divided into pickmen, smelters, washers, and labourers, besides carpenters and smiths.'[56] The account goes on to explain that, since they worked only six hours per day in the lead mines, they had a great deal of leisure time, much of which they spent in reading; a library, to which all subscribed, had been made available for their use.

Granite

Once again, it is the unexpected which provides interest. After examining a series of rural Aberdeenshire parishes, in which, apart from agriculture, the only occupations mentioned are fishing and knitting stockings, one comes across the account for Newhills in which 'the principal article of trade is the cutting and preparing of stones for the London market.'[57]

Lime

In Closeburn, Borders, lime was one of the principal products, as the account explains: 'The limeworks of Closeburn deserve particular notice. By improving the land, and exciting a spirit of industry in the people, they have proved a public blessing to the country, as well as a source of wealth to the proprietor.'[58] Small lime kilns were common all over Scotland by this time.

Copper

The account for Kilmartin, Argyll, offers this surprising comment: 'There is a copper mine, which has been wrought for some years, in the property of Mr Campbell of Kilmartin.'[59]

Tar

A long and detailed account of the method by which tar was extracted from coal forms part of the account from Cranston, near Edinburgh, where it was the district's main industry.[60]

Oil Cakes

In Monifeith, Angus, there was a mill in which the oil was extracted from lint seed. The principal trade seemed to be the making of oil cakes for cattle – a very early type of supplementary feeding – these being exported to England.[61]

Snuff

The account from Logie and Pert, Angus, explains at some length that the manufacture of snuff has declined considerably during the previous 30-40 years through a prohibition on the import of tobacco; at one time, when it was freely imported at Montrose, nearly 40,000lbs. of snuff had been produced annually, a figure which has now dropped to around 5,000lbs.[62]

Cabinet Making

Cabinet making is mentioned in the account for Greenlaw, Borders: 'Cabinet makers' work is extremely well executed here; eight or ten tradesmen are constantly employed in making household furniture for gentlemen in the neighbourhood; but none is made but what is commissioned.'[63]

Throughout the accounts, there are many examples of industrial ventures being introduced by local lairds. A few examples will suffice to illustrate this. One is described in the account for Cullen, Banffshire: 'Before the year 1748, the inhabitants of Cullen were as poor and idle as any set of people in the north. There was no industry, trade, nor manufacturing among them; their only employment was to labour a few acres of land, and to keep tippling houses; and often to drink with one another, to consume the beer for want of customers.

'The late Earl of Findlater, that true patriot, pitying the situation of the people, resolved to introduce the linen manufacture among them. And here, perhaps, it may not be improper to mention the method he adopted to promote this purpose. He brought two or three gentlemen's sons from Edinburgh, who had been regularly bred in the business, and who had some patrimony of their own; but, for their encouragement to settle so far north, he gave to each £600 free of interest for seven years; after which, the money was to be repaid by £50 yearly, the remainder in their hands to be always free of interest. Besides this, he built excellent weaving shops, and furnished every accommodation at very reasonable prices . . . So good a plan, and so great encouragement, could not fail of success. In a few years, the manufacture was established to the extent desired. All the young people were engaged in the business; and even the old found employment in various ways by the manufactures; and thus a spirit of industry was diffused over the place and neighbourhood in a very short time, which soon appeared in their comfortable mode of living, and their dress.'[64]

In Longside, Aberdeenshire, a woollen industry was set up: 'A manufacture of woollen cloth has, of late, become very considerable for an infant manufacture. It is conducted by Messrs. Thomas and Robert Kilgour, and deserves to be particularly mentioned. About 40 families are employed by them constantly; to whom they give houses and gardens. But far the greater number whom they employ, are scattered in this and the neighbouring parishes, and work for the company only occasionally. The articles manufactured here are woollen cloths . . . It is with pleasure the writer of the present article adds, from his own observation, as well as from the express testimony of their employees, that both men and women are peaceable, sober, and attentive. As a proof of this, it deserves to be mentioned, that during the space of 15 years, not a single person has been dismissed. Living in a healthy county, and not crowded together, as in towns; and having, moreover, all gardens for the employment of their spare hours, they, in general, enjoy good health, and have numerous families.'[65]

An interesting snippet showing something of the beginnings of unions comes from the account for Bonhill near Dumbarton, where there was by this time a thriving cotton industry. 'They appointed a committee of their number from the different printfields in the West of Scotland, to meet and regulate the prices, which they were to oblige their masters to give for the different pieces of work. They were to allow no persons to be employed, but such as came under certain regulations which they had framed . . . These measures obliged the masters to commence prosecutions, and to imprison some of their hands last summer, and a kind of compromise has been made between the masters and servants for a time; but it will be easily foreseen, that one of the parties must be in complete subjection to the other, before the trade can be upon a proper and sure footing.'[66]

Occupations

The range of occupations listed in the accounts, especially in the smaller towns, seems nothing short of astonishing today.

The following are examples from all over Scotland, covering a wide variety of parishes – rural areas, small towns, larger towns. Those accounts offering what seemed either the most varied or the most interesting lists are detailed here. It is of particular interest to note how not only the number of, for example, butchers and bakers increases in the more sophisticated places (such as Inveresk in the vicinity of Edinburgh), but also that of non-essential occupations – hairdressers, mantua-makers and perfumers among them.

Sandwick and Stromness, Orkney [67] *(village of Stromness)*

Blacksmiths	15	Seamen	60
Clergymen	1	Ship carpenters	18
Coopers	7	Shoemakers	13
Customhouse boatmen	6	Shop-keepers	25
Customhouse surveyors	2	Surgeons	1
Day labourers	22	Tailors	11
Female servants	118	Tide waiters	3
Flax dressers	3	Weavers	15
Joiners	8	Writers	2
Masons	13		

Kippen [68]

Antiburgher ministers	1	Merchants	10
Apprentices	14	Millers	8
Bakers	1	Ministers	1
Butchers	2	Physicians	1
Carters	7	Publicans	8
Coopers	4	Saddlers	2
Day labourers	47	Schoolmasters	2
Distillers	4	Sheriff officers	4
Dyers	1	Shoemakers	14
Excisemen	1	Smiths	10
Farm servants	88	Tailors	18
Farmers	100	Tanners	3
Hecklers	4	Weavers	37
Journeymen	5	Writers	1
Maltmen	6	Wheelwrights	2
Masons	7		

South Knapdale, Argyll [69]

Boat carpenters	3	Millers	6
Bounty fishers	51	Publicans	9
Clergymen	2	Schoolmasters	3
Cottagers	158	Shepherds	16
Dyers	1	Shoemakers	13
Female servants	29	Smiths	5
Gardeners	2	Soldiers	4
Improvers, English	2	Tacksmen	7
Joiners	19	Tailors	12
Male servants	14	Tenants	89
Masons	9	Weavers	19

Thurso [70]

Alehouse keepers	20	Goldsmiths	1
Bakers	2	Innkeepers	3
Barbers	1	Kirk officers	2
Blacksmiths	6	Mantua makers	3
Bleachers	1	Masons	23
Boat makers	3	Merchants	3
Butchers	2	Messengers	2
Carpenters/wrights	69	Millers	9
Chelsea pensioners	12	Physicians & Surgeons	3
Clergymen	2	Poor	120
Clerks	3	Saddlers	3
Clock makers	3	Schoolmasters	2
Coopers	13	Sheriff officers	6
Curriers	2	Shoemakers	40
Dyers	3	Shopkeepers	30
Excise officers	9	Tailors	29
Farmers	84	Tanners	3
Ferrymen	2	Weavers	73
Gardeners	3	Writers & Attorneys	8

Kirriemuir [71]

Bakers	7	Gardeners	9
Butchers	4	Innkeepers	14
Carpenters	50	Male domestic servants	4
Clergymen	2	Male farm servants	290
Day labourers	47	Masons	28
Farmers	78	Merchants/shopkeepers	30
Female domestic servants	96	Millers	25
Female farm servants	96	Schoolmasters	7
Flaxdressers	18	Shoemakers	56

Smiths	12	Tailors	39
Surgeons	2	Weavers	516

Inveresk [72]

Bakers	44	Masons	40
Carters	63	Milliners	2
Fishermen	49	Perfumers	2
Fishwives	90	Salt wives	50
Fleshers	50	Shoemakers	96
Gardeners	16	Tailors	30
Grocers	10	Weavers	140
Hairdressers	6	Wine merchants	4
Mantua makers	10	Wrights and smiths	70

Elgyn [73]

'in the country'		**'in the town'**	
Blacksmiths	7	Bakers	4
Shoemakers	5	Barbers	6
Tailors	9	Blacksmiths	16
Weavers	19	Glovers	8
Wrights	9	Physicians	2
		Shoemakers	55
		Surgeons	2
		Tailors	32
		Tin men	3
		Weavers	70
		Wrights ★	70

★ incl. plough & waggon makers

Inverness [74]

Apprentices	3	Messengers at arms	3
Bakers	34	Millers	16
Barbers	25	Perfumers/wig-makers	14
Brethren of the Guild	70	Physicians & surgeons	4
Butchers	14	Sheriffs	2
Clergymen	4	Shoemakers	78
Customs officers	8	Skinners	12
Dyers	12	Tailors	50
Excise officers	8	Weavers	131
Farmers	270	Wrights	104
Gardeners	13	Writers	10
Hammermen	53		

Irvine [75]

Bakers	7	Maltsters	10
Barbers	6	Master butchers	6
Carters	60	Physicians	1
Chandlers	2	Saddlers	2
Cloth merchants	6	Surgeons	3
Coal hewers	150	Tinkers	4
Coppersmiths	3	Writers	5
Druggists	2		

Carriers		**Incorporated trades**	
to Kilmarnock	2	Coopers	7
to Paisley	2	Masons/wrights	80
to Glasgow	2	Shoemakers	56
to Greenock	2	Smiths	24
		Tailors	27
		Weavers	116
		Also sailors	(no no. given)

Kelso [76]

Bakers	32	Midwives	6
Booksellers & printers	2	Optician	1
Brewers	2	Plaisterers	6
Butchers	24	Saddlers	12
Carpenters	60	Schoolmasters	7
Carriers	3	Shoemakers	147
Carters	40	Shopkeepers	30
Clergymen	7	Skinners	20
Copper & white ironsmiths	6	Smiths	15
Dyers & Clothiers	3	Staymakers	3
Glovers	4	Stocking weavers	7
Housepainters	2	Tailors	47
Inn & alehouse keepers	40	Upholsterers	2
Labourers	162	Weavers	60
Masons	40	Writers or attorneys	11
Medical practitioners	6		

Crieff [77]

Apothecary/physician/surgeon	4	Clergymen	3
Bakers	4	Clockmakers	4
Barbers	2	Coopers	4
Butchers	8	Distillers/brewers	3
Carriers	9	Dyers	4
Carters	29	Excise-officers	4

Farmers	40	Midwives	4
Fiddlers	2	Millers	3
Gardeners	2	Saddlers	2
Gentry	11	Schoolmasters/mistresses	6
Hecklers	7	Shoemakers	29
Innkeepers	17	Smiths	8
Labourers	111	Spinsters	159
Mantua makers	11	Stockingmakers	6
Manufacturers	6	Tailors	30
Masons and slaters	16	Weavers	92
Merchants/Shopkeepers	49	Wrights	20
(of whom 19 retail tea)		Writers/notaries	1
Messengers	2		

Cupar [78]

Attorneys & writers	12	Mantua makers	10
Bakers & servants	9	Masons	21
Barbers	7	Medical practitioners	5
Brewers	5	Messengers	3
Butchers & servants	16	Midwives	4
Candle makers	2	Milliners	6
Carriers	4	Private teachers	4
Clergymen	3	Saddlers	5
Clerks to above	20	Schoolmasters	3
Dyers	5	Shoemakers	35
Excise officers	3	Shop keepers	31
Footmen	20	Smiths	24
Glovers	5	Stationers	2
Hatters	2	Tailors	29
House painters	3	Watch makers	3
Linen merchants	6	Wrights	48

Leith [79]

In 1784 the trade of Leith was estimated at half a million sterling, according to the following statement:

8 traders or companies dealing in grain	£161,000
8 dealing in flax, hemp, iron, ashes, tar etc.	£160,500
10 dealing in teas, spirits and groceries	£65,000
9 dealing in wine and spirits, hops etc.	£36,500
10 dealing in wood	£32,000
2 manufacturers of soap and candles	£13,000
Rope works, raw materials	£12,200
Labour	£14,800
Total:	**£495,000**

Kinnoul [80]

Bakers	10	Masons	18
Boat-carpenters	2	Nurserymen/gardeners	14
Boatmen	3	Saddlers	3
Butchers	6	Sailors	3
Carters	6	Schoolmasters	2
Chelsea-pensioners	2	Shoemakers	17
Clergyman	1	Shopkeepers/merchants	6
Coopers	2	Smiths	5
Dyers	2	Tailors	15
Excise-officer	1	Weavers/apprentices	57
Inn-keepers	16	Wheel-wrights	2

Kilmalie (including Fort William) [81]

Attorneys	4	Masons	26
Bakers	3	Merchants	2
Barber	1	Nailers	3
Boat-wrights	3	Sawers	6
Butchers	3	Schoolmasters	2
Carpenters	11	Seamstressess	4
Cart-wrights	2	Ship-wright	1
Comptroller	1	Shoemakers	18
Coopers	2	Shop-keepers	9
Dyer	1	Smiths	3
Excisemen	2	Surgeons	3
Farmers	10	Surveyor	1
Fiddlers	2	Tailors	12
Gardeners	4	Tide-waiters	2
Inn-keepers	2	Weavers	24
Mantua-makers	5	Wheel-wrights	3

Finally, there are a few occupations mentioned in the accounts which seemed worthy of special note. For example, the account from St Andrews and Deerness, Northern Isles, describes one which appears to have anticipated some of today's mountaineering skills: 'The people of this island get vast quantities of sea-fowls, eggs, and feathers; which last they sell for 9d. per lb. The method of getting them is this: a boy, having a rope tied round his waist, is turned over the brink of the rock, quite out of sight of those who support him, by holding in their hands the end of the rope. The boy, as soon as he comes where the birds or eggs are, secures them; and when loading, informs those above, by signs which they mutually understand, how to direct the rope, when to lower, and when to pull up. He has a staff to defend him from the rugged points and shelves.

'A human being, suspended from the top of a cliff 50 fathoms high, is, to the stranger, a dreadful sight; but the rockmen, as they are properly and significantly called, walk on the very edges of the shelves, in the very face of the rock, with the greatest unconcern.'[82]

One of the most intriguing descriptions comes from the Inveresk account and concerns what must arguably be the earliest record of Scots women in business. Many years before the time of the SA, Edinburgh seems to have been supplied with its vegetables by the people of the neighbouring village of Inveresk – a trade which was, however, largely superseded by new markets nearer to the city. All the produce was carried in creels on the backs of the women; they returned laden with goods, or else with dirty linen to be washed in the River Esk. This employment of women became a tradition, and in the area led to a reversal of the roles of the sexes. The account declares: 'This . . . has formed a character and manners, in the female sex, which seems peculiar to them, at least in this country. The carriers of greens, salt, etc., are generally the wives of weavers, shoemakers, tailors, or sievemakers, who, being confined by their employments indoors, take charge of the children and family, while the females trudge to Edinburgh about their several branches of business, long before day in winter, and return by midday or later, according to the time spent in selling their commodities. Their usual daily profits may be computed at from 8d. to 1s. 3d., which, besides the free, social, and disengaged life which they lead, is a greater addition to the income of the family, than they could earn by any other branch of industry.

'The fish-wives, as they are all of one class, and educated in it from their infancy, are of a character and manners still more singular than the former, and particularly distinguished by the laborious lives they lead.'[83] (See Fishing.)

The necessarily wide-ranging nature of the skills ordinary men were obliged to acquire in some rural areas comes across especially in some of the Highland accounts. The Applecross account, for example, states: 'In a country destitute of trade and manufactures, distinct occupations are not to be expected. All the inhabitants of a parish are, in some degree, farmers and fishers. Every man is the architect of his own house; and though there be a few nominal shoemakers, scarcely a boy of 15 but can make his own brogues.'[84] And in Kirkhill near Inverness: 'Frequently a man has three occupations; he manages his croft, works as a labourer in summer, or while the weather is good, and as a weaver, tailor, shoemaker or carpenter in winter, or when the weather is bad.'[85] This list, impressive though it may be, is resoundingly capped in a note from the Orphir, Orkney, account, which tells of a man who 'serves the parish in the different capacities of beadle, sexton, cooper, slater, plasterer, boat-beater, gardener, kelper, mason, quarryman, labourer, thatcher, and farmer, and the most fortunate begetter of boys of any in the parish, for his wife bore him three at one birth, and most of his children are boys.'[86] Possibly each of them succeeded his father in one of his branches of trade!

One more noteworthy snippet, which may serve as a suitable ending for this chapter on the diverse range of occupations in eighteenth-century Scotland, comes from another Orkney account: 'There are two fiddlers, and one piper, who professes by means of his music, to banish the rats from their habitations.'[87]

1. IX, 290
2. IX, 335
3. VII, 773
4. VII, 821
5. VII, 827
6. VII, 6
7. VII, 460
8. IX, 177
9. XII, 34
10. XIII, 401
11. XIII, 61
12. XIII, 253
13. IX, 12
14. XI, 527
15. XVII, 492
16. XII, 645
17. VII, 157
18. VI, 157
19. VII, 676
20. XIX, 490
21. X, 310
22. II, 162

23. IX, 680
24. IX, 220
25. VI, 29
26. IV, 35
27. VII, 714
28. XI, 619
29. II, 14
30. XVI, 668
31. XVI, 434
32. XVI 668
33. XVI, 434
34. XVII, 172
35. XIX, 125
36. XIX, 127
37. XIX, 28
38. XIII, 487
39. XVII, 675
40. XVII, 660
41. VIII, 60
42. II, 760
43. XII, 534
44. XI, 106

45. X, 335
46. X, 339
47. IV, 450
48. II, 569
49. II, 760
50. III, 280
51. VIII, 173
52. XX, 362
53. VII, 532
54. IX, 661
55. XVI, 50
56. VII, 209
57. XIV, 624
58. IV, 60
59. VIII, 254
60. II, 179
61. XIII, 524
62. XIII, 447
63. III, 205
64. XVI, 123
65. XV, 291
66. IX, 15

67. XIX, 238
68. XII, 636
69. VIII, 323
70. XVIII, 21
71. XIII, 367
72. II, 301
73. XVI, 599
74. XVII, 100
75. VI, 244
76. III, 512
77. XII, 285
78. X, 231
79. II, 2
80. XI, 299
81. XVII, 137
82. XIX, 207
83. II, 301
84. XVII, 289
85. XVII, 212
86. XIX, 165
87. XIX, 193

Life before and after the Improvements
(top) Woodhead Farm, the home of the Bairds of Gartsherrie
(bottom) High Cross Farm to which they moved
A. MacGeorge, *The Bairds of Gartsherrie*, Glasgow, 1875
(The Trustees of the National Library of Scotland)

14   AGRICULTURE

At the time of the publication of the SA, Scotland was predominantly an agricultural country, but until around the mid-eighteenth century, agriculture in Scotland had been in an extremely backward state. The picture which emerges from many of the accounts, as from other sources, is one of a land largely undrained and unfertilised, often choked with weeds; of crop rotations and planting dates firmly fixed by tradition, with all attempts at innovation met with deep suspicion or downright antagonism; of cumbersome, antiquated implements and malnourished livestock. Not surprisingly therefore, times of scarcity, even of actual famine, were by no means infrequent.

In the final quarter of the century, however, there had begun a gradual awakening of the agricultural mind, stimulated by the 'improvers' – principally enlightened proprietors, gentlemen farmers, and in many cases also the parish ministers, with much encouragement also from early horticultural and agricultural societies. What the writers of the accounts often call 'an improving spirit' had begun to percolate through to ordinary farmers. New methods were gradually being adopted; proper crop rotations were coming in; manageable modern implements were replacing the ancient, unwieldy ones. And with a general increase in wages, the hard-pressed working folk were at last finding themselves with a little cash to spend. The old ways were beginning to change all over the country.

It is this very period of transition which is recorded in the pages of the SA. Indeed, it is doubtful whether Sir John Sinclair could possibly have chosen a more significant time at which to capture for posterity the whole changing scene. On the other hand, nothing could better illustrate the truth that an 'agricultural revolution' does not happen overnight. The accounts correct any impression of steady, uniform changes taking place all over the country, since what they actually show is more like a patchwork. While in one parish all may seem to be bustling with energy and new life, in a neighbouring one things are apparently continuing as they had been for centuries.

The Scene Before the Improvements

Some of the accounts express, with devastating frankness, the pitiful state of the parishes – for example, the account for Glasford, Lanarkshire: 'The spirit of improvement has not yet reached this parish. There is in it only one man who deserves the name of a farmer. To improve land requires both industry and skill.

Few of the farmers here have a moderate portion of either, and many are defective in both.'[1]

From an altogether different part of Scotland – Longside, Aberdeenshire – comes a fairly similar picture: 'A person interested in the welfare of the country must be hurt, when he remarks the state of the corn farming; fields ploughed, from which scarcely twice the seed may be expected; and species of grain sometimes growing which require two bolls to produce one of meal. Nor will he be less hurt, when he remarks the necessary consequences of this management with regard to hay and pasture; extensive ranges of country, where these ought to be found in great abundance, yielding a scanty subsistence to a few sheep.'[2]

As for the livestock, their unfortunate state, especially during winter and spring, is highlighted in the account for the island of Tiree: 'The black cattle and horses are mostly in a starving condition. The latter, when their pasture is very bare in winter and spring, tear up the ground with their feet to come at the roots. Many tenants keep two or three cows, which have not had a calf for years together. One informed me of his having a cow 10 years old, that never had but one calf. Another, that he keeps three or four cows, but had not had a calf for six years.'[3]

The account from Eccles, Berwickshire, tells a different story, however: 'The farms are all inclosed in the very best modern manner, and on many estates, the hedge rows, which are all in a thriving state, when seen at a distance by the traveller, exhibit the appearance of a highly cultivated garden.'[4]

Ploughs

An interesting feature of the accounts is the detailed description offered by many writers of the antiquated, and almost unbelievably cumbersome, Scotch plough – an implement which seems to have been perversely designed to accomplish the least possible work with the maximum labour. Although the type of plough seems to have varied to some extent, in most cases several men were required as attendants, not to mention up to eight or ten horses or oxen, and the ploughman usually walked backwards! Out of a large number of equally intriguing examples, two will sufficiently illustrate the point. From Kintail, West Highlands: 'The plough with which these horses labour the ground is of a singular construction. The two handles are almost perpendicular; the ploughman therefore stands in an erect position. Four horses all in a breast pull against the beam in thongs of leather cords, generally made of the skins of deers. Behind the ploughman, a man follows with a spade to compress the strong furrows which resisted the side boards. The driver confronts the ploughman, holding the reins of the horses collected in a cross stick 3 feet long; in this awkward position, the driver moves backward; and neither example nor precept can convince the people of a better mode of culture.'[5] Out of many examples from the Hebrides, the account from Tiree is fairly typical: 'The method of ploughing by one man, two horses, and long reins, is used only by two in the parish, but might very easily be practised by getting a stronger breed of horses. Instead of this, 4 men and 7 horses often attend the same furrow. When in one farm 4 or 13 ploughs are set agoing, and 30 or even 96 horses with creels sent to carry sea-ware off the shore, besides some idle mares and followers, such a farm takes many hands and horses, and labouring must prove dear. A change of method is indeed required.'[6]

From some parts of the east coast the picture is not much different – for example the account for Keith, Banffshire, states that 'agriculture is here just in its infancy; the long drawling team of 8 or 10 oxen in yokes, sometimes preceded by a couple of horses, is yet often to be seen creeping along, dragging after them an immense log of a clumsy Scotch plough.'[7]

In many parts of Scotland, however, the much-needed change had already come, following the invention of the light, efficient chain-plough (later replaced by the swing-plough) by James Small of Berwickshire in 1765. The account for Borthwick declares: 'One ingenious mechanick, indeed, we must not omit to mention. At the village of Ford . . . lives James Small, the best plough-maker in Scotland. In this particular department, indeed, he is perhaps second to none in the island. He makes 300, 400, and sometimes 500 ploughs in a year, and by his acknowledged and decided superiority, such is the demand, he might make his own terms, and increase the sale of his ploughs to an incredible extent. His chain plough is now in general use, and well known.'[8] Certainly in a large number of accounts 'Small's plough' is mentioned as the only one worthy of consideration. But some parishes remained, at least in part, true to the old ways. In Covington, Lanarkshire, the account asserts that 'every farmer keeps two ploughs at least; one of them is the old Scotch, and the other Small's.'[9] Rutherglen farmers went one better: 'There are three kinds of ploughs used in the parish; the Scotch, the chain, and the Rutherglen plough. The last was, for the first time, made here about 50 years ago, and consequently, according to Lord Kames' account, must have been among the first improved ploughs in Scotland. The plan after which it was constructed, was proposed by a Lady Stewart, grandmother to the present Earl of Buchan. She came from Goodtrees to the Farme, and was uncommonly active in promoting agricultural improvements.'[10] And from Erskine comes this comment: 'About 20 years ago the two-horse plough, with the curved mould and feathered sock, was introduced into this country by Mr George Orde. The use of it is now become universal.'[11]

Generally speaking, the lighter ploughs using horses rather than oxen were gaining in popularity. However, not all were convinced of their superiority, as seen for example in this account from Stobo, Peeblesshire: 'The Scotch plough is chiefly used in this parish, as it is best adapted to the nature of the ground. The practice of ploughing with oxen was for several years almost totally given up, till of late, that some of the farmers have begun to revive the ancient practice. In strong stoney land, which is frequently to be met with in this parish, oxen are preferable to horses . . . The oxen have also the advantage of the horses in point of economy, being maintained at much less expense.'[12]

From remote Glensheil comes this description of a very different kind of plough: 'In some places, particularly along the coast, the arable ground is so steep, and frequently so small in extent, that either the horses cannot stand firm, or have not room enough to turn round upon it with the draught; in which case, the ground is turned with a machine, called the crooked spade, in a man's hand.'[13] This is mentioned too in some other accounts, generally by its Gaelic name, cas chrom (crooked foot). In Snizort, Skye, both the old and the new ploughs are in use: 'About two years ago, Mr McDonald of Lindle introduced Small's ploughs from the south country; their utility in the great saving of labour in men and horses being soon observed, they were readily adopted by the principal farmers, not only of this district, but also of the neighbouring ones; some of the smallest tenants too use the common plough, for their weak ground, in the latter end of spring; yet the chief instrument they use in cultivating the ground, is the common spade.'[14]

A surprisingly modern note ends the subject of ploughing, with this account from Alloa: 'Just as the spirit of improvement was beginning to show itself, an intelligent East Lothian farmer took a farm in this parish, who was remarkable for his good ploughing, draining, and dressing of his grounds. His example quickened the diligence of his neighbours. A few years after he was settled here, he proposed to his landlord and brother farmers, to have trials of skill among the ploughmen; which scheme was eagerly adopted, and plowing matches were first established in 1784. Last spring (1791), 40 ploughs appeared . . . The improved chain plough, on Small's construction, was the only one used.'[15]

Carts

It is clear from the accounts that these, formerly the prized possession of the few, were becoming common in at least some areas by the last decade of the eighteenth century. Generally speaking, the southern part of Scotland seems to have been ahead in this respect – for example, the account for Colmonell, Ayrshire, declares that 'the home consumption of wood is greatly increased by the building of better houses, and by better implements of husbandry, particularly carts, of which, 30 years ago, there were only two in the parish; but now there is scarcely a farmer who has not one, two, three, and some even more in his possession.'[16] And in Torthorwald, Dumfriesshire: 'About 1750, there were very few carts in the parish, trail cars being then generally used for leading goods; dung was carried out in creels; hay led in trusses; and peats in large sacks, upon horses' backs; but, for a considerable time past, carts have been used for all these purposes, so that there are now 88 in the parish.'[17]

Not so, it would seem, further north. The Dingwall account states that 'there are only 24 carts, properly so called, in the parish . . . The farmers collect their manure into dunghills, and spread it on the fields, by means of a kind of carts called kellachies.'[18] An explanation of these is provided in the account from Kiltearn, Ross: 'There are about 10 oxen wains now in this parish. Besides these there are about 300 small rung carts, which are employed in leading home the fuel from the moss . . . These carts have, instead of wheels, small solid circles of wood, between 20 and 25 inches in diameter, called tumbling wheels. It is also very common to place a coarse, strong basket, formed like a sugar loaf, across these small carts, in which the manure is carried from the dung-hill to the field. These kinds of carts are called kellachys; and are not only used in this district, but over all the north country.'[19]

Rotations

One of the worst features of the old-style agriculture in early eighteenth-century Scotland, later challenged by improvers all over the country, was the lack of a proper system of crop rotation. The traditional farm was worked by several families who paid rent to the proprietor. Rents were generally paid in labour and produce – a system which meant the accumulation by the landlord of large numbers of stringy fowls and inferior grain, and labour carried out by resentful tenants who deeply grudged the enforced time spent away from their own holdings. The farm was commonly divided up into what was termed croft or infield – the few acres nearest the dwellings, which received all the manure from the farm – and, surrounding it, the outfield or open pasture beyond, which was generally ploughed in patches, with barley and oats being sown until the ground was exhausted. It then lay fallow until it was judged to have recovered. Beyond it there often lay an area of rough pasture land.

That division of land known as 'run-rig' was at one time practised all over the country; this system, by which all the cultivated land was divided into strips or ridges separated by 'balks' of earth often covered with grass or bracken, distributed among the tenants and usually re-allocated every year or so, meant that no tenant held land long enough to make it worth his while to spend either money or labour in improving it.

The absence of proper systems of rotation clearly irked many of the writers of the accounts in no small measure. One who professed himself actually ashamed of the local mores was the minister of Wamphray, Borders: 'I almost blush, to mention rotations. A favourite piece of convenient land has a great deal of indulgence shown it, when it is put under the following; viz. after manure, three crops of oats; dung, and drilled potatoes; nay, twice or thrice cut, and two or three years pasture . . . Lime is at present a new manure, and does wonders; but our soil will not stand repetitions of these rotations.'[20] The Halkirk, Caithness, account states: 'The great, and indeed the only vegetable produce, are bear and oats. These are sown in continuous alternate rotation, without the intervention of any other crop. This practice must surely be unfavourable to the field, the crop, the quality of the grain, and expose the farmer to more trouble and expense, for reasons well known. No great attempts have been made yet to raise pease and green crops, such as turnips etc.'[21]

It is clear from many other accounts, however, that in different areas superior systems had been in operation for some time, and indeed that the whole question was being given much consideration by the farmers – and frequently by the ministers. A short, and extremely informed, dissertation on the subject is offered, for example, by the Renfrew minister: 'There is no part of Scots agriculture more difficult to determine than what crop should precede wheat. Fallow ought if possible to be avoided, as it is losing a year. Wheat after turnips (unless spring wheat) is liable to the same objection, at least, if the turnips are suffered to come to perfection. The crop of potatoes being ready for gathering, when the wheat ought to be sown, is a strong temptation to make the one follow the other; but potatoes, instead of enriching, rather exhaust the soil, and make the ground too loose and open, which endangers the crop of wheat during the frosts. Oats –

barley – clover – wheat, would perhaps be the best rotation where the ground was rich enough for it.'[22]

There is in fact such a plethora of material on rotations in the accounts that a few have been selected for comparison of the different regions:

EAST: CRIMOND, ABERDEENSHIRE [23]

Year 1: turnips, potatoes, pease or fallow
Year 2: oats or barley along with artificial grasses
Year 3: hay
Years 4, 5, 6, 7: pasture
Years 8, 9: oats or bear

WEST: MONKTOWN AND PRESTWICK, AYRSHIRE [24]

'Two years oats, then bear or barley laid down with grass-seeds, sometimes pease and beans, and afterward a crop of oats. When the ground is laid down with grass-seeds, or, after cutting one or two years, in hay, it usually lies in ley four or six years.'

CENTRAL: GARGUNNOCK, STIRLINGSHIRE [25]

(This is an example of the typical rotation followed by the Carse farms):
'A farm ought to consist of 12 enclosures, and be managed as follows: summer fallow, wheat, beans, barley, hay, pasture three years, oats, beans, barley, summer fallow.'

BORDERS: CAERLAVEROCK, DUMFRIESSHIRE [26]

'The following rotation of crops is pursued with little variation. The ground is broken up for oats, two crops of which are taken in succession. Then follows a green crop, generally potatoes, seldom turnips, pease, or naked fallow. After this the ground is sown with clover and rye-grass, and is then mown for the first year, and pastured for the first two or three years. After which, it is again broken up to undergo the same course.'

Manures

The importance of manure can scarcely be over-estimated. It was a crucial factor in the production of crops which were vital in ensuring the survival of people who lived uncomfortably close to famine.

One of the fertilisers mentioned most often and most enthusiastically is lime produced from shell marl. This had given rise to small industries in some places – for example in Kilmuir, Easter Ross: 'There is an extensive level bed of shells, of diverse kinds, in the lands of New Tarbat and Nigg . . . manufactured into lime by persons trained up in the business from their infancy. There are 20 men, with their wives and children, who are employed in this trade. At full sea, they go from the shore in boats, cast anchor over the bed of shells and remain there till the sea ebbs; then all hands begin to dig up the shells and freight the boats.'[27] In the account for Logie and Pert, Angus, the extensive use of marl is made clear – the local quarries produced 16,000 bolls of shells in a year, each boll yielding three bolls of finely powdered lime, 'fit either for building or manure.'[28] Following an enthusiastic essay on the uses and action of marl, the minister of Kinloch, Perthshire, writes: 'In two of these lakes, there is a valuable treasure of rich shell marl. In the moss or marsh which is connected with the Rae Loch, there is a marl-pit, the first that was opened in this country. It was partially drained, and opened for public sale, about the year 1734.'[29]

Inevitably, however, there are conflicting views. The account from nearby Lethendy expresses disenchantment with the marl: 'Rapid as the improvement has been, it was much longer of having reached its present state, than a judicious treatment of the soil would have brought it . . . Experience has now proved, that there is no nutritive quality in marl, that it acts only as a stimulus to the soil, which, if not enriched with different manure, it soon exhausts, and reduces to a state of absolute sterility.'[30]

Seaweed is another fertiliser mentioned in a great many of the accounts. From the account for Cockburnspath, on the south-east coast, comes this reference: 'The lands of the lower division of the parish are very much benefited by the use of sea-ware as a manure . . . Ware-barley is much esteemed by the brewers, and is in great request for seed.'[31] The account for Sandwick and Stromness, Orkney, includes this observation: 'In parts near the sea, they principally depend on sea-ware or weed, which, with some little dung and house manure, raises excellent crops.'[32] Often it is used in conjunction with other substances, as in Portree, Skye: 'The principal manure used is the dung of housed cattle, mixed with straw, and sometimes with mud; and sea-weeds, cast in great quantities in some places, in the winter and spring, on the shore.'[33]

Poverty-stricken Highlanders and Islanders managed to coax meagre crops out of virtually barren land thanks to 'lazy-beds' (a misnomer if ever there was one). A most moving description of the almost unbelievable toil involved is given in the Harris account: 'Deep black moss is the only soil to be found along the east coast. It is curious to observe how the inhabitants of these creeks labour to cultivate it. The first operation in this tedious process is cutting of the sea-ware for manure, each colony having a portion of shore allotted to it for this purpose . . . Having carried up his share of the sea-ware, he spreads it very thick on the surface of a narrow rigg, disposed as the nature of the ground (than which nothing can be imagined more irregular) may chance to admit, either in a straight, circular, serpentine, or zig-zag direction, round the intervening rocks, pools, or bogs. Then he begins to labour with his casdireach, an implement of husbandry like that known in some parts of the south of Scotland by the name of the lugged spade. With this he cuts in the furrow all the turf, fit for his purpose, that he can collect. The clods so cut are taken up by the hands of a second person, who lays them closely over the manure on the rigg . . . As the surface is very strong, and the soil by nature absolutely barren, an immense quantity is necessary to force from it a tolerable crop. It generally takes no less than 200 large creel-fuls . . . The lazy-bed thus roughly covered with such sod or turf as the ground supplies, is left in this state till the time of sowing, generally very late in the spring; when, previous to its receiving the seed, another operation of considerable labour is found necessary to pulverise it, that is, breaking down through clods with a heavy kind of hoe, which, in the toughest parts of the soil, takes up nearly as much time as the first operation of covering the lazy-bed. Then the seed is sown; if with barley, pretty thin; if with potatoes, the cuttings are planted with a dibble, not many inches asunder. The finishing operation is harrowing, which is done with a hand rake, having six timber teeth about two feet long . . . The farmer, who toils so hard for bread, would surely require ample returns to compensate his labour. There are some instances of a rich increase from this mode of cultivation, but the vast expense of time and labour bestowed on the ungrateful soil in which it is used, cannot be said to be generally repaid. The returns from barley seed are in a good year from 16 to 20 fold . . . The returns from potatoes are from eight to ten fold only.'[34]

There is no lack of descriptions of the use of dung from the growing towns and cities for the production of crops such as potatoes, and for market gardens in the vicinity of these centres of population. Two examples from the outskirts of Edinburgh are North Leith, the account for which states that 'the face of the country is flat, and its soil light and sandy; but with the dung procured from the town, it produces wheat, barley, clover and potatoes . . . The whole lands do not exceed 170 acres, of which there may be about 20 in kitchen gardens;'[35] and Collington (Colinton), from which the observation is made that 'there is no manure but what each farm affords, excepting the Edinburgh dung, on which the farms chiefly depend for their cultivation and their crops. This is purchased at about 10d. or 1s. each double horse-cart.'[36] Smaller towns like Inverness also made use of this, the account stating that 'seaware, street, and stable dung, and lime, are all used for manure.'

The wide range of materials employed as fertilisers demonstrates a considerable knowledge of composting – for example, in Nigg, Kincardineshire, it is 'animal dung and ashes, and that manure produced in the fishing villages from the mixture of all oily and fishy substances . . . Another manure is ware and sea-weed.'[37] In Dyke and Moy 'there are no manures in common use but compost dung-hills, in which they intermix earth, clay, or water-sand from the burns, with stable dung and ashes.'[38] In Essie and Nevay, Angus, it is 'dung of the farm-yards, and compost consisting of weeds, ditch-scourings, ruins of mud walls etc.'[39]

The dung of livestock was never wasted; but the accounts at times give cause for concern about the care accorded to the unfortunate beasts themselves – as in this excerpt from the Tingwall, Shetland, account: 'Instead of carrying the dung daily from the byres, it is allowed to remain there as long as there is room for it, and it is every day mixed with black mould brought from the hills. After the byres are full, and the cattle raised to the very roof, the whole mixture is carried to the dung-hill; and then the operation within begins again and goes on daily as before.'[40]

Sometimes an interesting variant is added – as in Kilmarnock, where the account remarks that 'as no marl of any kind has as yet been found, the manures made use of are only the dung collected in the town, or at the different farms, together with coal-ashes and lime: small quantities of horn shavings have occasionally been brought from Ireland, and raise good crops for two or three years, without injuring the soil.'[41]

This chapter ends on a decidedly enigmatic note – the magic ingredient which apparently caused ample crops to be produced with no manure at all! For example, in Kilmorack near Inverness: 'New experiments are frequently made in the culture of potatoes, and many of them have succeeded beyond expectation. The present incumbent has had 11 successive crops from one field without a particle of manure, and all, except the last, equally good. He has now the satisfaction to see many of his parishioners following his example. The potatoes thus raised are, in number and size, at least equal, and in quality far superior, to those laid down with the richest manure.'[42] The same enigmatic situation seems to have prevailed in Dalmeny, Lothians, where a phenomenon known as 'perpetual soil' is described: 'In this parish are a few spots of what is called perpetual soil, exceedingly fertile, and which have had no dung, it is said, in the memory of man. Part of the minister's garden is of this kind, which has been long known to produce great crops; and, of late, surprising ones of potatoes have been reared. For experiment's sake, potatoes were lately planted on a portion of it, six years running, and the last crop was as good as the first. Dung was applied one year, but the plants ran to stalks and leaves; the roots were numerous, but very small.'[43]

Oats

There are so many references to oats, a staple food, (along with barley in most places) that it would be impossible to include even a tenth of these. One will suffice – from Kilmuir, Skye, a parish which grew so much corn that it was able to make up for the deficiencies of neighbouring ones:. 'In the particular district in which the incumbent lives, the eye can at one view see four miles, which look like one continued field of corn, there being not the smallest portion of muir within that extent.'[44] This must certainly have been unusual in the Highlands and Islands, where oats commonly had to be imported.

Potatoes

Introduced to Britain during the seventeenth century, from Virginia, the potato had, by the time of the writing of the SA, spread all over Scotland; its immense importance to the poorer folk is made clear in many accounts. The reasons for this can readily be seen. It gave good yields even in poor soil; it was an acceptable and nourishing addition to the diet; and, most importantly, it had already brought to an end the common necessity of buying oatmeal at often exorbitant prices when the stock in the barrel had been exhausted. These points are amply illustrated in the accounts.

'With regard to potatoes,' declares the Peebles account, 'first imported into Britain by Sir Walter Raleigh, and the most useful root that ever was imported into this or any other country, they are nowhere cultivated with more care, and raised in greater excellence, than at Peebles.'[45]

'This root has proved more beneficial to the country than perhaps any other production of the land, lint excepted,' affirms the Little Dunkeld, Perthshire, account in similar vein. 'It has saved the tenants from the ruinous necessity of purchasing meal for their families to a prodigious amount. It is not above 22 years since potatoes were introduced into the field, and cultivated by means of the plough . . . This vegetable may be reckoned a full third of the food of the common people; yet they are as healthy and vigorous, at least, as before; and instead of involving themselves in inextricable debt and difficulties, by purchasing meal as formerly, they can afford to sell part of their barley to the distillers. They eat potatoes for the most part with milk, but sometimes with a little animal food from their flocks and herds. By means of this root the produce is fully adequate to the maintenance of the inhabitants.'[46] The great benefits which could accrue from the frequently prolific crops is the main point made in the account for Dalry, Ayrshire: 'I have known a large family, not under 15, plentifully supplied for six months of the year, with a large quantity given every day to two or three horses instead of corn in the winter months, and also to cows and poultry; and after all, selling £5 worth of them that remained, and all from the produce of one acre.'[47] The introduction of this humble root had indeed brought a revolutionary range of benefits to a poverty-stricken people.

Yet with hindsight there can also be seen from the accounts something which is nowhere even hinted at – the growing tendency to be too dependent on potatoes which would culminate some 50 years later in the disastrous potato famines, when the crops were ruined by the blight.

Wheat

That little wheat was grown in Scotland in comparison to oats and barley is evident from the paucity of references to this cereal in the accounts. The main exceptions were the Lothians, the Central Belt and Morayshire, where it had been grown since the days of the Cistercian monks. The preference for raising potatoes is explained in the account for Kilmadock or Doune: 'There is no wheat raised, except in the carses on the banks of Forth; though the most of the lands on the south side of Teith . . . are capable of producing it. A potato crop is accounted better husbandry, when the grounds are free and dry. This root enriches the land, in place of exhausting it, like wheat.'[48] And from the fertile lands of Morayshire comes this observation: 'For centuries past, they have raised wheat; and until lately, a considerable proportion of their rents was paid to the Earl of Moray in that grain. This his lordship has now converted into money, as the tenants found it more advantageous to cultivate barley; but wheat is still sown, though not to so great an extent.'[49]

Lint

Prominence is given to lint-growing in the account for Little Dunkeld, Perthshire: 'Lint is another article of great importance to the inhabitants of this country. Potatoes and lint may be called the two feet that support them. Lint-seed is more generally sown after barley, but very often after potatoes . . . There are 1,375 pecks of lint-seed sown in the ordinary economy of the farms, and their produce is 4,125 stones, besides which, 51 pecks are sown by adventurers for premiums etc., producing 171 stones; in whole 4,296 stones of flax. All this is made into yarn by the women of the parish (12 years old and upwards), and affords them constant employment for six months in the year, and not a little in the remaining months. The yarn, all but a small part of it manufactured for domestic purposes, is sold to hawkers and others who purchase it for the great manufactories.'[50]

Horses

One of the most striking things about the SA is its record of the very large numbers of horses which seem to have been kept. On the island of Tiree, for example, the number is given as 1,400. In the parish of Sandwick, Orkney, there are over 500, the writer of the account suggesting that prestige was involved: 'The number of horses in the following list will appear great, when compared to the number of acres cultivated, and the quantity of grain raised. It is the pride of the farmers to keep as many, and as good horses as they can afford; and therefore they give them a considerable part of the oat crop. It is usual at a marriage, when returning from church, to try who can ride foremost to the wedding house, and they are as keen in the race, and perhaps as much elated with the victory, as those of higher rank at Newmarket.'[51]

That the horses were generally rather small by modern standards, however, is made clear in many accounts, and not least by an amusing anecdote from the Tiree account: 'A country man, who died last year, about 5ft 10ins. high, was employed by the Laird of Coll as post to Glasgow or Edinburgh. His ordinary burden thence to Coll was about 16 stone. Being once stopt at a toll near Dumbarton, he humorously asked whether he should pay for a burden, and upon being answered in the negative, carried his horse in his arms past the toll.'[52]

Horses receive mention too in the account for Kildrummy, Aberdeenshire: 'The horses, though of a small size, are of a fine figure, spirited and hardy. They appear to be an unmixed breed, that has for ages past been raised in this quarter of the country. If properly broke, and well kept, they would make fine pownies for ladies, and for an airing in the country.'[53]

'Shelties' were used in Shetland, then as now. The Unst account states: 'The horses are well known for their small size and hardiness. They are called shelties in Britain. Though they measure only from nine to eleven hands high, they are fit for riding, and all the ordinary services of husbandry, and are now frequently used in noblemen's and gentlemen's carriages. Of these there may be nearly 1,000 in the island.'[54]

It emerges from the Caithness accounts that horses are commonly sold when young to Orkney, only to be bought back, at considerable expense, later. The irrationality of this is mentioned in the Wick account: 'Horse coupers or dealers buy up in summer all the year-old garrons or colts they can find, which they send over to Orkney, and sell with profit. These the Orkney men, after keeping and working for three or four years, resell when fully grown, perhaps at double the price, according to their age and appearance; so that when they are brought back to Caithness, the farmer must give such a price for them that he pays for their keeping in Orkney, more than they would have cost had they remained in Caithness.'[55]

This section ends on a sad note with a description of cruelty to horses which prevailed in certain places. The writer of the account for the islands of Gigha and Cara is deeply concerned about practices in his area: 'The barbarous practice of working with horses four abreast, which still prevails in some parts of the Highlands, is said never to have obtained here. But another practice, no less barbarous, is sometimes used, though not so common as in other places, that is, tying the harrow to the horse's tail. This is often done to save the expense and trouble of harness, and sometimes to tame young horses, as they term it, which, indeed, it does with a vengeance. For the honour of human nature, as well as from a regard to the safety and ease of that noble animal, to which we are indebted for a great share of the pleasures and conveniences of life, it were to be wished that other proprietors would form a resolution, as is now the case in Gigha, to put an effectual stop to such cruelty. "A merciful man hath compassion on his beast".'[56]

Weeds

The writers of the accounts are not slow to point out that, however poor some of the crops may be, there is never any scarcity of weeds. Certainly there is no shortage of evidence that under the old-style system of agriculture, slovenly methods meant that crops were frequently over-run with weeds.

One which receives special mention is the wild chrysanthemum, known as gool, which seems to have spread over large areas of Scotland, and which was particularly difficult to eradicate.

Centuries before the SA, indeed, reference is made to regulations dealing with farmers who permitted this noxious weed to grow on their lands. 'Gool courts' were established to inflict fines on those tenants who permitted even a single head of gool to pollute their fields.

Traces of the survival of this practice are to be found in some of the accounts. The Torthorwald, Dumfriesshire, account, for instance, states: 'The late Sir William Grierson, of Lag, was so attentive to have his lands clear of weeds, that he held gool courts as long as he lived, for the purpose of fining the farmers, on whose growing crop three heads or upwards of that weed were found.'[57]

The Cargill, Perthshire, account offers this fuller description: 'An old custom takes place in the parish, called gool-riding, which seems worthy of observation. The lands of Cargill were formerly so very much over-run by a weed with a yellow flower that grows among the corns, especially in wet seasons, called gool, and which had the most pernicious effects, not only upon the corns while growing, but also in preventing their winning after being cut down, that it was found absolutely necessary to adopt some effectual method of extirpating it altogether. Accordingly, after allowing a reasonable time for procuring clean seed from other quarters, an act of the baron-court was passed, enforcing an old Act of Parliament to the same effect, imposing a fine of 3s.4d. or a wedder sheep, on the tenants, for every stock of gool that should be found growing among their corns on a particular day, and certain persons, styled gool-riders, were appointed to ride through the fields, search for gool, and carry the law into execution when they discovered it. Though the fine of a wedder sheep, originally imposed for every stock of gool found growing in the barony, is now commuted and reduced to 1d. Sterling, the practice of gool-riding is still kept up, and the fine rigidly exacted. The effects of this baronial regulation have been salutary, beyond what could well have been expected. Five stocks of gool were formerly said to grow for every stock of corn through all the lands of the barony, and 20 threaves of barley did not then produce one boll. Now, the grounds are so cleared from this noxious weed, that the corns are in high request for seed; and after the most diligent search, the gool-riders can hardly discover as many growing stocks of gool, the fine for which will afford them a dinner and a drink.'[58]

Cattle

At the time of the writing of the SA, cattle – principally the small, black breed for which Scotland was best known – were still the main cash crop, especially in the Highlands and Islands. From these areas, huge droves made their way each year to Falkirk, which by this time had taken over from Crieff as the main trysting-place: 'Till near the middle of this century, Crieff had continued to be the great mart to which the dealers in England annually resorted, to purchase, for the English markets, the droves of black cattle reared in the Highlands of Scotland. And old people here sometimes speak with deep regret of the glorious scene displayed to view, when 30,000 black cattle, in different droves, overspread the whole adjacent country for several miles around the town . . . But the principal sale and meeting has since that time been removed to Falkirk, and not a single head directly from the Highlands ever appears now in the market here.'[59]

The entry for Kintail is of interest in that it could be considered a typical Highland area which depended heavily on the sale of its cattle in the grim struggle for survival: 'It is not size, but shape and figure, that gives the Kintail cattle the claim to preference in the opinion of drovers, who always expect to meet with three good properties, a choice pile, weight, and short legs, in the true breed of cattle in the soil.'[60]

In the opinion of the writer of the Halkirk, Caithness, account, too many of these beasts were being reared. It is evident from many of the accounts that the livestock of the time were frequently under-sized and under-nourished – it has been said that livestock, like crops, had to be good survivors rather than simply good producers – a fact which this account attributes to over-production: 'There is a great number of cattle reared in this parish, being well calculated for it, as being furnished with good pasture, both lowland and highland. But yet I am persuaded, that the number reared is near a third more than it ought to have been, or the parish can well maintain. This is the cause why our cows do not usually yield so much milk as might be expected; why cattle are in general more poor, and of less size than they might have been; and consequently, why they fetch such low prices at markets. But what is the motive for this unfrugal and mistaken plan? Why, because the commerce in that cattle is a principal and necessary article of credit, and consequently, they calculate their stock, according to their number, and not according to their quality . . . Thus it happens, that they themselves, and their cattle, are half starved, and their ill founded expectations often times frustrated.'[61]

The beginnings of the dairy industry are also recorded, mainly in the Ayrshire accounts, and to a lesser extent in those of the Borders. The Kirkoswald, Ayrshire, account states: 'The dairy was in a most neglected state in this parish 40 years ago. Good butter and cheese were scarcely to be found. Now the milk cows are changed for the better, are put into parks sown down with white and yellow clover . . . Every steading of farm houses has an apartment by itself for a milk house, and every convenience suited to it. Both butter and cheese are now exported from the parish.'[62] And in another Ayrshire parish, Tarbolton, the situation is similar: 'The capital species of industry followed by the farmers is the management of cattle for the uses of the dairy . . . The cows are of a race famous for the abundance of their milk. They are frequently brindled, and have short heads, straight backs, and square ribs. A prodigious quantity of butter and cheese is annually made here for sale. And in the preparation of these articles, the people of this parish, as well as the other inhabitants of this middle district of Ayrshire, are well known to excel the farmers of every other part of Scotland.'[63] That this state of affairs is not general, all the same, is apparent from the account for Kirkmichael, Ayrshire, which states that 'the common breed of cows are not remarkable for the quantity of the milk they give, nor is the dairy, as an article of export, much attended to in this part of the country.'[64] The Beith account draws attention to the beginnings of commercial cheese-making: 'The tenants in this parish pay their rents chiefly from their dairy. They almost universally make sweet milk cheese. The method of making this cheese was first introduced into this country by a farmer's wife in the parish of Dunlop, about the beginning of this century; and from this circumstance, it has got the name of Dunlop cheese . . . About 100 cows are kept for the purpose of making cheese . . . the quantity of cheese sent to the market annually, from this parish, should bring to the farmers about £3,500.'[65]

But Peeblesshire too had its dairy industry, as the Newlands account explains: 'Almost the first dairy farming in Tweeddale was begun in Wester Deanshouses by Thomas Stevenson, the present tenant . . . The farmer had the advantage of a house fitted up for himself by the Lord Chief Baron, when Sheriff of Peebles, with more conveniences than usual for farm houses. Tempted by these advantages, and the vicinity to Edinburgh, the farmer turned his attention to cows, and found the scheme profitable. His example was soon followed; and except in the sheep farms, all the farmers pay either the whole, or a considerable part of their rent, by their milch cows.'[66]

The actual quantity of milk to be expected from dairy cows – making an intriguing comparison with modern production – is given by the writer for Ormiston, Lothians. 'Our cows are a mixture of the Holderness kind, with that of the country. They are short horned and handsome, fatten well, and give much milk. We have had frequent instances of 20 Scotch pints in the day. That quantity indeed is rather extraordinary, but from 10 to 15 is common.'[67]

Sheep

To anybody brought up in the Scottish Highlands, with the Clearances still held in bitter memory, the subject of sheep is almost inevitably an emotive one; so it is of maximum interest to look in these accounts for early signs of removal of people in favour of the more lucrative sheep. The Walls and Flota, Orkney, account contains this statement: 'What accounts for an increase [in population] is the settlement of a colony of Highlanders, who had been forced to emigrate from Strathnaver, where their farms were converted into sheep pasture. These people, it would appear, had been comfortably situated in their former residence, as they all brought with them, to this place, a very considerable stock in horses, cows, sheep, and goats; and also in grain.'[68] At least it would seem from this description that this early clearance was carried out less brutally than the more notorious evictions from that same strath in the following century.

From Boleskine and Abertarf, Inverness-shire, the account declares: 'The principal tacksman, finding the returns from his holding not to bear proportion to his wants, bethought himself of a different plan of management, and exchanged his former tenants for a flock of south country sheep . . . Formerly, Abertarf was inhabited by the numerous and hardy race of the names of Macdonalds, Magruers, Kennedies, and Frasers . . . but this part of the parish having, within these 30 years, exchanged its proprietors, it is now almost totally under sheep, and hardly contains the tenth part of its former inhabitants, and some parts of the country of Stratherrick, having been converted into sheep-walks, has considerably reduced the number of its people.'[69] From Kilmallie near Fort William comes the following observation: 'The great augmentation of rents must be attributed, principally, to the mode adopted, of stocking farms with sheep. They require a smaller number of hands to tend them, than black cattle; can graze in places where these would not venture, and yield a greater produce. This, it will be acknowledged, is a strong temptation to proprietors, who value money more than men, to encourage sheep-farming.'[70]

References to sheep are in fact rather patchy – in some areas there is no mention of them at all – and, as was noted with cattle, it is clear from some of the accounts that they were generally small in size by today's standards. The account for Barvas, Lewis, points out that 'all the sheep, except a few of the black-faced kind introduced by the minister, are very small.'[71] One tends to imagine that on the Islands the black-faced breed would have predominated; yet the account from South Uist states: 'There was an attempt made some years ago, by some gentlemen, to import some black faced sheep; but a disorder, well known by the name of braxy, got among them.'[72] On the mainland, the Speymouth account has this to say: 'The sheep are generally of a very small kind. Some time ago, the Linton breed [the usual name for black-faces] was sought after, as being of a larger size. But their wool was found to be much coarser, and they were not found to thrive so well with our pasture, as the old native breed of the country; nor was their flesh thought so delicate. The old native breed is therefore now preferred here, and almost all over Murray.'[73]

Many of the accounts illustrate the fact that the sheep were not looked after very well. In Orkney especially, the accounts find much to criticise, as in the account from Hoy and Graemsay: 'The sheep run wild in the mountains, and are never got until they run them down with their dogs, and by that means they are much abused. Some of these sheep will run with 3 or 4 years' wool upon them, and when hounded by their dogs, they run generally to the rocks, where there is no possibility of access to them. Many of their young lambs are devoured, and picked up by eagles and other kinds of prey.'[74] From Shapinsay, too, comes a report of ill-treatment of the unfortunate animals: 'Instead of their being directed by the tender and attentive care of a shepherd, they are then attacked with sticks and stones [when they encroach upon farmland] and hunted by dogs, with more fury than is commonly used to ravenous beasts in other countries. Hence these animals, which under proper management might be a source of wealth to the proprietor, and a benefit to the country at large, are decreasing in number, and degenerating in quality so fast, that in a short time, if the mode of treatment is not altered, they will not be worth raising.'[75]

A different picture is painted in the account from Delting, Shetland: 'The hills, in general, are covered with heath, and afford good pasturage for sheep, which roam wild without any herdsman to attend them. They are in general, however, so tame, that they can be driven into punds or small enclosures, where the wool is pulled off, the young lambs marked, and such ram lambs cut as are not intended for tups to the flock.'[76]

From much further south, in Aberdeenshire, comes a description of poor management of a different sort: 'As we have no shepherds, nor even good sheep dogs, so there are no divisions of the stocks . . . In this season, they are turned out upon the arable lands of the farm, which have not been in corn crop; and seldom sent to the hill, unless the weather is very mild; but during storms and falls of snow, their subsistence must depend very much upon heath and broom, or any thing else, which can be reached by scraping. No salve or smearing is used in this country; and if a farmer's stock is not very numerous, the sheep are crammed into small houses, built for the purpose, during the night, and what with the alternate heat and cold they thus undergo, and the poor scanty feeding of this season, they are in spring reduced to a very lean weakly state, which it requires a considerable part of the summer to restore.'[77]

Unlike the Alford sheep, flocks in most other parts of mainland Scotland do seem to have been smeared: it was considered important to keep parasites at bay by treating them with a mixture of butter and tar – for example in Glendevon, Perthshire: 'The principal article attended to is sheep, in the management of which the farmers are much improved . . . The number of sheep in the parish, at present, may amount to 8,000. They are of the black-faced kind, the farmers giving preference to this species, both on account of its size and its hardiness . . . They smear with tar and butter, mixed together, their hogs and sometimes their ewes; and it is imagined it would be profitable to smear the whole, since it is an effectual preservative against the scab.'[78] A recommendation for the practice comes also from the Lothians: 'Smearing is a practice, which universally prevails throughout all Lamer-moor. A compound is made of tar and butter, or oil; and this mixture is laid on, or spread over the whole body, soon after the separation of the fleece, or at the commencement of winter. It is thought, that this greatly contributes to preserve the animal from vermin.'[79] The account for Closeburn, Borders, provides another variation: 'The sheep generally kept are the short black-faced kind. It is computed that every score of such sheep will yield fully 3 stone of wool. The wool is generally sold at 6s. or 7s. the stone; but it has lately become a practice with several of the farmers in this and the neighbouring parishes to wash their sheep before they are clipped. This no doubt lessens the weight of their wool, but brings them a price for it so much higher, as more than to compensate for the loss of weight, and for the trouble of washing.'[80]

Finally, an interesting snippet from the Edinburgh report: 'In 1790 a society for the improvement of wool was instituted by Sir John Sinclair. This constitution has had the effect of rousing attention to this valuable article of manufacture; and has excited much emulation among the farmers and gentlemen. Much labour and expense has been bestowed in collecting the best breeds of sheep, foreign and domestic, and spreading them over the country.'[81]

Veal

Despite a heartening absence, in general, of today's distressing methods of intensive food production, there is one reference to veal in the account for Avendale, Strathaven: 'The practice of bleeding calves, so common in England, is hardly known here. The only arts used to make them fatten fast, are bringing them on gradually to take a great deal of milk, keeping them in a dark place, and amidst plenty of dry litter. Unless they are fed moderately at first, they are apt to loathe the milk in a short time.' The calves were inconsiderate enough, however, to prefer play to getting on with the job of providing food, and the account continues: 'Like most other young animals, they are sportive, and apt to take too much exercise, which is best prevented by shutting them up from the light.'[82]

Turnips

It has been claimed in some of the accounts that the introduction of this humble vegetable actually heralded the advent of the Agricultural Revolution. Up to this time, owing to lack of winter feeding, most of the cattle had been slaughtered at Martinmas, the meat (known in Scotland as 'the mart') being salted and kept for occasional winter use, and for payment of rents. This scene changed when the turnip – previously cultivated only in the gardens of the rich, and used by them mainly as a dessert – became a field crop, providing good winter feeding for livestock and a valuable addition to limited crop rotations.

'Ten years ago,' declares the account from Symington, Lanarkshire, 'there were no turnips to be seen; and now, everyone who is not doing more or less in that way, is considered as void of all spirit and skill.'[83] This statement is typical of many in the SA. And from Kinnellar, Aberdeenshire, comes this advice on hoeing of this crop: 'The culture of turnips was unknown at the settlement of the present incumbent. A few only were raised by some gentlemen in their gardens, for kitchen use. In the year 1758, the minister, unwilling to be at great pains in weeding a bed which he had sown in his garden and did not expect to succeed well, tore out the greater part with a hoe, leaving only a few scattered here and there upon the bed; but was much surprised, to find his crop of turnips turn out much superior to any of the same plant, that he had ever before seen. After this, he continued to hoe and thin all his subsequent growths of turnips in the same manner. In the next year, a neighbouring gentleman sowed some turnips in a field, and although he did not use a hoe in weeding them, yet thinned them so as to leave about a hand-breadth of ground around each plant. His crops answered equally well. In 1760 or 1761, the practice of hoeing was generally adopted by all who sowed turnips through the parish.'[84]

Pigs

Although a certain prejudice against eating pork had existed in some areas, notably in the Highlands, the rearing of pigs did become more common after the introduction of the potato. The account from Kirkpatrick-Durham, Borders, highlights this fact: 'Great quantities of potatoes are annually raised, and a considerable proportion of them is used as food by the inhabitants; and what is not necessary, for the purpose of internal consumption, is either sent to market, or employed in feeding hogs, which by many, is considered as one of the most lucrative branches of rural attention.'[85]

Surprisingly large numbers are referred to in some places, notably in the Orkney parishes. 'The number of swine may be about 400 or 500,' asserts the account for Evie and Rendall, 'of a very diminutive species . . . They go at large from the end of harvest till the month of May, and being never ringed, and getting no food from their owners, do incredible mischief with their snouts both to corn and grass grounds.'[86] The writer of the account from Shapinsay, Orkney, complains that despite their destructive habits, pigs are treated rather better than the poor harmless sheep which, as he describes elsewhere, are hunted by dogs. He continues: 'To the regret of all good farmers, swine are raised here in vast numbers; and what adds much to the evil, they are under the very worst of management. In the summer seasons they are driven to the hill with the sheep and young cattle, where they commit depredations without molestation; and at the end of harvest, when the fruits of the earth are removed, they come down in legions, fierce and hungry, and are allowed to roam at large around the shores, to the almost utter destruction of some of the best land of the island.'[87]

Tobacco

An unexpected crop makes its appearance in the accounts for Crailing and Gordon in the Borders. The former account states that 'in one season, a tenant, in this district, drew £115 for tobacco plants, and afterwards raised a crop on 12 or 13 acres which he sold upon the ground, for £320; but an act of parliament intervening, (the policy or the justice of which, need not be entered into) the purchaser was unable to fulfil his bargain, and the farmer was compelled to dispose of his tobacco to government, at only 4d. the pound; at which rate, it brought him only £104. It appeared, from the trials made at that time, that tobacco would thrive well in the southern parts of Scotland.'[88] And from Gordon: 'A rage for raising tobacco prevailed in 1782, and many acres of the best land were occupied with it, which diminished the crops of corn. But a bill, passed in parliament in 1783, cured the frenzy.'[89] So ended a lucrative trade – perhaps just as well, for this was in fact the very time of great scarcity in other areas.

Goats

In the light of today's accent on the use of goats' milk in preference to that of cows in treating certain disorders, it is interesting to find that practically all the references to it in these accounts have a medical note. The Glensheil account, for example, declares that 'goats are reared in the height of the parish. Their flesh and milk are believed to be of a medicinal quality, and to contribute not a little to prevent and remove many complaints, particularly those of a consumptive type.'[90] Similarly in Aberdeenshire: 'A great many goats are kept, and persons afflicted with consumptions frequently resort to goat-whey quarters in that parish. Goat milk is sold from 4d. to 6d. per pint. It is also made into cheese; and is much esteemed by connoisseurs.'[91] Dunkeld was another place to which 'consumptives' were sent for the goats' milk cure.

Agricultural Experiments

The number and range of agricultural experiments, no less that the scientific approach often displayed, is cause for admiration. The modern concept of a 'controlled' experiment, for example, is demonstrated in the account for Strathblane, Stirlingshire, where a local farmer took 100 lambs of the same stock and divided them equally, smearing 50 and leaving 50 unsmeared. At sheep-shearing, he found it took seven unsmeared fleeces to weigh one stone, whereas it took only four of those smeared. Continuing his experiment for five years, and finding the difference even more marked, he continued to smear all his sheep. He then carried out tests to reduce the costs of smearing, and found that two pints of buttermilk mixed with six Scotch pints of tar and 12 lbs Tron of butter would smear four sheep more than tar and butter alone![92]

In Colvend and Southwick, Borders, an intriguing experiment in stock-breeding was carried out: 'About 6 or 7 years ago,' says the account, 'a gentleman of this parish, then master of a vessel in the Baltic trade, purchased from some Laplanders he saw at Stockholm, a Lapland ram with 4 horns, of about the size and weight of the common black-faced sheep of this country; but his great excellence was his fleece, which was very abundant, and remarkably fine and silky. He brought him home to this country, with which he seemed to agree very well. He was observed to delight much in cropping the heather, and to prefer it to every other plant the climate produced. He lived 18 months in the country, and experienced all our variety of season. He propagated with ewe of this country; but both he and his offspring were killed by some other animal, by which means the breed was unfortunately lost.'[93]

Not far away, in Borgue, much cross-breeding of sheep was going on, no less than six breeds being mentioned: 'the Spanish, the Shetland, the Cheviot, the common muir or black-face, the mug, and the Bakewell.'[94] The same Border area also tells of an experiment that went wrong: 'A few sheep of the Yorkshire and Northumberland breed, kept on the low lands, produce fleeces which weigh from 6-10lbs. English each, of excellent wool. These sheep do not thrive upon the hills; nor are the hill-sheep any thing improved by being crossed with the English rams. The late Sir John Dalziel of Barncroth, a gentleman who bestowed great pains in improving the breed of black cattle and sheep in this country, tried the experiment in a farm he possessed in this parish; but it had a very different effect from what he expected. The wool of the brood of these English rams was coarse and shaggy, and the sheep themselves ill-shaped and unhardy.'[95]

Greater success attended the experiments of a Moffat farmer: 'An intelligent farmer in the parish,' states the account, 'has tried a very important and successful experiment. In the years 1787, 1788, and 1789, he put Eskdale and Teviotdale rams, of the white-faced, polled kind, the same with the Cheviot breed, to his ewes of the horned, black-faced kind . . . Should his plan of improvement be justified by further experiments, it would double the value of the wool produced in the parish, by increasing the weight a seventh part, and the price more than a third.'[96]

Fewer experiments involving cattle seem to have been recorded, but there are some mentioned. In Killearn, Stirlingshire, 'attention is beginning to be paid to the breeding of milch cows by crossing the Ayrshire with the native breed, which approaches nearly to the Highland.'[97] Another controlled experiment, too, is reported from Twyneholm and Kirk-Christ, Borders: 'A gentleman in this country, who had a large dairy, remarkable for rearing the best cattle, and who kept and fed them till a proper age, when he sent them with other cattle which he bought from his tenants, to the English market, to try an experiment, bought one of Mr Bakewell's bulls. He put the half of his cows to this, and the other half to a Moorland bull, bred upon his own estate. He fed the product equally, till they were sent to market at Norfolk, when those bred from the Galloway bull, brought considerably more money than the others, besides being easier to feed.'[98]

The Improvements

Pioneers

It is clear from these accounts that there were a great many 'improvers', apart from Sir John Sinclair himself, in Scotland at the time.

The Kilsyth account has this to say of a local pioneer of potato culture: 'If the name of any man deserves to be handed down to succeeding ages, with honour and gratitude, it is that of Robert Graham Esq., of Tamrawer. He, with a spirit truly patriotic, and a mind active and indefatigable, set vigorously to work in the cultivation of potatoes, in the year 1739 . . . Had the people known the amazing benefit that was to accrue to the nation, from his fortunate attempt, they would have doubtless hailed the auspicious event, and erected a monument to Mr Graham, on the spot . . . he raised the culture of potatoes in the neighbourhood of Kilsyth to a pitch scarcely yet, if at all, surpassed anywhere.'[99]

The next extract is of interest in that it shows that Sir John Sinclair was not the only improver to be a politician as well. 'These lands might have perhaps remained in their original state,' declares the account from Ecclesgrieg or St Cyrus, Kincardine, 'had not the late Robert Scott, Esq., of Dunninauld, been induced, from the lime rocks within the flood mark at Milton, to rent the farm bearing that name. As he was representative in parliament for the county of

Forfar, which his son now represents, in going up and coming down from London, he was not inattentive to the system of agriculture followed in England. Finding it superior to any hitherto practised in Scotland, he tried to follow it, first upon his own estate and afterwards upon the farm of Milton. He set the example of draining, stoning, liming, fallowing, cleaning, manuring, and properly dressing the fields on this farm. The consequence was, he raised great crops of all sorts of grain, as well as of grass. The farmers who at first held his plans in derision, and were unwilling to leave their own old beaten track, began to be surprised at his great crops; and when experience demonstrated to them the success of his scheme, they gradually turned round to imitate them. Hence arose a spirit of agriculture, and even of emulation of it, which has produced the happiest effects.'[100]

Another example is provided by the account for Duddingston, Lothians: 'There is not a more highly cultivated spot in Scotland, nor one which more resembles the rich champaign of England, than that which the general aspect of this parish displays . . . The lands of Prestonfield were the first that were improved in the parish, or probably in the county. The proprietor of that estate was Lord Provost of Edinburgh, about the time of the Revolution in 1688. At that period, the fulzie or sweepings, and manure from the streets of the city was so little understood, that instead of drawing revenue from it, a considerable sum was paid to some of the farmers in the neighbourhood for removing it. The then proprietor of Prestonfield availed himself of the opportunity to enrich his estate. He undertook to empty or to scour the streets; and he applied the manure thus obtained, to improve the lands of Prestonfield. These he laid down in the most favourable condition, inclosed and subdivided. And as it is believed, that these were the first inclosed lands in the vicinity of Edinburgh, so it is certain, that they were the first improved . . . It was rather a matter of wonder, that such an example was not immediately followed by many of the neighbouring gentlemen, who must quickly have observed the singular effect which resulted from this experiment.'[101]

As an example of a different kind of pioneering, there is the intriguing story of a farmer whose invention – a threshing-mill – seems to have brought help to many but, at least at the beginning, only scorn and derision to himself. It is included in the account for Kilmadock or Doune: 'This is one of the most ingenious and most useful inventions that has, perhaps, ever appeared in the world. The first inventor was Michael Stirling, farmer in Craighead, in the parish of Dunblane, who died in the 89th year of his age, in 1796. This venerable old man, when in the prime of life, had a strong propensity to every curious invention; and, after much thought and study, he prepared and finished a machine for thrashing his corn in the year 1748, having employed tradesmen to execute the work under his direction . . . Mr Stirling's ignorant neighbours were, however, no way struck with the invention, but laughed at it, and called him a maggotty fellow. In short, like Noah with his ark, poor Mr Stirling was surrounded only with mockers, and at length he concealed his operations altogether. The wonderful powers of the machine, however, soon drew the attention of strangers, who came and picked up models, and who were able to erect others, both in Scotland and England. Mr Stirling's machine, in one short winter day, thrashed 50 threaves of stiff outfield corn, yielding 16 bolls of oats, which would have taken 16 days of one man to thrash with the flail.'[102]

The Hawick account tells of another inventor: 'The winnowing machine, or corn fanner, from the best information, made its first appearance in Hawick. Accounts, well authenticated, state, that Andrew Rodger, a farmer on the estate of Cavers, having a mechanical turn, retired from his farm and gave his genius its bent . . . The descendants of Andrew Rodger, residing in Hawick, at present supply the whole country around, and continue to send many of them into Northumberland.'[103]

The Landlords

Two outstanding grievances aired repeatedly in the accounts are, firstly, the deeply-resented 'servitude' – by which precious days of labour had to be spent, often in all-too-scarce spells of good weather, on the landlords' farm or fuel supply. Secondly, there is much distress at the woefully short leases granted – a mere 19 years in most cases – which effectively stifled any 'improving spirit' in the tenants.

In his introduction to Vol. XIV of the modern edition of the SA, Donald J Withrington (general editor) stresses the prime importance of the proprietors and sums up the situation thus: 'The heritors in some parishes displayed generosity, goodwill and a sensible paternalism towards their tenants, working towards the goal of improvement – generally – with the grudging support or easy co-operation of the leaseholders. Elsewhere, landlord policies were brutal and often short-sighted, and the landlords might be more tied to the old ways than their tenants.'

This is an important aspect of the study of agricultural reform in the late eighteenth century, and both positive and negative examples have been included.

The parish of Glen Urquhart, Inverness-shire, is a prime example of what Dr Withrington calls 'sensible paternalism'. 'Lime has conduced very much to the improvement of Urquhart,' states the account. 'There is abundance of limestone on Sir James Grant's estate, and to encourage its use, he not only gives his people quarry-leave free, but it is at the expense of quarrying the stones. He also gives manufactured lime for new ground, as a premium to the industrious tenant and cottar, at the rate of from 60 to 80 bolls an acre.' This generous landlord did much more – he encouraged the growth of lint, and its manufacture into linen by the women and girls, and gave rye-grass and clover seeds to his smaller tenants gratis, which 'has greatly encouraged the culture of these most useful plants.' It emerges, as in every parish in which the landlord can be seen to put the welfare of his tenants above self-interest, that the people are much more comfortably-off than many others in less fortunate situations. Glen Urquhart's produce is listed as 'grain, potatoes, lint, hay, timber, black cattle, sheep, horses, goats, butter and cheese,' and that not only is sufficient grain produced to feed its own people, but that it sends a considerable quantity of seed-oats and meal to neighbouring districts. Finally, the account declares that 'most people have a small piece of land, which yields them the comforts of a milch-cow,' and that 'the country contains all the necessaries, and many of the comforts of life, in abundance. It has been considerably improved already, and improvement is progressive. The situation of the people becomes daily better, their living and clothing is much meliorated, and by perseverance in the same line of conduct, which distinguishes the superior and inferior, their mutual interest and comfort will, under providence, be still further promoted and increased.'[104]

Another outstanding example of the transformation due to a benign proprietor comes from the account for Tyrie, Aberdeenshire: 'About 40 years ago, a great part of the lands in this parish lay in their natural uncultivated state, and such of them as were in culture produced poor starved crops . . . What has been done for promoting the industry, prosperity, and happiness of this parish and neighbourhood, must reflect great honour to the memory of the late Alex Fraser of Strichen. He first introduced improvements; gave lime to his tenants, gratis, and, in spite of their prejudices, prevailed with them to use it as a manure; brought skilful men from the south country, who taught them how to grow grass seeds, and raise turnips, cabbages and potatoes in their fields. He gave them leases, during their lives, at a reasonable rate; and did not think his interests hurt when he saw his tenants enjoying the comforts of life; nor did he treat them like cattle, as occasions offered. The good effects of these encouragements are, extensive fields regularly laid out, fine stone fences, good houses built with stone and lime, excellent crops of turnips, sown grass, and almost all sorts of grain, stocks of cattle, full corn yards, and everywhere the appearance of plenty . . . and all ranks of people are more industrious than formerly.'[105]

The satisfaction of seeing such a transformation must surely have rewarded this generous proprietor for his altruism; but for a great many tenants in Scotland at the time, no such benefits were on offer – as the account for Buittle, Galloway, makes clear: 'It is probable that longer leases than those of 19 years would be favourable to permanent improvements, such as hedges etc., and it must be owned, that as the lease draws near a close, the tenant is often found comporting himself, as if under a conviction that he inhabited hostile ground. To say the truth, however, that narrowness of mind, or aristocratical pride, which adjusted every manner of lease, to the visible purpose of keeping tenants in abject dependence upon their landlords, has of late been put very much to the blush.'[106] At least a note of optimism appears here, but in many accounts, notably those of Highland parishes, even this is missing. A good example comes from Killearnan, Ross-shire. The writer, after a lengthy dissertation on the difficulties of effecting improvements when landlords neither set good examples themselves nor offer any help to their tenants, finishes thus: 'The agricultural state of this parish will farther be accounted for, when it is mentioned, that leases are, with very few exceptions, unknown. The farms on the most considerable property have been held only from year to year . . . What inducement does this present for improvement?'[107] Similarly devoid of any evidence of forward movement is the brief comment from the writer of the account for Auldearn near Nairn. He says of the tenants: 'They are tenacious of antiquated practices', and of the proprietors: 'None of them have inclosed any of their grounds, nor give encouragement to their tenants to do so.'[108]

The Agricultural Societies

The important part played by these is well documented; what is more enlightening than the already well-known societies in these accounts is mention of those which began in very small places – for example in Stronsay and Eday, Orkney: 'With a view to guard against disappointments in reference to agricultural improvements, to communicate the success of experiments, and to remedy certain inconveniences to which this district is liable by its social circumstances; the principal farmers in the island of Stronsay, most chearfully concurred to form themselves into a society.'[109] And in Rosemarkie, Black Isle, the 'Ross-shire Farming Society' was established: 'In a little time,' the writer hopes, 'it may excite emulation among the practical farmers, who will thus have an opportunity of communicating to one another their observations and experiments, which may be the means of introducing valuable improvements.'[110]

The Agricultural Scene

The account for Birse, Aberdeenshire, illustrates within itself the fascinatingly variegated nature of the 'agricultural revolution' of the time. While some in the parish were enthusiastically improving their ground, others were opposing just as vigorously: 'Some are clearing their ground by fallowing by a little green cropping, and by laying it down with artificial grasses; others are going on taking two or three successive crops of oats and of bear (when they give the ground a little dung), without allowing some portions of their ground any rest in a century. Indeed when the poorer sort of it is completely exhausted, by successive crops, they must let it rest; but for years it is almost useless. Some are going on with spirit, inclosing and clearing the ground of stones. Others are throwing every impediment in the way of the improver, by trampling down the fences, and by not only neglecting to remove the stones from their fields, but even by alleging, that the stones are beneficial to the soil, and tend to nourish the crop.'[111] In contrast, the account for Airlie, Angus, seems to describe a uniformly improved rural scene: 'About 26 years ago, it was almost in a state of nature, with scarcely an inclosure in it. Now, the greatest part is cultivated to a high degree, and about two-thirds of it is substantially inclosed, either with stone dikes, ditch and hedge, or ditch and paling; which fences, with the stripes and clumps of planting, well dressed fields, and handsome farm steadings, make a most beautiful appearance.'[112]

In the general euphoria – in which most of the ministers certainly joined – it is only extremely rarely that any note of doubt can be discerned. One who does voice misgivings, however, is the writer of the account from Auchtertoul, Fife. He views with concern the beginnings of the enforced drift from the countryside to which the fashion for enlarging farms would give rise; and while many writers plead eloquently for 'manufactures' in their areas, he seems to be keenly aware of the loss of human dignity and wholesomeness of rural life which would be the fate of the dispossessed in the rapidly-growing industrial towns and cities – fears which were to be realised to the full with the coming of the Industrial Revolution. 'This taste for enlarging and uniting farms,' he writes, 'which seems to be on the increase throughout Scotland, will perhaps, eventually, be unfavourable to the population of the country, and most undoubtedly to the personal character and morals of its inhabitants. It forces people from the active, healthy employments of a country life, to take refuge in manufacturing towns and populous cities, which may literally be said to be the graves of the human species.'[113]

From the majority of the Ayrshire reports, the impression is that this county's agricultural state was fairly advanced by this final decade of the century. A typical one is from Kirkmichael: 'About 30 years ago, the country was for the most part unenclosed: low ill-paid rents, poor farmers, starved cattle, puny horses, no carts, and scarcely a tolerable instrument of husbandry, prevailed everywhere. Now the reverse of all these is the case.'[114] From the North-East, in which many parishes were bustling with activity, comes this brief comment: 'The farms in general are in no better state than they were 100 years ago.'[115]

To end, however, on a more optimistic note – the brevity of the Kirriemuir account has much to commend it: 'What is wet, they are draining; what is uncultivated and arable, they are bringing into tillage; what is not arable, they are planting.'[116] The last word has to be given to the description of the improvements from the account for Clunie, Perthshire: 'It is only of late years that the knowledge of agriculture, and the spirit of improvement, began to display themselves in this parish. The people in general having no prospect of emolument to rouse their attention, and no example of industry set them by their superiors, squandered away their time, either in doing nothing at all, or in doing nothing to the purpose. Their grounds scratched over once a-year, without receiving half the necessary manure, and perpetually crossed with oats and barley alternately, were reduced to a *caput mortuum*. The lands were nowhere subdivided nor inclosed. The farmer, if he may be called so, had his crooked ridges everywhere warped through the crooked ridges of his neighbour; and the country being open in winter as well as in summer, all things were common, and men and beasts were at liberty to prey one upon another. Happily for the place, the pleasure, and the advantage of the people, the scene has now assumed another and better appearance. Commonties and runrigs are done away; the farms begin to be reduced to some form, and the marches to be straightened. Each man begins to know his own, and to have it in his power to improve it. Wet grounds are drained; rough grounds are cleared; stone-fences are built, and hedges are planted. Marl is brought from the neighbouring parishes of Kinloch and Caputh; lime from the shore of Perth; rich clays are applied to sand, and a good soil formed, where there was no soil before; green crops begin to be raised and a regular rotation of crops begins in some places to be understood. Many new implements of husbandry, common in the low country, are now introduced here; many old prejudices, that had long retarded the progress of improvement, are laid aside; and here, as in other places, the farmer begins to find his account, in following the good example of those who are wiser and more experienced than himself. In the course of the last 40 years, (during which there has been a considerable revolution of the property) the rents are in most places doubled, and in some places tripled, and, which was not the case before, regularly paid on a certain day. The farmers are more independent of their landlords on that account; and though in every respect the expense of living has more than kept pace with the rise of the rents, it is a fact, that both themselves and their families are better lodged, better dressed, and better fed than ever.'[117]

Mosses

No more fascinating story emerges from the pages of the SA than that of the clearing of the great swamps on the edge of Scotland's Central Belt. In the earlier part of the eighteenth century, this whole area was still a bottomless, impenetrable bog, stretching approximately from Stirling to Aberfoyle, and often referred to as the Moat of Scotland. The reclamation of this area, and its subsequent transformation into prime agricultural land, must surely rank as one of the outstanding achievements of the agricultural improvements of the day.

However, it is of interest to note that mosses of much smaller extent did exist in other parts of Scotland. In Dunnichen, Angus, for example, the local moss was seen principally as a rich source of fuel; the account states that the moss had been drained about 30 years previously and adds that 'in all probability it will furnish the neighbourhood with fuel for about 30 years longer, and may then be made a rich meadow.'[118] In view of the chronic scarcity of fuel in many areas this moss must have been an essential resource for the local people.

The moss of Torthorwald, Dumfriesshire, thought to have been at one time an inlet of the Solway, had yielded some very interesting finds, as noted in the Dumfries account: 'A stratum of sea sand is found at certain depths, and pieces of vessels, dug up in various parts of it, have been seen by persons who are still alive.' It also states that 'many large trees, chiefly fir, have been found in this moss, and uniformly laid with their tops to the NE.'[119] This moss too was a valuable source of fuel for the people.

The minister of Torthorwald quotes an ancient saying:

First a wood and next a sea
Now a moss, and ever will be.[120]

This seems indeed to have been the rather fatalistic attitude which prevailed in some places, for example in Shotts, Lanarkshire: 'The fields of moss with which, for two miles on each side of the great road, this parish is intersected, are a disadvantage from which the proprietors of Shotts can promise themselves no deliverance. The flatness of the fields, and the barren hill, which lies at the bottom of the moss, exclude the very idea of cultivation, from the mind even of the most adventurous improver.'[121]

A landowner in Kilbarchan, Renfrewshire, had found one method of tackling the problem: 'Mr Napier of Blackstone,' runs the account, 'has planted about 15 acres of moss bent, that is, the stuff left over after the peat is taken off, with trees of all kinds. They have been planted about 17 years, and are in a thriving condition, although growing upon 4 feet of moss.'[122]

But it was the clearing of the moss of Kincardine, a plan already renowned for its scope and audacity, which had clearly caught the imagination of many by the time the accounts were written. The writer of the Gargunnock, Stirlingshire, account states with undisguised admiration: 'The beauty of the landscape is greatly increased of late, by the very extraordinary improvements in the moss of Kincardine.'[123]

Certainly the detailed description found in Volume XII (pp. 574-604) in the Kincardine report is well worth reading in full, but here a summary must suffice: 'The mosses of Kincardine and Flanders cover more than 2,000 acres of the Carse ground in this parish,' writes the minister, the Rev. Christopher Tait. He begins by describing the methods formerly employed in the attempt to clear the giant moss. 'Some persons ploughed, and when it became dry, set fire to it. By repeating this operation, as often as their convenience or the season permitted, such a quantity of ashes was procured, as being incorporated with the remaining bog-earth, produced a coarse grass.' Another method was 'to dig ditches, or goats, as they are called, at such distances, and of such depths, that the clay dug from them was sufficient to cover the intermediate spaces of moss to the depth desired.'

All such attempts were abandoned, however, when the revolutionary method of floating off the deep surface moss was conceived through the genius of Lord Kames, a Court of Session judge who was married to the heiress of the Drummond Estates. In 1766 Lord Kames and his wife took up residence at Blair Drummond. Realising that much of their land comprised unproductive peat bog under which lay potentially fertile alluvial clay, Lord Kames carried out experiments which led him to conclude that a powerful stream of water could be employed to carry off large quantities of unwanted moss as quickly as labourers stationed at strategic intervals could throw the moss into it. What he had to find, therefore, was a work-force willing to face the daunting labour involved, and the miserably wet conditions of working. And find them he did, in those poverty-stricken Highlanders who had been dispossessed in favour of sheep, in some of the very early clearances.

The scheme began with a single tenant in 1767. At first, settlers were slow to offer themselves. Then, in 1774, after a road was opened up through the swamp, people began to come more readily. By 1782, we read, there were 42 tenants in all, occupying 336 acres. The account states that 'in the year 1783 Mr Drummond [Lord Kames' son, Henry Home Drummond] entered into possession of the estate of Blair Drummond, and went fully into the plan adopted by his predecessor for subduing the moss.'

Some neighbouring landowners had by this time adopted the scheme. The minister continues: 'The encouragements given for removing the moss are different with different proprietors. The most common method is to let a portion, commonly from 6 to 8 acres, to a moss tenant (or 'laird', as in contempt he is styled) for 36 years. In money and timber for building his hut he receives from the proprietor to the amount of £3-£4 sterling. No rent is exacted for the first 7 years. On the 8th he pays a merk Scotch, advancing a merk each year, until the 20th year. For this, and the remaining 18 years, he pays at the rate of 12s. yearly for each acre cleared, and 2s. 6d. per acre for what is not cleared. This last obligation is considered merely as a spur to the tenant to reclaim the ground; for the moss, in its original state, is not worth 3d. an acre.'

The minister has no hesitation in condemning the outrageous exploitation which this scheme involved. 'The ardour of the tenant,' he declares, 'to reclaim the high moss, is greatly checked. It costs him labour worth £10 or £12 or from 17-20 years purchase, to clear it, and he is to possess it, free of rent, only for 6 years. Whatever part of this sum is not recovered before the end of these 6 years, may be considered as lost to him. If this be the case, during the latter part of the first term of 19 years, folly alone can prompt him to continue his operations.'

Fortunately not all of the proprietors involved followed this selfish course. 'Some proprietors, of more liberal and enlarged views, pay to the tenant from £3 to £12 for each acre reclaimed, according to the depth of the moss, or bog earth removed from it.' The account continues: 'In some cases, this is paid when the work is executed; in others, it is paid at the end of the lease.' The Drummond family themselves did much to encourage their new tenants, offering for example a new plough as a prize to the labourer who cleared the largest area in a year. They also provided roof timber for the tenants to build their huts, and two bolls of oatmeal to sustain each family until they could grow their own crops.

The method by which the vast moss was cleared is next described in detail. Back in 1766, when Lord Kames acquired Blair Drummond, he decided to 'sweep off the whole body of moss. That moss might be floated in water, was abundantly obvious; but to find water in sufficient quantity was difficult.' The only available stream was employed in turning a corn mill. Lord Kames made an agreement with the mill tenant to demolish it so that the water could be used for his new purpose. His plan was nothing if not ingenious. It is described thus: 'A stream of water sufficient to turn a common mill will carry off as much moss as 20 men can throw into it, provided they be stationed at the distance of 100 yards from each other. The first step is to make, in the clay, alongside of the moss, a drain to convey the water . . . The drain being formed, the operation marks off, to a convenient extent alongside of it, a section of moss 10 feet broad; the greatest distance from which he can heave his spadeful into the drain. This he repeatedly does until the entire mass be removed down to the clay.'

Vital to the operation, clearly, was a powerful stream of water to carry the debris away. Not content with the original mill stream, Home Drummond later commissioned an engineer to build a large pumping wheel: 'Water is raised from the Teath to the height of 18 feet by a Persian wheel, and conveyed about 300 yards in a pipe of 18 inches diameter, which discharges it into an aqueduct that reaches the moss at the distance of 800 yards.'

The labourers, apart from enduring such exacting toil, were constantly soaked to the skin. But they were no strangers to hardship. 'A large number of the settlers in the moss of Kincardine, were people of the lowest rank in the Highlands, who were expelled from their native residence in consequence of the extensive sheep farms which have been established of late. Had opportunity offered, they would have removed to America. Fortunately, however, they have here found, not only an asylum, but a comfortable settlement, in which they are usefully employed for themselves, and with great benefit to their country.' An asylum doubtless; but the word 'comfortable' is surely a little euphemistic, since there could have been but scant comfort in the rude huts, some of which are said to have actually floated on the morass. The writer takes a rosy view of the workers' life, continuing thus: 'Though moss-work be laborious, it is at the same time amusing. The operator moves the moss 5 feet only at a medium; and the water, like carts in other cases, carrying it off as fast as it is thrown in, excites him to activity. Still he must submit to be wet from morning to night. But habit reconciles him to this inconvenience; while his house and arable land fill his eye and cheer his mind. Nor is it found that the health of the inhabitants is in the smallest degree injured either by the nature of the work or the vicinity of the moss.'

Admittedly, as time went on conditions clearly improved for the moss settlers, stated to comprise 764 men, women and children, with 54 carts, 201 cows, and 102 brick houses: 'In a favourable day there may be seen hundreds, men, women, and children, labouring with the utmost assiduity. The women declare they can make more by working at the moss than at their wheel; and such is their general attachment to that employment, that they have frequently been discovered working by moonlight.'

Of their character, the minister writes in glowing terms: 'Of the whole inhabitants, full 9/10 are Highlanders, from the neighbouring parishes of Callander, Balquhidder, etc., a sober, frugal and industrious people. Neither ought it to be forgotten, that, from their settlement to the present day, not a single instance has occurred among them of theft, bad neighbourhood, or of any other misdemeanour, that required the interposition of the civil magistrate. Nor, however poor in circumstances, has any one of them, ever stooped to solicit assistance from the parish funds appropriated to that purpose.'

Ostracised at first by the people around, and known derisively as 'moss lairds', the labourers were further isolated by the fact that they spoke only Gaelic.

Whatever the cost in human terms – and this aspect cannot be ignored – it has to be said that the feat of transforming the vast bog into some of Scotland's finest agricultural land is impressive, a fact which the writer of the account is at pains to emphasise: 'The following full and accurate account of the moss of Kincardine, must no doubt be acceptable and useful to the public, as it describes the rise and progress of the most singular and considerable piece of improvement that has yet been executed in any parish in Scotland. There is probably no tract of land of the same extent, equally unprofitable and useless, that has ever been rendered so productive and populous, in any part of the three kingdoms.'[124]

FOOTNOTE:

Although several other schemes were later started to reclaim some of the Flanders Moss area, from 1865 all further work was prohibited because the Forth had become silted up with moss and peat.

1. VII, 276
2. XV, 289
3. XX, 274
4. III, 152
5. XVII, 524
6. XX, 274
7. XVI, 249
8. II, 72
9. VII, 199
10. VII, 557
11. VII, 667
12. III, 891
13. XVII, 405
14. XX, 215
15. IX, 669
16. VI, 84
17. IV, 500
18. XVII, 362
19. XVII, 483
20. IV, 531
21. XVIII, 89
22. VII, 869
23. XV, 69
24. VI, 462
25. IX, 358
26. IV, 17
27. XVII, 447
28. XIII, 142
29. XII, 606
30. XII, 697
31. III, 85

32. XIX, 224
33. XX, 196
34. XX, 59
35. II, 13
36. II, 135
37. XIV, 219
38. XVI, 542
39. XIII, 233
40. XIX, 486
41. VI, 301
42. XVII, 170
43. II, 727
44. XX, 171
45. III, 871
46. XII, 408
47. VI, 150
48. XII, 491
49. XVI, 454
50. XII, 409
51. XIX, 234
52. XX, 276
53. XIV, 540
54. XIX, 502
55. XVIII, 259
56. XX, 424
57. IV, 500
58. XI, 59
59. XII, 292
60. XVII, 524
61. XVIII, 86
62. VI, 401

63. VI, 646
64. VI, 377
65. VI, 66
66. III, 832
67. II, 539
68. XIX, 344
69. XVII, 20
70. XVII, 141
71. XX, 5
72. XX, 129
73. XVI, 658
74. XIX, 108
75. XIX, 275
76. XIX, 408
77. XIV, 391
78. XII, 454
79. II, 645
80. IV, 57
81. II, 29
82. VII, 3
83. VII, 594
84. XIV, 559
85. V, 240
86. XIX, 78
87. XIX, 276
88. III, 193
89. III, 415
90. XVII, 408
91. XIV, 371
92. IX, 639
93. V, 89

94. V, 40
95. V, 219
96. IV, 407
97. IX, 393
98. V, 357
99. IX, 475
100. XIV, 94
101. II, 224
102. XII, 522
103. III, 450
104. XVII, 265
105. XV, 544
106. V, 61
107. XVII, 418
108. XVI, 722
109. XIX, 312
110. XVII, 615
111. XIV, 417
112. XIII, 7
113. X, 66
114. VI, 376
115. XVI, 438
116. XIII, 358
117. XII, 236
118. XIII, 200
119. IV, 125
120. IV, 498
121. VII, 581
122. VII, 755
123. IX, 347
124. XII, 574

15   EMIGRATION

Much of the attraction of the SA lies in the fact that it covers a period of significant change in Scotland. In agriculture especially, crop rotations, implements and husbandry were all undergoing unprecedented change; in industry, a great variety of new processes – or modifications of old ones – were coming into use. And in medicine, the revolutionary technique of inoculation was being either welcomed or stubbornly resisted.

In investigating the accounts for records of emigration, however, one is rather looking at a process which had already been going on for a long time, but which was to reach its culmination in the early decades of the nineteenth century with the most notorious of the Highland Clearances in the county of Sutherland. There is thus much interest in noting those accounts in which emigration is highlighted, frequently along with the reasons for it; and as always, there is interest in identifying the varying perspectives of the writers – what one sees as a downright evil, another may perceive as merely inevitable, yet another as a positive boon.

Seasonal migrations had been common long before this. From many of the Highland and Island parishes in particular, young people had been accustomed to make their way south, to work either in the cities or, more usually, at the harvest or the shearing on Lowland farms, returning, according to some of the accounts, richer financially if not necessarily in character. 'Most of our young women go to the low country for some weeks in harvest,' asserts the Small Isles account. 'This they spend in shearing; and with the money, they endeavour to dress after the low country fashion; the fashion, thus introduced, raises an emulation among the women in general, and, of course, merchants are encouraged to import like articles. The periodical migration of our young women to the low country in harvest, is entirely with a view to dress.'[1]

In the Highlands and Islands, from where the accounts show most emigration took place, the principal factor to be observed is the demise of the old paternalistic clan system. In attempting to describe this process, one would be hard put to better the telling account from North Uist: 'The gentlemen farmers are for the most part the descendants of the different branches of the families of the chieftains, on whose estate they live . . . The chieftain prided himself upon the number of his gentlemen so much, that he looked upon himself as their common father. In their distress he relieved their wants; and when one of them died, he became the guardian of their children, and the executor of his will; which trust was in general executed with fidelity. On the other hand, when the chieftain was threatened with danger from the invasion or encroachments of his neighbours, his gentlemen flocked to his castle to assist in his deliberations, and to offer their services. If war was determined upon, they, with their adherents, followed him to the field, to support his pretensions, and share his fate. By this means the strongest attachment was established between them, partly on the ties of consanguinity, and partly on mutual services. This attachment continued unimpaired, till the rebellion in the year 1745, which, though attended with the happy consequence of civilizing the Highlanders, and making them good and loyal subjects, yet was attended with this disadvantage, that it weakened the attachment between the chieftains and their people; for since that period, the chieftains, from different motives, have withdrawn themselves from their estates, have become unacquainted with their people, whom they visit but seldom, are not so attentive to the ties of consanguinity, and are become less scrupulous in removing the tacksmen from their farms, if a higher offer is made than the possessors can afford to pay.'[2]

In short, the encroachment of an altogether more materialistic set of values is apparent, and this seems to have spread very widely. There are exceptions, though. Just one of these may be quoted in contrast; the minister of Lintrathen, Angus, describes the patriarchal system which was still prevailing in the House of Airlie: 'It does not become a clergyman to enter into controversy, but it is an undoubted fact that the tenants of the noble family of Airly, both here and in other parishes, have always been remarkable for ease and opulence. Few of the old residenters or their tenants have ever been removed, a confidence between the landlords and tenants having prevailed from time immemorial.'[3]

In the less fortunate areas, the weakening of the ancient ties can be seen to have led to much exploitation, probably the worst example being the kelp industry; the pursuit of profit to the total exclusion of the people's welfare is highlighted in several of the accounts. Because of the vast fortunes to be made, many landlords actively opposed emigration when the rates being paid for the product in this highly labour-intensive industry were high, but made haste to be rid of their tenantry when the trade ceased to be lucrative.

The introduction of sheep-rearing will forever be associated with forced emigration. The older, traditional sheep in the Highland area were small and white-faced, with long, silky wool. The blackface (Linton) breed displaced it because of its ability to survive in a harsh climate, as well as its superior yield of wool and mutton; the Cheviot sheep was also introduced in some areas. For those landlords who valued profit more than people, removing tenants to make way for sheep proved a temptation too strong to resist, as the account from Kilmallie near Fort William illustrates: 'The great augmentation of rents must be attributed, principally, to the mode adopted, of stocking farms with sheep. They require a smaller number of hands to tend them, than black cattle; can graze in places where these would not venture, and yield a greater produce. This, it will be acknowledged, is a strong temptation to proprietors, who value money more than men, to encourage sheep-farming.'[4] (Later, the year 1792 was to be called 'the year of the sheep'.)

The main emphasis, therefore, in the Highland accounts, is on sheep, and it seems not inappropriate to include a number of excerpts on them at this point, so as to demonstrate differing shades of opinion on this emotive subject.

From Lochbroom, Wester Ross, comes an unfavourable account: 'The oppression of the landlords is a general complaint in the Highlands; and the consequence is, that great numbers of the people are forced to emigrate to America, while others go to service in the low countries and manufacturing towns. Thus the population is not near so great as might be expected in such an extent of territory. Another circumstance, which is unfriendly to population, is the engrossing of farms for sheep-walks. This mode of farming has been introduced lately into some parts of the parish, and proved the occasion of reducing to hardship several honest families, who lived tolerably happily on the fruits of their industry and frugality. Whoever would wish to see the population flourishing, should do all in their power to put a stop to the sheep traffic, and to introduce manufactures among the people. Whole districts have been already depopulated by the introduction of sheep; so that, where formerly hundreds of people could be seen, no human faces are now to be met with, except a shepherd attended by his dog.'[5]

In similar condemnatory vein the account for Abernethy and Kincardine states: 'It is to be regretted, that so many thousands of these loyal brave people have been forced to a foreign shore by necessity, for want of employment, habitation, or ground to subsist on. However advantageous the sheep-farming may be, it is possible it may be overdone; and if ever that happens, it will be found to be impolitic in every sense, as it is cruel in many places at present.'[6]

A vivid picture of depopulation emerges in the report for Boleskine and Abertarf, Inverness-shire: 'Formerly, Abertarf was inhabited by the numerous and hardy race of names of the Macdonalds, Macgruers, Kennedies, and Frasers . . . but this part of the parish having, within these 30 years, exchanged its proprietors, it is now almost totally under sheep, and hardly contains the tenth part of its former inhabitants, and some parts of the country of Stratherrick, having been converted into sheep-walks, has considerably reduced the number of its people.'[7]

Further south, from Strachur, Argyll, comes a very similar account of depopulation: 'The district is now thinned of its inhabitants. The people have been forced to leave their native hills. The sheep have banished the men. Where, in 12 or 16 families, a hardy race was reared, an opulent tacksman, with a shepherd or two, occupy the lands. The Highlanders of old did not live either in plenty or in elegance, yet they were happy. They prided themselves on their capacity of enduring hunger and fatigue. They were passionately fond of music and poetry. The song and the dance soon made them forget their toils. The sound of the bagpipe is now seldom heard. With the modes of life that nourished it, the vein for poetry has also disappeared. The deer have fled from the mountains. A forest, in the close neighbourhood of this parish, where several hundreds of them roamed at pleasure, is now converted into a sheep-walk.'[8]

However, there were contrasting views; the account for Cromdale, Morayshire, finds the numerous flocks of sheep a positive improvement: 'The hills and level grounds are generally covered with black heath, having scarce any mixture of grass connected with it. Though these circumstances quickly discover themselves to the stranger and traveller, from the unpleasant aspect the country at first exhibits, yet these prejudices are soon removed, when a person adverts to the utility and consequence of places, formerly, in a great measure, thought barren and useless, now rendered productive of the greatest source of natural wealth, by the flocks of sheep, which every where cover the face of the country.'[9]

The extremely small size of the poor people's holdings is the subject of some accounts; and it has to be said that over-population was clearly a pressing problem in some areas, including the county of Sutherland. The Golspie account takes the proprietors' side, asserting that 'the multitude of small farms in this, and in almost all the parishes in the country, are much against the interest of proprietors; because, were several of them conjoined, the lands being contiguous, they would fetch a much better rent.' In a statement which makes strange reading in the county most notorious for the Clearances at a later date, he goes on to say: 'These gentlemen would not sacrifice their humanity to the most advantageous consideration of interest.'[10]

When one reads the Walls and Flota, Orkney, account however, an example comes to light which belies these sentiments. Writing of a notable increase in population, the account explains: 'What accounts for this increase is, the settlement of a colony of Highlanders, who had been forced to emigrate from Strathnaver, where their farms were converted into sheep pasture.' To those familiar with the history of the Clearances, the name of this place is synonymous with all that is worst in that cruel episode in Scottish history. The account continues: 'These people, it would appear, had been comfortably situated in their former residence, as they all brought with them, to this place, a very considerable stock in horses, cows, sheep, and goats, and also in grain.'[11] Although displaced, these folk were among the more fortunate; no doubt they were able to rebuild their lives on the Orkney Islands. Later on, this chapter will examine the fate of many who were not so well settled.

The problem posed by over-population comes across especially in the Western Isles accounts. In Tiree, for example, the numbers seem staggering: 'It is too much for this parish, without manufactures, and without greater improvements in agriculture, to support 3,457 inhabitants.'[12] The sheer impossibility of supporting the population is illustrated graphically in the account for Duirinish, Skye: 'Of late, the inhabitants have multiplied so much, that from August 1771, to October 1790, eight large transports have sailed from this island with emigrants, to seek settlements in America. These eight ships have, at a moderate computation, carried away from this island 2,400 souls, and £24,000 sterling, ship-freights included . . . The utmost that the whole island can do in the very best seasons, is to serve the inhabitants with meal. In unfavourable seasons they buy large quantities of imported meal.'[13] The enforced division of land into ever-lessening holdings is stressed in the Small Isles account: 'In the years 1788 and 1790, 183 souls emigrated from this parish to America, and 55 to the mainland of Scotland and to neighbouring islands; and of these 176 left Eigg. A principal cause of this emigration was, that the country was overstocked with people, arising from frequent early marriages; of course, the lands were able to supply them but scantily with the necessaries of life. It is not unfrequent on such occasions, for a parent to divide with his newly married son, the pittance of land (sometimes a very small portion of a farm) possessed by him, which must reduce both to poverty and misery.'[14]

The writer of the North Uist account is at great pains to describe what he sees as the principal causes underlying the trend towards emigration; not only that, but he offers very practical suggestions as to how it may be reversed: 'The sudden rise of the land-rents was certainly the original cause of emigration from the Isle of Sky and Uist to America. Those who found a difficulty in supporting their families when the rents were low, could not be persuaded that any exertions in industry would enable them to live with any degree of comfort, when raised a third more at least. This determined some of them to look out for asylum somewhere else. Copies of letters from persons who had emigrated several years before to America, to their friends at home, containing the most flattering accounts of the province of North Carolina, were circulated among them. The implicit faith given to these accounts made them resolve to desert their native country, to encounter the dangers of crossing the Atlantic to settle in the wilds of America . . . Other causes have concurred with that already mentioned. The sense of grievances, whether real or imaginary; the fear of having the fruits of their industry called for by the landlords, many of whom think they have a right to the earnings of the tenants, except what barely supports life; the want of employment for such as have no lands to cultivate . . . and the facility of procuring a property for a small sum of money, the produce of which they can call their own, and from which their removal does not depend on the will of capricious masters. These are the principal motives that determine people now to emigrate to America, without at all attending to the difficulties and discouragements in their way, arising from the danger they must encounter in crossing the seas.'

There then follows the writer's recommendations as to how these evils may be combated: 'To put a stop to the present rage for emigration requires very nice management in the proprietors.' Primarily, he wanted to see the old attachment between them and their tenants renewed; secondly, long leases should be granted; thirdly, help should be given to the people so that improvements might be carried out; next, manufactures should be established; lastly, villages should be erected.[15]

So far, the focus of attention has been on the causes of emigration from the Highlands and Islands parishes. Although to some extent the same factors operated all over the country (for example, the introduction of black-faced sheep on the Campsie and Ochil hills led to wholesale removals of small tenants, and indeed of tacksmen as well), in the southern parts, what might be called the negative side of the agricultural improvements appeared; the amalgamation of many small units into very large farms led to the dispossession of huge numbers of people who had been living on smallholdings. Predominantly in such counties as Ayrshire, Lanarkshire and Renfrewshire this process caused the virtual elimination of the cottar class, and forced the people to migrate in search of work to the great industrial centres – Glasgow, the Vale of Leven, Paisley and Greenock – often to quite abysmal conditions.

Various views are offered in the accounts, but the following statement is typical of many. 'Within these two or three years,' declares the account from Ardchattan and Muckairn, Argyll: '140 persons emigrated from hence to America; and this year more are preparing to follow, being much encouraged by the flattering accounts of the former emigrants. Several families have removed to the low country, where wages are high. The principal cause of the decrease of population is the engrossing and uniting of several farms, and turning them into sheep-walks. Farms that formerly supported eight or nine families are now occupied by only two or three, and, in some places, solely by one shepherd.'[16] And in Tinwald, Borders: 'The inhabitants were more numerous years ago, by some hundreds, than at present; ten or more tenants sometimes being turned out with their cottagers to make way for one. In some instances, only the herdsman is retained in the farm.'[17]

The Selkirk writer makes his feelings clear when he declares with heavy irony: 'To restore this country to its former state of respectability, as well as beauty, it must be indebted to the proprietors of the soil, for replacing not only the woods, but the inhabitants, which the impolitic practice of adding farm to farm, and the fatal operation of poors' rates, have compelled to leave their native home. It is painful to see (as in this parish) one person rent a property, on which one hundred inhabitants were reared to the state, and found a comfortable subsistence. It adds to the bleakness of the scene, to see a few shepherds strolling about the face of a country, which formerly was the nurse of heroes, who were justly accounted the bulwark of their native soil.'[18]

In another Eastern Borders account, that from Broughton, it is the demolition of cottages which excites the writer's wrath: 'The throwing down of cottages must be one principal reason of the decrease of population in country parishes, and of the increase of population in towns and villages, and a principal reason of the scarcity of servants, and the increase of their wages; the poor people being banished from the country, take up their residence in towns, and breed their children to manufactures, who would otherwise have been bred to the plough.'[19]

The recorder from Lochgoilhead and Kilmorich, Argyll, however, finds nothing at all wrong with this situation. 'It is frequent with people who wish well to their country, to inveigh against the practice of turning several small farms into one extensive grazing . . . But the complaint does not seem to apply to this country. The strength of a nation cannot surely consist in the number of idle people which it maintains . . . Such of the people as went to towns, and had no stock to lay out in trade, found employment, partly as day-labourers, porters, barrowmen, boatmen etc., but the greatest number of those who left the country for fifteen years past, support themselves by working in bleachfields, printfields, cotton mills, and many other branches of manufactures, in which much previous instruction or preparation is not required. So that the former inhabitants of this country have been taken from a situation, in which they contributed nothing to the wealth, and very little to the support of the state, to a situation in which their labour is of the greatest public utility.'[20]

Accounts from some parishes show a trend contrary to the depopulation of those already examined; in the Lothians parish of Humbie, for example, the introduction of turnips on a large scale had saved the inhabitants from the necessity of leaving their native soil: 'The improvement of two horses instead of four in a plough, which was introduced in the year 1768, evidently lessened the number of farm servants; but this effect of it seems to have been counteracted, by the additional work occasioned by the preferable modes of agriculture, and particularly that of raising turnips, which commenced exactly at the same period: for upon one large farm, on which about 100 acres of turnips are raised annually, the numbers are increased, and more still could find employment.'[21]

The account from Dalmeny, Lothians, also contends that depopulation is not necessarily a consequence of the amalgamation of farms: 'The union of farms has often been stated as a cause of depopulation; but the fact seems disputable. In many instances population has been known to increase, on a great farmer's succeeding to a number of small ones. And the reason is plain to those who make an attentive observation. A small farmer has seldom any cottagers, his men servants are unmarried, and lodge in his house or offices. The reverse is the case of a great farmer; almost the whole of his men servants have separate houses, are married, and have a numerous and healthy progeny.'[22]

Undoubtedly the building of villages did much to combat forced migration and emigration in some districts, a practice which is strongly advocated in the account from Scone: 'If the proprietors of the soil, who dispossess the small to make room for the greater farmers, would build villages on their estates, the population would seldom be diminished in any situation; the wealth and comfort of the people would increase in proportion to the superior cultivation of the land; the farmers would find a market for the great part of their produce at home, and would have day labourers at command; and the proprietors themselves would derive advantages from the villages, far beyond the expense of erecting them.'[23]

These excerpts deal largely with people's departure to the industrial centres to find work. Where else did they go? A variety of locations are mentioned in the accounts. In the far north, especially Orkney, the Greenland fisheries and Hudson's Bay Company tended to draw away many of the younger men. Some of the accounts express vigorous opposition – to the latter in particular – for example the Orphir account: 'The greatest number enter into the service of the Hudson's Bay Company; and instead of offering an honourable service to their king and country, or staying at home to cultivate their lands, and protect their wives, their children, and their parents, for the sum of £6 per annum, hire themselves out as slaves in a foreign land, where, in the language of Scripture, they are literally employed as hewers of wood and drawers of water; or, what is a still more distinguishing badge of slavery, in dragging large loads of timber, yoked in the team like beasts of burden . . . Many of those men, at their return, after eight or ten years exile, bring home with them all the vices, without any of the virtues of savages; indolence, dissipation, irreligion, and at the same time a broken constitution.'[24]

In much the same vein, the account of Firth and Stenness declares: 'Nothing contributes so much to the hurt of this place, as the resort of the Hudson's Bay Company's ships to Stromness, and their engaging lads from this country. A few lads returning with some money make excellent recruits for the Company's service; and the report of a war makes great numbers solicit to go out to their settlements. The farmers' servants and sons leave them, to spend the prime of life in cold and drudgery in the North-West; from whence such of them as are not incapacitated by diseases contracted there, return to be farmers, their skill in that line not improved by their absence . . . Young lads, however, who have married before they have any stock, or can get small farms by going into the Company's service, are able to remit a trifle to their families.' Only one other benefit, according to this account, accrues from this particular form of emigration: 'When a man and his wife cannot live in peace together, the parties and the parish are relieved from such disquiets, by the husband's retreat to the Hudson's Bay settlements.'[25] The Sandwick and Stromness account bewails the shortage of men in proportion to women which is 'occasioned by the young men going abroad to various parts of the world; to the Greenland Fishery, Hudson's Bay, and His Majesty's Navy.'[26]

It is clear, therefore, from accounts from all over Scotland that emigration took place to quite a variety of places. Two from the North-East also illustrate this. From Duffus, Morayshire, comes this comment: 'About the end of last century, some individuals went to North America, a few of whom returned and settled at home, bringing bad tidings of the country, which their imaginations had figured to be a fairy-land of wealth. Since that time, those who would have gone to America, had the prospect been favourable, have preferred a home emigration to the southern parts of Scotland, particularly Glasgow, Paisley etc. And from this part of the North, there is, and always has been, a constant succession of adventurers issuing forth to the British capital, the East and West Indies, and other parts of the Empire.'[27] From the Aberlour account some similar comments were expressed: 'Since the year 1782, when there were whole families emigrating from the neighbouring parishes to North America, none, except a few aspiring young men, have left this parish, and gone, some to London, some to the West India islands.'[28] That these aspiring young men frequently returned in vastly improved circumstances is made clear in some accounts, for example that of Kells, Galloway: 'Several young men of spirit go to the West Indies as planters and merchants. Some go to England to push their fortunes, as pedlars, and, when sober and industrious, return, after ten or twelve years, with £800, or £900, or £1,000. Several return from the West Indies, after 16 or 17 years, with genteel fortunes; and some young men choose a sea-faring life.'[29]

The Duffus account quoted above makes it clear that there could be disenchantment on the part of those who had taken the step of leaving their native land. But in the Western Isles in particular, the people often had very little choice; in addition, some of the writers do not mince their words in asserting that they were at times lured abroad by false promises. The Barra account, for example, states: 'Upwards of 200 left this country within the last two years; some emigrated to the island of St John's, and Nova Scotia, in North America, being inveigled thither by a Mr F., upon promises of the undisturbed profession of their religion (being all Roman Catholics) and of free property for themselves and their offspring for ever; but how soon they were landed, he left them to their shifts, and returned back to his native country. These poor people were left in the most deplorable situation. If the inhabitants of the different places in which they landed, had not exerted themselves for their relief, many of them must have perished, for want of the common necessaries of life.'[30] Interestingly, the Newabbey, Borders, account, although supplying no details, mentions a similar experience from a totally different area of the country: 'There has been little or no emigration from this parish within the last 20 years, excepting a few ill-advised people, both married and single, who went to St John's in North America, and, in the issue, had abundant reason to repent leaving their native country.'[31]

While forced migration is mentioned from time to time – for example, that of Highland folk from inland parishes to the coast after they had been displaced in favour of sheep – only one mention of another kind of removal on an altogether smaller scale is particularly noticeable. From Hutton in the Eastern Borders, the account describes a pattern of living which may, in pre-holiday days, have been occasioned by sheer boredom: 'There is no other kind of emigration but that which takes place at the Whitsunday, when there is a removal of many hinds, herds, cottagers, into neighbouring parishes; whose places are, at the same time, filled up by many of the same description, who are actuated by an unaccountable desire to change their habitations, though they seldom ameliorate their situations. Nothing but the expectation of better pasture for their cow, can be assigned as a reason; for their gains, as they are called, which are, so many bolls of corn planted and linseed sowed, etc., are the same everywhere in this corner of the country.'[32] This would appear to be an early example of what would become a way of life in the agricultural areas in the nineteenth century, when labourers would 'flit' on the term days – 28th May and 28th November – after being hired at the 'feeing markets.'

Occasionally, an account mentions a parish in which the people are exceptionally fortunate. These folk have no desire to move, either to the manufacturing towns or abroad. Invariably the reason is that they have landlords who care about their welfare – for example in Athelstaneford, Lothians: 'The increase of buildings and inhabitants in the village is owing to the liberal encouragement given by Sir David Kinloch of Gilmerton, the proprietor, to people to settle on his estate. The houses are built upon a feu-tack of 38 years, at the expense of the people, who pay to the proprietor a trifle annually for the ground on which the house stands. They have large gardens of excellent soil, at the same proportion of rent which a farmer would cheerfully pay for it. Besides this, the feuers of these houses hold, in a conjunct lease, about 100 acres of good land at a moderate rent. This land is divided among them in small lots. Two of their number have each a pair of horses. With these they labour the land for the community at a reasonable hire, and drive coals and carriages that are necessary for the village. With the produce of this land the inhabitants supply themselves with meal and potatoes, and many of them have it in their power to keep a cow. In this manner they are enabled to live comfortably, to clothe and educate their children decently, and to assist in setting them out in the world. There is no village in the country where the people have improved more of late years in comfort and convenience than in the village of Athelstaneford. Formerly, their dwellings were no more than small, dirty, dark hovels; now they are all neat, commodious houses, generally with two apartments, and well lighted . . . While many villages in Scotland are deserted, and permitted to go to ruins, the worthy proprietor of Athelstaneford has the pleasure of seeing a flourishing village on his estate, the numerous inhabitants of which look up to him with gratitude as their guardian and benefactor, always ready to advise, protect, and assist them.'[33]

That this utopian picture is in stark contrast to the norm scarcely needs to be pointed out; nor does the flattering description of this particular landlord come across as in any way sycophantic – on the contrary, it seems to be substantiated in the rest of the account, as a true description of one who took genuine pleasure in seeing his tenants flourish.

Undoubtedly the Western Isles suffered more than most, not only on account of the problems of over-population and under-production, but also in the matter of negligent and oppressive landlords. Despite the known disenchantment of some who had left their native land, despite the known rigours of the voyage, with the appalling conditions on board the emigrant ships, the people still left in droves. Even there, however, a single cheering example of a more enlightened regime shines out amid the general gloom. The altogether happier life enjoyed by the people of Kilchoman, Islay, not surprisingly induced them to leave their roots firmly planted in their native soil: 'They are so sensible of the advantages they enjoy, and are in general so contented with their situation, that very few have emigrated from the island. And the farms of those who have, have never continued long unpossessed. When tenants are emancipated from the avarice of monopolisers, they seem to breathe a purer air, and improvements go on rapidly; for nothing has tended more to excite the spirit of emigration, than the Demon of Monopoly; which leads the avaricious to add land to land, and farm to farm . . . If the moderation and lenity, that have hitherto been observed in Islay, continues to be adhered to, we may venture to promise, that the people will rather stay at home, to improve the lands of their native island, than go abroad to cultivate the wilds of America. Amen!'[34]

1. XX, 251	10. XVIII, 425	19. III, 741	28. XVI, 5
2. XX, 109	11. XIX, 344	20. VIII, 349	29. V, 148
3. XIII, 421	12. XX, 266	21. II, 506	30. XX, 140
4. XVII, 141	13. XX, 160	22. II, 728	31. V, 290
5. XVII, 562	14. XX, 239	23. XI, 572	32. III, 213
6. XVI, 450	15. XX, 117	24. XIX, 616	33. II, 448
7. XVII, 30	16. VIII, 5	25. XIX, 93	34. XX, 394
8. VIII, 417	17. IV, 489	26. XIX, 236	
9. XVI, 36	18. III, 707	27. XVI, 493	

15   THE CHURCH AND ITS MINISTERS

It might well be expected that these parochial accounts written by nearly a thousand ministers of the Kirk would be heavily biased towards theology, or would at least yield a wealth of ecclesiastical anecdotes. This is far from being the case. Most of the writers confine themselves to fairly terse replies to Sir John's queries on the subject. Surprisingly, too, there are few references to church discipline, possibly because this was uniform throughout the Church – the stool of repentance, for example, being taken for granted at the time.

What does bulk large in the accounts, on the other hand, is discussion of the various dissenting bodies which by then had broken away from the established Church.

Today it is quite difficult to appreciate fully the important role of the Church in eighteenth-century Scotland. While an overwhelming majority in most areas adhered to the national Church, there were – notably in the central and more urbanised districts – various groups of 'dissenters' who, although no longer persecuted for their refusal to accept the established form of belief, were still frequently regarded with suspicion or active dislike by their fellow-citizens, and could be excluded from certain official posts.

In order to illustrate something of the degree of dissension, a few statistical tables from parishes around the country have been selected; first, though, it would seem helpful to include a very brief explanation of the origins of the principal factions of which mention is made most often in the accounts.

For around two centuries before these accounts were written, profound controversy had existed in Scotland over the question of who should have the right to elect and call parish ministers. 'Patronage' – that right vested in patrons, or heritors – eventually gave rise to a secession from the national Church led by one Ebenezer Erskine in 1733, he and three colleagues forming themselves into a separate presbytery which by 1742 comprised 36 congregations and 20 ministers.

As was the tendency in such situations, this new presbytery was itself split again in 1744 over the issue of the Burgess Oath, disagreement having arisen over whether it was lawful for a seceder to take the oath required of burgesses in certain cities, whereby they acknowledged that religious belief which was publicly preached and legally authorised. Thus two ecclesiastical bodies emerged, known as the Burghers and the Antiburghers; both factions grew steadily at the expense of the established Church, attracting for example those alienated either because of patronage, or else laxity, as they saw it, in church discipline or doctrine.

In the accounts, Burghers and Antiburghers receive frequent mention; so do the Cameronians – a strict presbyterian body owing their origin to a preacher named Richard Cameron some 100 years earlier, and loyal to the National Covenants. The rather strangely named 'Presbytery of Relief' ('Relief' for short) appears also in some accounts; it too was opposed to patronage, and had been constituted in 1761 'for the relief of Christians oppressed in their church privileges.' This faction was said to be free of the animosity towards the establishment which had characterised the earlier secession.

In addition to the main bodies, some smaller splinter groups formed around a single minister – for example the Glassites (later known as Sandemanians) following John Glas, and the Bereans, founded in the last quarter of the eighteenth century by a Mr Barclay in Crieff.

It has to be stressed that all of the parties mentioned above were orthodox Christian believers who simply deviated in certain points which, surprisingly as it may seem today, were warranted sufficient to call for the establishment of a new denomination. In contrast, one of the Ayrshire accounts offers a colourful description of a strange dissenting body, known as the Buchanites, which went badly off the rails. When a Mr Whyte was minister of the Relief congregation there, the account, from Irvine, states, a Mrs Buchan was received in the parish as a kind of prophetess. 'Her time was wholly employed in visiting from house to house and in making family worship, solving doubts, answering questions, and expounding the Scriptures.' Later, however, her orthodoxy began to be questioned – as well as that of the minister himself for having accepted her principles; he was deposed, and for some time after preached in a tent. Mrs Buchan began to make strange claims for herself, so much so that 'she drew on herself and her party the indignation of the populace.' Finally, we read, they hounded her out of the town, where she was joined by the Rev Mr Whyte and others, and the whole party (of about 40 people) 'proceeded on their way to Mauchline, and from thence to Cumnock and to Closeburn in Dumfriesshire, singing as they went, and saying that they were going to the New Jerusalem.'[1]

Stirling is credited with having been the first to experience divisions, as the account from Lecropt, Perthshire, states: 'The town of Stirling was the original seat of the secession from the Established Church; and from a variety of causes, the peculiar tenets of that persuasion took early a deep root in that neighbourhood. A great variety of opinions have sprung up since that period. We have Burghers, Antiburghers, Cameronians, Bereans, and persons who adhere to the Presbytery of Relief. But it ought to be remarked to their credit, that persons entertaining all these different opinions live with those of the Established Church, and with one another, in friendship and brotherly love.'[2]

Stirling [3]

Established Church	2,795
Burghers	1,415
Antiburghers	172

Cameronians	120
Episcopalians	89
Relief	74
Bereans	33

Kilmarnock [4]

Established Church	5,716
Burghers	540
Antiburghers	480
Cameronians	40

Barony of Glasgow [5]

Established Church	12,369
Relief	2,793
Burghers	1,564
Antiburghers	1,054
Cameronians	220
Episcopalians	171
Independents (Congregationalists)	162
Methodists	64
Baptists	25
Roman Catholics	20
Quakers	4
Bereans	3
Glassites	2

Buittle [6]

Established Church	678
Cameronians	67
Seceders	34
Roman Catholics	75
Episcopalians	1

Bendothy [7]

Established Church	696
Seceders	143
Relievers	32
Episcopalians	3
Roman Catholics	2

Perth

Here the minister does not quote actual numbers, but mentions that while there are three established congregations, there are no fewer than nine groups of dissenters. He then lists these in some detail:

'The different dissenters are as follows:

1. Scots Episcopalians.
2. An English Episcopalian chapel.
3. A small society of Cameronians, who affect to be called the old Scots Presbyterians.
4. A small society of Anabaptists. The principles they entertain are not well known.
5. A congregation of Burgher Seceders.
6. A congregation of Antiburgher Seceders.
7. A congregation of what are called Relief people.
8. A small congregation of Balchristy people, who are a species of Independents.
9. A pretty large church of that kind of Independents, who commonly are called Glassites, or Sandemanians.'[8]

The writer of this account ends by saying: 'A gentleman in Dundee, some years ago, wrote to his correspondent in Perth, that if it were agreeable, an Unitarian minister, who was then residing in Dundee, would come to Perth, to give a sermon and an explanation of his principles. The Perth gentleman very properly replied, there were already too many religions in Perth, and he did not wish to see any more.'

One wonders whether the minister of Innerleithen, Borders, was being deliberately obtuse when he stated: 'What proportion the Dissenters may bear to those who are of the Established Church is beyond the power of man to determine'[9] – strange, if he refers to his own parish of only 560 souls!

The neighbouring minister of Linton with a total population of 1,003 does not seem to share his confusion. He offers this table:

Burghers	339
Antiburghers	2
Relief	35 [10]

In many of the accounts, it is the character of the Dissenters which comes under scrutiny. In some, a tolerant view is taken; in others, they are regarded with suspicion, intolerance or downright antagonism. It emerges fairly clearly that much of the bad feeling is engendered by the Dissenters' failure to contribute to poor relief; this was the responsibility of the Established Church, the funds coming from the weekly church collections and from various charitable endowments. One example of this failure comes from the Penpont, Dumfriesshire, account: 'The poor belonging to the Cameronians and Seceders receive supplies from the parochial funds; yet not one of these sects contributes a farthing to the maintenance of the parish poor. Moreover, many of the established church attend their meetings on particular days, which adds to their collections.'[11] There were exceptions, however, for example at Abernethy, Perthshire: 'The Antiburgher Kirk-session distributes £20 Sterling annually among the poor in this parish, besides contributing to the relief of others that attend their meeting-house from neighbouring parishes.'[12]

Two Lothians accounts offer, on the subject of dissenters, an example of that diversity of attitude which is typical of the accounts. The Corstorphine account declares: 'It would be improper, were I not here to take notice of that liberality of sentiment which Dissenters also discover in matters regarding religion. Difference, in religious opinion, excites no discord or strife between them and their brethren of the Establishment: they exercise acts of mutual kindness, and live in the bonds of charity and fraternal love.'[13] Not so, it would appear, in nearby Kirknewton: 'These Seceders must be a heavy burden on poor people; but they are productive of worse consequences, indirectly counteracting the design of Christianity, which is to make men live together as brethren; and in supporting superstition and fanaticism, which are mistaken by many for religion, and maintained with a violence and flaming zeal proportioned to the ignorance of their deluded votaries.'[14]

A similarly irritable note creeps into the account for Killbrandon and Killchattan, Argyll: 'There are no sectaries except a few, whose charity is not very extensive. Charity with them is confined to the household of faith; the members of which they are at no loss to distinguish, and evidently find them to be few.'[15]

To round off the question of the character of the Dissenters, the account for Avendale or Strathaven seems to offer a balanced view, especially in a parish where, the minister states, only about half the people still adhere to the Established Church: 'Divisions which were formed in anger redound to the increase of knowledge and forbearance; time moderates the fierceness of wrath; the multitude of sects abates their animosity; principle is respected, mistakes pardoned, and they are drawn together again by the bonds of humanity.'[16]

Patronage – that custom by which unwanted ministers were often foisted on the people by the will of the local heritors – was always responsible for much unrest and anger. The writer of the account for Bothkennar, Stirlingshire, raises his voice against the practice: 'The late Mr Graham, who had a particular pleasure in promoting the happiness of those around him (although not a member of the Established Church), was accustomed to indulge the people with the choice of their own pastors; by doing so, he obtained just and universal esteem while he lived, and on this account his memory will long be highly respected. If other patrons were of the same disposition, the law of patronage, so long complained of, would cease from being a grievance; and instead of that frequent discord and animosity, which are so destructive of the civil and religious interests of our country, peace and harmony would everywhere prevail.'[17] It may perhaps be added here that the very fact that so many of the common people were at this time setting up their own breakaway churches must be seen as a significant pointer to a new trend towards their grasping of initiative in their own affairs.

So far this chapter has tried to assess something of the character of those who had found the national Church in some sense wanting. What of the writers of the parochial reports? What can be gleaned of the character of the ministers themselves by a close perusal of what they have recorded? In a sense – although they appear to have much in common – just as great a diversity as has been observed throughout the preceding chapters, especially if one is to judge by the quantity as well as the quality of their replies to Sir John's questions. Some, for example, offer accounts of such great length and erudition that they could very well stand as books in their own right; one is astonished at the laboriously produced statistical tables – of the numbers of men, women and children of different age-groups; of horses, cattle and even sheep; of diseases; of trades and wages and prices; of births, marriages and deaths. Others, albeit a minority, appear to have dashed off hasty, ill-considered answers to the 160 queries, in the manner of lazy schoolboys – not that one can altogether blame them!

An example of this latter group comes from the account for Careston, Angus; here, even the most charitable might be likely to feel that the writer could have put a little more effort into his researches: 'The only conjecture that can be formed, respecting the number of parishioners, arises from the tokens, struck for the use of communicants, in the year 1709, when this parish was under the care of an Episcopalian clergyman, which number was 200.'[18]

The great majority of Scotland's ministers at the time belonged to the party known as 'Moderates'. In reaction to the doctrinal controversies which had caused bitter division in the country for centuries, and with its roots firmly in the spirit of enquiry and criticism of the Enlightenment, Moderatism tended to focus strongly upon culture and scholarship rather than 'enthusiasm' – the derogatory term of the day for religious fervour or evangelistic zeal – generally considered the precinct of the Seceders. One principle of the Moderate regime was that the law of patronage must be obeyed; patrons being on the whole men of education and position, they were held to be better judges of ministerial quality than the unlettered populace.

All of this is clearly reflected in the accounts. It would be hard to deny that most of the writers appear to be concerned with morality rather than doctrine, and that they are comfortable with parishioners who are law-abiding and respectable rather than filled with religious fervour. 'Sober and industrious', 'peaceable and contented' are terms of approbation used over and over again in the accounts. Altogether typical is the description of the character of his parishioners by the minister of Ecclesgrieg and St Cyrus, Kincardineshire: 'The religious character of the inhabitants of this parish is moderate. They neither run into the extreme of superstition on the one hand, nor of fanaticism on the other. In truth, their religion is of the calm mild cast; and they make no great noise or bustle about it, though they are very regular in attending its institutions.'[19] This actually paints a fairly accurate picture of the attitude of many of the ministers; the 'noise and bustle' are left to the dissenters.

It is strange to find some ministers pouring scorn on their parishioners for excessive seriousness in their views and pursuits – for example in Llanbryd, Morayshire: 'Almost the only pleasure they indulge in is meeting occasionally for the purpose of conversing about some of the abstrusest doctrines of Calvinism, in which they display their eloquence in the only kind of spouting in which they have any notion.'[20] One reason, of course, was that dissension could be caused only too easily. Awareness of this danger is clear in this excerpt from the account from Kirkpatrick-Juxta, Borders: 'The vulgar read almost nothing but books on religious subjects. Many of them are too fond of controversial divinity; a taste which the dissenters are very diligent in promoting, and which the few books they are acquainted with are rather calculated to confirm.'[21]

Other accounts express different attitudes; that from Mid-Calder, Lothians, declares: 'The great bulk of the inhabitants of this parish have a considerable share of religious knowledge, and a becoming fervency in their devotion. It is hoped that they will not be charged with singularity of manners, when we mention, that there are not perhaps six families in this parish, who do not daily, and in a family capacity, assemble together to acknowledge the Author of their mercies.'[22] Very different also is the picture presented in the Kilsyth account. In this parish, a religious revival had taken place some 50 years earlier, and – doubtless in the face of some scepticism – the writer is clearly at pains to substantiate the validity of that experience, and its continuing effects: 'If strife and contention, wrath and malice ceased, and love, and peace, and forbearance, and long-suffering, and forgiveness of one another prevailed; if the thief stole no more, but made restitution; and a whole parish at once, became decent and devout, sober and serious; and that they did so, is attested by pastor and heritors, elders and magistrates, in 1742, and by all the wise and worthy men of the congregation of Kilsyth, who were eye-witnesses to the events of that year, and are still alive; call this enthusiasm, or call it by any other name, I pray God, that I may ever feel its influence, and bear testimony to its power among the people!'[23]

Some of the accounts, while concise and eminently readable, give away little about the writers themselves; others tend to skimp on many of the questions, majoring instead on pet subjects such as archaeology, place-names, botany, or agriculture. A few are obsequious towards the local landowners; a far larger number are in no way afraid to attack them, frequently on account of their non-churchgoing habits, but very often also on behalf of people they feel are being exploited.

The majority of the writers of the accounts appear to be strongly conservative in character; yet some are keen protagonists of economic development. Extolling the merits of a paper mill which had increased the local population by 200, the writer of the Currie, Midlothian, account declares: 'While the advantages of manufactures in Scotland cannot be too strongly inculcated, those, in particular, that employ the very young and the aged, ought to meet with every encouragement. The paper trade employs children from 10 to 12 years of age, a period when they can do nothing very laborious, and when their morals, from idleness and neglect, are very apt to be neglected.'[24] Similarly, the Blantyre, Lanarkshire, writer seems to see little but good in the gigantic cotton mills which swallowed huge numbers of children to labour in terrible conditions and for very long hours: 'The employment in cotton mills, has, in general, been accounted unfavourable to health; and yet, what is singular in the present case, is, that out of a great number, employed at work within the mill, only two have died since it was erected. Great care indeed is taken, to keep both the house and the machinery as clean as possible; fresh air is carefully thrown in; and tar is burnt, to remove or counteract the noxious smell of the oil, that must necessarily be used about the machines.'[25]

Needless to say, the opposite view can be found without any difficulty; of these same cotton mills the Paisley minister asserts: 'The numbers that are brought together, the confinement, the breathing of an air loaded with the dust and downy particles of the cotton, and contaminated with the effluvia of rancid oil, arising from the machinery, must prove hurtful, in a high degree, to the delicate lungs of children.'[26] For the majority of the ministers, concern centred upon the moral degradation consequent on industrial development, rather than upon health hazards – as at Neilston, Renfrewshire: 'It is apprehended, that the rapid increase in manufactures, is neither friendly to the health nor morals of the people. In cotton mills a multitude of children are employed, before they receive even common education. They there spend, perhaps, a considerable part of their life, without any other principles in the direction of their conduct, but those which natural conscience dictates. The lower ranks of mankind, however, when collected and confined together, are too apt to corrupt one another.'[27]

Of agricultural matters many display an impressive knowledge. Some indeed are known to have excelled in this; one, the Rev. Robert Rennie of Kilsyth, was even invited by the Tsar of Russia to become professor of agriculture at St Petersburg University – an offer he declined. In the account for Kilmadock or Doune we meet another keen agriculturalist; this minister expands on the subject for a total of eighteen pages, under the following headings: draining, levelling, stone-clearing, trenching, straightening marches and burns, dividing runrig lands and commons, inclosing, rotation of crops, size of farms, leases and rents, implements of husbandry, threshing-mills, sales of grain, agricultural wages, black cattle, horses, sheep, markets, and prices of provisions.[28] One wonders when this minister found time to prepare his sermons or visit his congregation.

A great many others also exhibit a lively interest in the agricultural scene, and seem as practical as they are knowledgeable. For example, the Foveran, Aberdeenshire, writer suggests modifications in the granting of leases; reasonable rents; the establishment of 'parochial clubs' (comprising lairds, farmers and the minister) to plan agricultural policy; and collections from these to set up 'funds for encouraging industry among cottagers' – one example being a prize of 5s. for the best turnips or grass.[29] In the case of the Innerleithen writer it is the viability of his own glebe which mainly occupies his attention. 'If it is asked, will the minister of Innerleithen have a profitable occupancy? No. The land he possesses will not enable him to employ his man and horses half the time they ought to be employed. Ground cannot be laboured without two horses. Two he must keep, for the hiring of his ploughing he cannot obtain. One horse he ought to keep for parish duty; and when this requires one horse, the other is thrown idle as to the tilling the ground, and many other farming purposes. Should he, apostle like, abjure the use of horses for his own convenience, he may then drive in his fuel, and have his little farm cultivated in proper season; but every year he must go to market for fodder to maintain his horses; and this the late incumbent considered as an average expense of £5 per annum; which, added to the wages and maintenance of a ploughman, renders the glebe a loss rather than a profit to any incumbent.'[30]

It is noteworthy from a great many accounts that the writers are not at all afraid of speaking out strongly against a wide range of social evils. The gentry – some of whom of course were their patrons – are by no means spared, especially, as has been noted earlier, in the matter of their failure to set a good example in church-going. A stern rebuke on this account is delivered by the minister of Redgorton, Perthshire: 'If the gentry could be induced to attend the worship of the established church; if the churches were rendered more comfortable, and the roads and avenues leading thereunto were kept decent and dry, public worship would be more generally attended, the collections for the poor would be increased, and assessments rendered unnecessary in most country parishes; the gentlemen would thereby become more patriotic, and their influence greatly enlarged.'[31] In contrast, the broadside in the Borthwick, Lothians, account is brief and to the point: 'In many parishes not a single proprietor resides; and where he does, gives not himself the smallest trouble about the poor.'[32] Nor does the minister of Towie, Aberdeenshire, think highly of the general character of the heritors in his area: 'A generous mind will never think without indignation on the desire which some proprietors of land in this Highland part of the country, have to keep their tenants in a state of slavish dependence. That the latter should presume to think for themselves, and the former have no other coercion but what reason and the laws of the country allow them, is a sentiment so little realised by many of the lairds, that a poor tenant, if he is disposed to cringe, will often be preferred to one whose spirit and circumstances lead him to think of a manly independence.'[33] And in the Fala and Soutra, Lothians, account the writer resorts to sarcasm, this time again on the subject of church-going: 'It is only fashionable for the lower classes of people to attend the church. The higher orders are above the vulgar prejudice of believing it is necessary to worship the God of their fathers.'[34]

The ministers' ire is also frequently directed against the landlords on account of the short leases granted to tenants; on this particular subject, the writer for the Kirkmichael, Perthshire, account seems to sum up the situation admirably: 'Few of the tenants enjoy leases of their farms. Holding their small possessions by a short and uncertain tenure, they are continually in a state of abject dependence on their landlords . . . Is it that landlords are apprehensive of obtaining no benefit to themselves from granting leases, or of their tenants not having money or skill, or industry, for making improvements? Or is it that the tenants are unwilling to bind themselves for a number of years, to modes of cultivation, with which they are but little acquainted? Or is it that men, on whom wealth and power have conferred one kind of superiority, find, in the exercise of that superiority, and in receiving that servile dependence of their inferiors, a gratification which they cannot be persuaded to relinquish?'[35]

Another very real cause of grievance was the quasi-feudal state of affairs in some parishes; tenants were to a large extent prevented from keeping their own smallholdings of land properly because of the arduous services demanded of them by their landlords. The Bressay, Burra and Quarf, Orkney, account states:

'Few leases are granted. Many services, the sad marks of slavery, are demanded. They must fish for their masters, who either give them a fee entirely inadequate to their labour or their dangers, or take their fish at a lower price than others would give. It is true, that, in years of scarcity, they must depend on their landlords for the means of subsistence, and are often deep in their debt. But why not allow them to make the best of their situation? Why not let them have leases on reasonable terms, and dispose of their produce to those who will give them the best price? Why not let them fish for themselves? Why should the laird have any claim except for the stipulated rent?'[36]

In contrast, sometimes what appear as possibly over-obsequious remarks may be made in an account, and it is natural to wonder whether these were fully deserved. One such occurs in the account from Scone, Perth; after describing a monument erected by the Earl of Mansfield in honour of Lady Stormont, including 'a remarkably elegant and pathetic Latin inscription,' the writer adds that it 'does much honour, not only to the genius and erudition, but to the heart, of its noble author.'[37] On the other hand, the fulsome praise offered to the wife of a landowner in Lochs, Isle of Lewis, is clearly explained. Mrs Mackenzie is described as a true friend to the people, having obtained supplies of flax and encouraged the teaching of spinning to young girls, as well as having paid for two schoolmistresses, and given much financial help to the poor of the parish. The warm comments of the minister are therefore understandable: 'The memory of the haughty, and of course, the cruel-hearted daughters of dissipation, shall be utterly forgotten, or if mentioned, shall be mentioned with abhorrence; whilst that of the generous, whose kind efforts are well directed for the permanent good of mankind, shall be blessed on the earth for many succeeding years.'[38]

The truly lamentable situation of Scotland's schoolmasters at the time, and the fairly general refusal of the heritors to do anything to ameliorate their lot, is perhaps the single most frequent reason for the ministers speaking out. Not surprisingly, many of them also complained – some bitterly – about the state of their own manses and churches; unless the writer of the account for Orwel, Kinross-shire, greatly exaggerates, it is not that surprising: 'The manse is built in a temporary manner; the walls being insufficient to hold out rain, the house is often filled with water, and the ceilings destroyed.'[39] Similarly, in the account from Primrose, Lothians: 'The church was built in 1711. Its form is regular and convenient, and its walls well built and substantial. But as the roof is much decayed, as the windows are shattered, the walls rough from the hand of the mason, the seats crazy and irregular, its internal appearance is the very reverse of that simple elegance which befits a place of public worship. The manse was built in 1790; but the offices are paltry and ruinous.'[40] Worst of all, it seems, was the church in Heriot, Midlothian: 'The church is an old and infirm building. It is scarcely safe to perform public duty in it. It is neither dry above, nor decently seated. It is, perhaps, the most shabby and miserable place of accommodation for divine service in Scotland.'[41]

However, a contrast is available not far away, in Lasswade, Lothians, where: 'The manse, one of the best in the country, was built in 1789 and cost £500. If the sum expended in building the manse is a proof of the liberality of the heritors, they deserve no less credit from the church just now erecting, which, in point of accommodation, and magnificence of structure, will far exceed any modern country church in Scotland.'[42]

The writer of the Clunie, Perthshire, account has some wise words on the subject: 'It would be a credit to this country, if all the old crazy kirks and manses in it were razed to the foundation, and new ones built in a workmanlike manner, on a decent and convenient plan, and of the most substantial and permanent materials. This would occasion some expense to the present proprietors of the country, who in general are opulent and liberal; but what it would take out of their pockets, it would put into those of their posterity to the 13th and 14th generations. The kirk of Clunie, though one of the best in the neighbourhood, has neither comeliness nor proportion . . . the manse, like the church, is a bungled piece of architecture.'[43]

The last word on the subject comes from Glasford, Lanarkshire: 'The church was built in 1663. It never was elegant or convenient. Its present uncouth appearance fixes the attention of every beholder; and scarce a stranger passes by without making it a compliment. It is not in good repair. The heritors, unlike the ancient Jew, love not to decorate the temple; though it would be doing them an injustice not to observe, that they love to attend it. Matters are so managed here, that the manse is like the church. Though repaired five years ago, the manse needs again to be repaired. After a thaw or a smart shower of rain, the inside walls and timber exhibit a scene wonderfully striking. The pearly drops meet the eye from every point of view; so that, amid the rigours of winter, its inhabitants enjoy some of the pleasures of a May morning. The situation of the manse accounts for this. It lies in a swamp.'[44]

Some of the things which irritated the writers are less predictable; the Barra minister, for example, is annoyed by an error in a certain prestigious publication: 'The main island of Barray is eight computed miles in length, and from two to four in breadth, being intersected in different places by arms of the sea. The compilers of the Encyclopaedia Britannica will do well to correct their error in calling Barray a rock half a mile in circumference, inhabited only by solan geese and other wild fowls.'[45]

Repeatedly in the accounts the pastoral concern of the ministers is demonstrated. The injustice suffered by the poor in the loss of their precious crops to their landlords' marauding pigeons is the theme of a complaint in the account for Auchterderran, Fife: 'It has been doubted whether our law authorising pigeon-houses is not, in some degree, contrary to natural equality; as it does not seem reasonable that any one should keep a house furnished with a multitude of animals, over which he has no government, and which prey on his neighbour's corn as freely as on his own, while he alone has the profit.'[46]

The sheer moral courage of some of the clergy is nowhere more clearly illustrated than in the matter of inoculation for the smallpox; in the face of many of the people's strongly held prejudices, they not only championed its use, but even, in some cases, dared to inoculate their own children. As many examples have been quoted in the chapter on inoculation, a single excerpt, from the Tough, Aberdeenshire, account will suffice here: 'The prejudices of the people in this neighbourhood, are strongly bent against inoculation for the smallpox. Some months ago, when the present incumbent had a child inoculated, one man, who has a numerous young family by a second wife (his children of the first marriage having suffered extremely by the smallpox), was desirous that his young family should undergo that operation. They were accordingly inoculated, and got through remarkably well; but so violent were the prejudices of the people, that, it is said, some of them declared, if the inoculated children had died, they would have considered it as a just dispensation of Providence.' This writer later adds a comment demonstrating the high value he places on the SA: 'If the more discerning heads of families were attentively to read the *Statistical Survey*, it might be of considerable service to them, in that as well as in many other respects.'[47]

The ministers are by no means lacking in humour. Usually this is of a dry ironic type, a good example of which comes from the account by the minister of Montquhitter, Aberdeenshire: 'Those who have been born in the parish are fondly attached to their native soil. "How can I live?" said a poor fellow, not destitute of genius, who had wandered to Edinburgh in search of business, "oh, how can I live, out of the sight of the bonny parks of Auchry?" To the bonny parks of Auchry his predominant passion obliged him to return, and he is now active in increasing the population by a numerous family.'[48]

It is of interest to note here that the ministers themselves frequently had numerous progeny. In his introduction to Vol. XI, Professor Bruce Lenman describes them as 'a professional group with a strong tendency to self-perpetuation, much given to marrying ministers' daughters and begetting future ministers.'

Another historian, John R. Hume, has this to say of the ministers in his introduction to Vol. V: 'Throughout their reports the sound of axes being ground can be heard, yet the abiding impression they give is of decent, well-educated men thoroughly involved with the secular, as well as the spiritual, lives of their parishioners.'

Since an attempt to build a picture of the authors of the accounts is limited to conjecture, it is a relief to find an actual testimonial to one of their number included in the account for Portree, Isle of Skye: 'Mr John Nicolson, the present minister, is a bachelor, in the 88th year of his age, and 39th of his ministry. He is a man of primitive manners and exemplary life; sincere, benevolent, and charitable, of untainted rectitude and uprightness, and of such indefatigable perseverance in the discharge of his pastoral office, that being appointed to preach in Kirktown of Raasay once a month, and once a quarter in another part of that island, of no easy access, he has not been absent above four times on the ordinary days, during the whole course of his ministry, till the beginning of spring last, when he got a fall that dislocated his shoulder, and confined him to the house for the rest of the season. Till that unfortunate accident he was never troubled with any sort of indisposition, and what is rather singular, never travelled on horseback for one mile in all his life.'[49]

From another part of the Highlands (Lochcarron) comes a whimsical entry with which to end this book; the minister finishing his report in verse:

'This same statistical account
Is sent to please Sir John,
And if it be not elegant
Let critics throw a stone.
We have not fine materials
And our account is plain,
Our lands and purling streams are good,
But we have too much rain . . .

Sir John send word, if you are pleased
With what I here rehearse,
Perhaps 'twere better had I told
My story all in verse.
The parson has no horse, nor farm,
No goat, nor watch, nor wife,
Without an augmentation too,
He leads a happy life.'[50]

1. VI, 252	14. II, 335	27. VII, 821	40. II, 122
2. XII, 691	15. VIII, 181	28. XII, 509–528	42. II, 347
3. IX, 617	16. VII, 9	29. XV, 163	43. XII, 244
4. VI, 288	17. IX, 188	30. III, 770	44. VII, 278
5. VII, 350	18. XIII, 108	31. XI, 536	45. XX, 135
6. V, 62	19. XIV, 101	32. II, 76	46. X, 52
7. XII, 74	20. XVI, 642	33. XIV, 740	47. XIV, 729
8. XI, 512	21. IV, 349	34. II, 252	48. XV, 324
9. III, 772	22. II, 110	35. XII, 678	49. XX, 198
10. II, 808	23. IX, 444	36. XIX, 394	50. XVII, 577
11. IV, 444	24. II, 203	37. XI, 584	
12. XI, 13	25. VII, 25	38. XX, 16	
13. II, 159	26. VII, 827	39. XI, 663	

Appendix

The following pages are a facsimile of the original questionnaire sent out to all the parishes in Scotland.

Copy of the QUERIES drawn up for the purpose of elucidating the Natural History and Political State of Scotland, which were inclosed in the preceding letter.

QUESTIONS *respecting the* GEOGRAPHY *and* NATURAL HISTORY *of the* PARISH.

1. What is the ancient and modern name of the Parish ?
2. What is the origin and etymology of the name ?
3. In what county is it situated ?
4. In what presbytery and synod ?
5. What is the extent and form of the parish ?
6. What its length and breadth ?
7. By what parishes is it bounded ?
8. What is the general appearance of the country? Is it flat or hilly, rocky or mountainous ?
9. What is the nature of the soil ? Is it fertile or barren, deep or shallow ?
10. What is the nature of the air? Is it moist or dry, unhealthy or otherwise ?
11. What are the most prevalent distempers ? and to what circumstances are they to be attributed ?
12. Are there any mineral springs ? and in what diseases are they serviceable ?
13. Are there any considerable lakes or rivers in the parish ?
14. What species of fish do they produce ? In what quantities ? What prices do they fetch on the spot ? And in what seasons are they in the greatest perfection ?
15. Are the rivers navigable ? or might they be rendered useful in navigation ?
16. Are there any navigable canals in the parish ?
17. What is the extent of sea-coast ?
18. Is the shore flat, sandy, high, or rocky ?
19. What sorts of fish are caught on the coast? In what quantity ? At what prices sold ? When most in season ? How taken ? And to what markets sent ?
20. What other sea animals, plants, sponges, corals, shells, &c. are found on or near the coast ?
21. Are there any remarkable sea weeds used for manuring land, or curious on any other account ?
22. Is there any kelp ? And what quantity, at an average, is annually made ?
23. What are the courses of the tides on the shore or at sea ? and are there any rocks, currents, &c. worthy of notice ?

24. Are

24. Are there any light-houfes, beacons, or land-marks? or could any be erected that would be of fervice?

25. What are the names of the principal creeks, bays, harbours, headlands, fands, or iflands, near the coaft?

26. Have there been any battles or fea fights near the coaft? and when did any remarkable wrecks or accidents happen, which can give light to any hiftorical fact?

27. Are there any remarkable mountains? and what are their heights?

28. Are the hills covered with heath, green, or rocky?

29. Are there any volcanic appearances in the parifh?

30. Are there any figured ftones, or any having the impreffion of plants or fifhes upon them?

31. Are there any foffil marine bodies, fuch as fhells, corals, &c. or any petrified part of animals? or any petrifying fprings or waters?

32. Are there any marble, moor-ftone, free-ftone, flate, or other ftones? How are they got at, and what ufe is made of them?

33. Are there any mines, particularly coal-mines? What are they? To whom do they belong? And what do they produce?

34. Is any part of the parifh fubject to inundations or land-floods? When did any remarkable event of that nature happen?

35. Hath there been any remarkable mifchief done by thunder and lightning, water-fpouts or whirlwinds?

36. Are there any remarkable echoes?

37. Have any remarkable phenomena been obferved in the air?

38. Are there any remarkable caves or grottos, natural or artificial?

39. What quadrupeds and birds are there in the parifh? What migratory birds? and at what times do they appear and difappear?

40. Is the parifh remarkable for breeding any fpecies of cattle, fheep, horfes, hogs, or goats, of peculiar quality, fize, or value?

II. Questions refpecting the Population of the Parish?

41. What was the ancient ftate of the population of the parifh, fo far as it can be traced?

42. What is now the amount of its population?

43. What may be the number of males?

44. What of females;

45. How many refide in towns?

46. ——————— villages?

47. ——————— the country?

48. What is the annual average of births?

49.

49. What is the annual average of deaths * ?
50. ―――――――――――― marriages ?
51. ―――――――――――― souls under 10 years of age ?
52. ―――――――――――― from 10 to 20 ?
53. ―――――――――――― 20 to 50 ?
54. ―――――――――――― 50 to 70 ?
55. ―――――――――――― 70 to 100 ?
56. Above 100 ?
57. Are there any inſtances of long lives well authenticated ?
58. What may be the number of farmers and their families ?
59. ―――――――――――― manufacturers ?
60. ―――――――――――― handycraftsmen ?
61. ―――――――――――― apprentices ?
62. ―――――――――――― ſeamen ?
63. ―――――――――――― fiſhermen ?
64. ―――――――――――― ferrymen ?
65. ―――――――――――― miners ?
66. ―――――――――――― houſehold ſervants, male and female ?
67. ―――――――――――― labouring ſervants, male and female ?
68. ―――――――――――― ſtudents at colleges and univerſities ?
69. ―――――――――――― merchants, citizens or tradeſmen ?
70. ―――――――――――― artiſts ?
71. ―――――――――――― Jews ?
72. ―――――――――――― negroes ?
73. ―――――――――――― gipſies ?
74. ―――――――――――― foreigners ?
75. ―――――――――――― perſons born in England, Ireland, or the British colonies ?

76. What

* It is of peculiar importance to have the queſtions 48 and 49 diſtinctly anſwered ; for it is generally underſtood, at leaſt on the Continent, that the population of any diſtrict or country, may be known with ſufficient accuracy, by multiplying the number of births by 26, or the number of deaths by 36. In Scotland, on the other hand, Mr Wilkie, miniſter of Cults, ſuppoſes, that the number either of births and burials, if they are equal, ſhould be multiplied by 40 ; or, if there is any difference, the half of the whole, (both the births and the burials), ſhould be multiplied by the expectation of an infant's life, adapted to the particular diſtrict, in order to aſcertain its population. See Statiſtical Accornt, vol. II. p. 415. It appears, from Mr Wilkie's calculations, that the expectation of a life in Scotland, is much greater than in England, or on the Continent.

76. What may be the number of perfons born in other diftricts or parifhes in Scotland?

77. What may be the number of the nobility and their families?

78. ———————————————— gentry?

79. ———————————————— clergy?

80. ———————————————— lawyers, and writers or attornies?

81. What may be the number of phyficians, furgeons, and apothecaries?

82. ———————————— the eftablifhed church?

83. ———————————— feceders?

84. ———————————— epifcopalians?

85. ———————————— Roman catholics?

86. Is the population of the parifh materially different from what it was 5, 10, or 25 years ago? and to what caufes is the alteration attributed?

87. What is the proportion between the annual births and the whole population?

88. What is the proportion between the annual marriages and the whole population?

89. What is the proportion between the annual deaths and the whole population?

90. What is the proportion between the batchelors and the married men, widowers included?

91. How many children does each marriage at an average produce?

92. What may be the caufes of depopulation?

93. Are there any deftructive epidemical diftempers?

94. Have any died from want?

95. Have any murders or fuicides been committed?

96. Have many emigrated from the parifh?

97. Have any been banifhed from it?

98. Have any been obliged to leave the parifh for want of employment?

99. Are there any uninhabited houfes?

100. What may be the number of inhabited houfes, and the number of perfons at an average to each inhabited houfe?

III. QUESTIONS *refpecting the* PRODUCTIONS *of the* PARISH.

101. What kinds of vegetables, plants, and trees, does the parifh produce?

102. What kinds of animals?

103. What at an average is fuppofed to be the number of cattle, fheep, horfes, hogs, and goats, in the diftrict?

104. Is there any map of the parifh? and has the number of acres in it been afcertained?

105. How

203

105. How many acres at an average may be employed in raifing corn, roots, &c.?

106. What number of acres to each fort refpectively, as wheat, barley, rye, oats, potatoes, turnip, cabbage. &c.?

107. Does the parifh fupply itfelf with provifions?

108. Does it in general export or import articles of provifion?

109. How many acres are employed in raifing hemp or flax?
110. How many in fown or artificial graffes?

111. How many in pafture?

112. When do they in general fow and reap their different crops?

113. What quantity of ground may lie wafte or in common?

114. What in woods, forefts, marfhes, lakes, and rivers?

115. Is there any chalk, marl, fullers earth, potters earth, ochre, &c.?

116. Are there any bitumen, naptha, or other fubftances of that nature found in the foil?

IV. Miscellaneous Questions.

117. Has the parifh any peculiar advantages or difadvantages?

118. What language is principally fpoken in it?

119. From what language do the names of places in the parifh feem to be derived?

120. What are the moft remarkable inftances of fuch derivations?

121. What may the land rent of the parifh be?

122. What the rent of houfes, fifhings, &c.?

123. What is the value of the living, including the glebe? and who is the patron?

124. Who is now minifter of the parifh?

125. How long has he been fettled in it?

126. What are the names of his predeceffors as far back as they can now be traced, and the time they refpectively held that office?

127. Is the minifter married, a widower, or fingle?

128. If with a family, how many fons, and how many daughters?

129. When were the church and the manfe built or repaired?

130. What is the number of heritors, or poffeffors of landed property in the parifh?

131. How many of them refide in it?

132. What is the number of the poor in the parifh receiving alms?

133. What is the annual amount of the contributions for their relief, and the produce of alms, legacies, or of any other fund deftined for that purpofe?

134. What are the prefent or ancient prices of provifions, beef, veal, mutton, lamb, pork, pigs, geefe, ducks, chickens, rabbits, butter, cheefe, wheat, barley, oats, &c.?

135. What

135. What is generally a day's wages for labourers in husbandry, and other work? and what *per* day for carpenters, bricklayers, masons, tailors, &c.?

136. What is the fuel commonly made use of? Is it coal, wood, heath, peat, furze, or whins? What are the prices paid on the spot; and whence is the fuel procured?

137. What, at an average, may be the expence of a common labourer, when married? and is the wages he receives sufficient to enable him to bring up a family?

138. What are the usual wages of male and female servants in the different branches of husbandry?

139. What the wages of domestic servants?

140. How many ploughs are there in the parish? and of what kinds?

141. How many carts and waggons?

142. How many carriages; and of what sorts?

143. Are there any villages in the parish? and how are they situated?

144. Are there any crosses or obelisks erected in the parish?

145. Are there any remains or ruins of monasteries or religious houses?

146. Are there any Roman, Saxon, Danish, or Pictish castles, camps, altars, roads, forts, or other remains of antiquity? and what traditions or historical accounts are there of them?

147. Have there been any medals, coins, arms, or other pieces of antiquity dug up in the parish? When were they found? And in whose custody are they now?

148. Are there any barrows, or tumuli? Have any been opened? And what has been found therein?

149. Have there been any remarkable battles fought in the parish? On what spot? At what time? By whom? And what traditions are there respecting the same?

150. Has the parish either given birth or burial to any man eminent for learning, or distinguished for any other valuable qualification?

151. Are the people of the country remarkable for strength, size, complexion, or any other personal or mental qualities?

152. What is the general size of the people?

153. What is the greatest height which any individual in the parish has attained, properly authenticated?

154. Are the people disposed to industry? What manufactures are carried on in the parish? And what number of hands are employed therein?

155. Are the people fond of a sea-faring life? What is the number of boats and of larger vessels belonging to the parish? And what number of seamen have entered into the navy during any preceding war?

156. Are

156. Are the people fond of a military life? Do many inlift in the army? And principally in what corps?

157. Are the people economical, or expenfive and luxurious for their circumftances? Is property, particularly in land, often changing? And at what prices is it in general fold?

158. Are the people difpofed to humane and generous actions; to protect and relieve the fhipwrecked, &c.? and are there any events which have happened in the parifh, which do honour to human nature?

159. Do the people, on the whole, enjoy, in a reafonable degree, the comforts and advantages of fociety? and are they contented with their fituation and circumftances?

160. Are there any means by which their condition could be ameliorated?

ADDENDA.

1. What is the ftate of the roads and bridges in the parifh? How were they originally made? How are they kept in repair? Is the ftatute labour exacted in kind, or commuted? Are there any turnpikes? and what is the general opinion of the advantages of turnpike roads?

2. What is in general the rent of the beft arable and the beft pafture or meadow grounds, per acre? What the rent of inferior?

3. What in general is the fize and the average rent of the farms in the parifh? And is the number of farms increafing or diminifhing?

4. Is the parifh in general inclofed, or uninclofed? And are the people convinced of the advantages of inclofures?

5. What was the fituation of the parifh anno 1782 and 1783? Pleafe ftate any curious or important circumftances connected with that era, or with any other feafon of fcarcity.

6. Are there any curious or important facts tending to prove any great alteration in the manners, cuftoms, drefs, ftile of living, &c. of the inhabitants of the parifh, now, and 20 or 50 years ago?

N. B. If you refide in a town or city, pleafe give an account of the hiftory and antiquities of the place; of its buildings, age, walls, fieges, charters, privileges, immunities, gates, ftreets, markets, fairs; the number of churches, wards, guilds, companies, fraternities, clubs, &c.: How the town is governed: if it is reprefented in parliament, to whom does the right of election belong, and what the number of electors? together with a comparifon between its ancient and modern ftate, in regard to population, commerce, fhipping, fifheries, manufactures, more particularly at the following periods, about the time of the Union, fince the year 1745, and at prefent.

INDEX